SPAIN - A NEW LIFE

Spain - A New Life

An Andalucian Odyssey

by

Toby Woolrych

with

occasional additions, disclaimers and general interference

from

Susan Woolrych

his wife

'Just when you think you have decoded life's messages, something or someone comes along to invert all your carefully built-up conclusions.' *Eric Lustbader*

Scotforth Books

Copyright © Toby Woolrych, 2002

First published in 2002 on behalf of the author
by Scotforth Books,
Carnegie House,
Chatsworth Road,
Lancaster LA1 4SL,
England
Tel: +44 (0) 1524 840111
Fax: +44 (0) 1524 840222
email: carnegie@provider.co.uk
Publishing and book sales: www.carnegiepub.co.uk
Book production: www.wooof.net

British Library Cataloguing-in-Publication data
A catalogue record for this book is available from the British Library

ISBN 1-904244-17-3

Printed and bound in the UK by
The Cromwell Press, Wiltshire

To George and Donella, for pointing the way

A Few Words in Advance

Every year, millions of people from all over Northern Europe travel to Spain for their holidays. Most congregate on the Costas, often for permutations of the themes of sun, sea, sangria, sex and, of course, golf. Some like the experience so much that they return year after year, and a whole industry has sprung up, renting or selling coastal properties to visitors from all over Europe and Scandinavia and even as far afield as Russia and the USA.

In addition to these temporary visitors there are those who, for any number of reasons, decide to quit their native shores and make their homes in Spain. Of these, many prefer to bring with them the customs and cultures of the lands of their birth, and there is now a whole infrastructure in the coastal resorts, catering for the needs of Northern expatriates, often provided by other expatriates, thus eliminating entirely the tiresome business of having even to learn Spanish, let alone of accommodating oneself to Spanish culture and customs.

This book isn't about any of this. It is the story of why and how an ordinary British couple decided to sell up and, at ages when sensible people are normally engaged in less foolish enterprises, with neither of them knowing anyone in the country, nor speaking a word of Spanish, nor having been to Spain since Torremolinos ceased to be a fishing village, and with one of them initially far from convinced about the wisdom of the idea, seek a home in the *campo* - rural, inland Spain - in Andalucía, a Region known to many only as the home of sherry, bull-fights, flamenco, Seville, Granada, and the *Costa del Sol*.

Despite its sub-title, this is not a do-it-yourself guide. It isn't even a *caveat* on how not to do it since, at the end of the day, we got most of it more or less right. It is simply a personal account of the experiences shared by a middle-aged husband and wife (with one of them bordering on the elderly) over the twelve months in which they sought for and bought a *finca* - a smallholding - renovated and modernised its *cortijo* - its farmhouse - and laid the foundations for a new enterprise in an area where, away from the coast, traditional customs and cultures prevail and most locals speak little Spanish, let alone English, but the unique dialect of 'Andaluz'.

The story has also been, at least for one of us, an unexpected voyage of self-discovery, a voyage which had evidently been in progress, undetected, since long before we arrived in Spain. Indeed it was only when I began to write this book that evidence of it started to surface. At first I rejected having anything to do with it, at least so far as the book was concerned, as I am extremely leery when such revelations are included in a book with a title like this one's, but as it is germane to the complete story I have cautiously given it some space.

The book comes in two distinct parts. The first sets out the reasons why we decided to leave England in the first place, and records the events and reflects the impressions gained during the course of our search for our new home and the subsequent wait until purchase could be completed; the second explores the joys and tribulations we experienced during our first seven months of occupation. Much of this information will not be found in guide books, but a lot will be relevant to anyone contemplating doing as we have done.* If any of our views cause affront or even outrage, then we apologise, unreservedly. We are also aware that the experiences of others who have trodden this path before us, the impressions they have gained and the wisdom they have acquired may well differ from ours; to them we can simply observe *lo que a uno cura a otra mata* (one man's - and woman's - meat is another man's poison), and of such is the spice of life.

---

* Author's note. Every effort has been made to ensure that information with regard to the laws, procedures, customs and traditions of Spain is accurate. However it would be profoundly unwise to regard the book's pronouncements on anything as 'gospel', as the laws in particular have a habit of changing without notice, and we take no responsibility for any actions taken by others based on our conclusions. Also, while the book is a miscellany of first and second-hand experiences, anecdotes and cautionary tales, to safeguard against possible future actions which may threaten the authors' physical and financial well-being, and to avoid embarrassment to the individuals concerned, the names of certain personalities portrayed herein have been changed.

Chapter 1

Do what you like before you like what you do.
(George Bernard Shaw)

It was quite a sizeable house, standing on its own in a saucer of land in the centre of the village. It was no better, and only marginally worse, than most of the other dwellings we had been shown. While we were looking at it we noticed that villagers, mainly male, had stopped on the track which ran round the saucer and were contemplating our reconnaissance with stolid curiosity. It was when we walked away from the house to look back at it from the perimeter of the saucer that I saw the possible reason.

'Sheri,' I said to the agent who had brought us there, 'could you please ask the *corredor* the meaning of the light over the front door. The <u>red</u> light over the door.' The *corredor's* immediate re-action to this query was to quickly point out various other features of the property, including the large tree which gave abundant shade.

I refused to be dist-racted. 'Please will you ask him to confirm, yes or no, whether this was a "cat-house", or whatever the equivalent is in Spanish.' The *corredor's*

1

face as he listened to her gave the expected answer. Now we understood the reason for the surprising number of beds in each room – clearly group sex was a feature in this village – and for the growing number of spectators, who now numbered around thirty; perhaps they hoped the mad foreigners were going to restart the enterprise. Sadly the building's position and condition ruled it out as a possible purchase so far as we were concerned, which was a pity really; buying it could have embarked us on a whole new adventure! The date was 3 January 1999 and we were well into our search for our new home in Spain.

We had arrived in Andalucía twelve days earlier, the day before Christmas Eve, having driven from England in 'the Duchess', our beloved sixteen-year-old Jaguar/Daimler Sovereign. We were staying in the small town of Colmenar, partly because it was central to la Axarquia, the area we wished to explore, and partly because it seemed, from what we could find out at long range (which was remarkably little), to be the only town for miles with anything that resembled a hotel.

Our first indication that house-hunting in Andalucía was going to be just a little different from the same activity in the UK came the evening we arrived, when we contacted the estate agents who had recommended the hotel where we were staying. Not only were they extremely reluctant to meet us, they didn't seem to want to talk to us at all. We were slightly nonplussed at this, but we put it down to their preoccupation with Christmas – these agents were British, not Spanish, and besides, we didn't know about Spanish Christmases at that point – and we arranged to meet them after Christmas, on Tuesday 29 December.

This still left Monday 28th, and as we <u>had</u> come to Spain to look for a new home, not sit around on the hotel veranda in the December sunlight enjoying *café y coñac*, no matter how agreeable that was, we tried, before everywhere shut down for the holiday, to arrange something for then. Accordingly I telephoned a Spanish agency, from whose British branch we had received a very comprehensive list of country properties before we left England, and which had urged us to phone their Spanish head office, 'as soon as you get there.' So, again, I was just a little surprised when I announced who we were and reminded them what we were looking for to be greeted with the reply, 'Well, someone will get back to you on Tuesday... perhaps.'

Now this was odd, because we should have represented an agent's dream: a couple, with available cash, who not only wanted to buy but they had so far committed themselves that they no longer had a home in England - they <u>had</u> to buy. Customers like us don't happen often - we know, having both been in sales in the past - and we had learned to treat people in positions like ours as the proverbial 'lodestone': nothing, absolutely nothing short of an avalanche or an earthquake, should take priority over devoting all one's attention to satisfying their requirements, because sure as fate, if you don't, someone else will. And in our case, they did.

However, before that happened, this 100% lack of enthusiasm from two agencies with which we had had prior dealings was distinctly off-putting, and we wondered whether it was going to be like this all the way. We discussed our misgivings with those other foreign residents in the hotel who were either also house-hunting like us, or were further along the chain of house purchase, and from their pooled experiences we learned that we had arrived at a boom time for the sale of properties in this part of Spain.

There appeared to be two reasons for this. First, because of the Spanish preference for conducting all private financial trans-actions in cash whenever possible, there had always been a good deal of 'invisible' money sloshing around. Now, with the impend-ing introduction of the Euro and the phasing out of national currencies, there was an urgent need to convert this cash into other forms of tangible asset and then dispose of it legally at a profit - and what better way to do this than to improve your home and sell it?

Secondly, because of the dramatic improvements to the infrastructure initiated by the *Junta del Andalucía* and the Regional authorities, more and more people were being attracted to Andalucía, and there had been a massive increase in the numbers of foreign 'hopefuls' looking for properties on the *Costas*. This was encouraging many Spanish house-owners, whether they had improved their homes or not, to put their houses up for sale to take advantage of the astonishing prices which foreigners seemed to be prepared to pay.

So this was a 'sellers' market', where agents really didn't have to go out of their way to obtain business; it literally beat a path to their doors. If they missed a buyer, it didn't matter that much; like the proverbial No 9 bus, there would always be another one along in a minute. As we were to discover, this induced not only complacency in some of those doing the selling, it also allowed scope for those whose standards of professionalism were possibly not entirely what a prospective purchaser might be expecting. In times of plenty, it is not only the lions that prosper: the jackals also thrive.

However our faith in human nature was restored when we telephoned another British agent whose card was pinned to a board in the hotel, as he not only called in to see us at 8 o'clock that evening, he left his family outside in his car and took time to discuss what we were looking for, finally leaving us with a portfolio of properties on his books, and arranging to meet us at 10 o'clock on Monday 28 December.

Kevin duly arrived in a substantial 4 x 4, which had us thinking a bit, and for the rest of the day he took us round a bewildering succession of properties, from which we learned a number of things. The first was that, without exception, any property we saw on his or any other agent's lists which both suited us and came within our price range was already sold. When we remonstrated with Kevin about this he explained, entirely reasonably, that attractive properties moved so fast through his hands, he didn't have time to keep amending his list to keep pace with the changes; he brought it up to date when there were fewer properties available than those already sold. Thus what we were left with were the rejects, unless we timed it right. This taught us our first rule in house-hunting in the *campo*:

Allow yourself sufficient time to be in the area of your choice when new properties become available. The best ones don't hang around long.

The second thing we learned was that what we saw often bore little resemblance to our ideas of what we were going to look at. This was because our mental pictures were based on our experiences of house-hunting in England, where a description 'This old country cottage can be restored with ease,' doesn't

4

usually mean that it is structurally unsound, and has no water, electricity or drainage; and where 'The property can be reached via a 5 km long track; the last 500 metres are a little rugged,' is unlikely to mean that there are times when the property cannot be reached at all via the 5 km long track because the last 500 metres are under water, being along a river bed which is not merely rugged, it is a raging torrent at certain times of the year! This taught us the second rule in house-hunting in the *campo*:

What you read about in the agents' portfolios will not necessarily resemble what you think you are going to look at on the ground.

And so it sadly proved with Kevin. At the end of a long, dusty and unproductive day, entirely at his expense except for the coffees we bought along the way, we had to mutually admit that there was nothing on his books which met our dream, not even the 'charming olive farm set in 11 acres of land with over 250 olive trees giving an income of around 700,000 *pesetas* per crop', as its six bedrooms were like shoe-boxes, its staircase was unlit, barely a metre wide, and had a clearance overhead of less than five feet, and the only room large enough to be considered anything more than a cell appeared to be used as a garage. It was also 7 km from the nearest metalled road, so we parted company outside the hotel, leaving him to seek more rewarding potential customers and us to move on to other agencies on our list.

Beware, too, of the photos!

We saw many photos that looked exactly what we wanted in the portfolio, but which proved very different in reality. 'Is that another house close behind?' 'Yes there is a house but it's only used at the weekends by the Spanish owner to tend his land.' Oh yeah? What about the rest of his family; do they come too? If so, what might it be like when dozens of men, women and children and even granny come along to enjoy the fresh air at the tops of their voices? And what about the gradient? That bit sloping out of sight on the photo, is it just an anomaly, or is the whole site on a 1-in-hell slope and needs crampons to reach it?

Our decision to move to Spain had been triggered by an event whose origins stretched way back to the early '70s. I was then acting as master of a garrison church choir in Germany in addition to my 'day job', when I gradually became aware that my throat was tending to close up when I was singing, especially on the lower notes (very helpful for a bass), thus preventing breathing. In the end I had to give up singing altogether, much to my disappointment, but no doubt to the choir's considerable relief.

This was hardly epoch-shattering, and as it didn't seem to affect anything else I paid it little heed until 1989, when matters suddenly took a turn for the worse. It was not an experience I was likely to forget. By now I had been out of the Army for some ten-odd years - some of them very odd - and was involved with a Canadian network marketing company. I had been attending a meeting with some of my business colleagues in the Post House Hotel outside Birmingham and we were all enjoying a glass of wine and an excellent meal before going our various ways.

I was eating a lamb chop when suddenly my entire gullet closed, leaving me gagging and rushing to the toilet with tears in my eyes. This was no fault of the chop, which was quite delicious; it was my old friend, which had decided to take this moment to move into a higher gear. After this, I learned to be circumspect about what I ate, especially in public, and I developed a bird-like swallowing technique which usually did the trick when I was faced with more challenging menus (older readers may recall an advertisement promoting a well-known Irish stout which featured an ostrich with a glass lodged in its throat. I knew just how that ostrich might have felt - but without the benefit of the stout) though it did attract some funny looks when a particularly difficult morsel showed a tendency to go the wrong way.

Toby's throat was causing me more than a few thoughts about how to spend our future. Not one for bothering doctors, he left things to clear up or get worse. This had already happened with three attacks of renal colic (kidney stones) which ended up with him being rushed to hospital, once with me not knowing where he had gone as I had been out visiting with my children. So when the throat problem started to get worse, not being one to keep anything to myself, I shared this thought with him: he was nearing retirement age, his National Insurance contributions were fully paid up, so why not consider a complete change of direction?

At the time I gave this suggestion little serious consideration. I had worked all my life and, being of a generation which expected to have to do so to put bread on the table instead of standing with its hand out hoping that the benevolent State would put something in it, hadn't ever contemplated doing anything else. However at this point Fate took a hand and matters came to a head, so to speak, in June 1998. By now I was a professional teacher of English as a foreign language, and I had been engaged to run a week's residential course in southern Germany for a group of engineers from a large, well-known German engineering firm. I was lunching with the said engineers when, without warning, my throat closed completely and I regurgitated part of my excellent meal under the horrified gaze of my students, causing my immediate neighbour to leave the table in a hurry and me to resolve to seek professional help!

While Toby was away in Germany I took the bull by the horns and sat down with reasonably up-to-date figures relating to tax, cost of living and any other financial aspects which might need to be taken into account and listed them for Britain, France and Spain. I also researched the rules and provision of each of those countries to do with taxes, inheritance and so on. France on the whole was only marginally cheaper than the UK but Spain, Wow! So with a head full of facts and a paper full of figures, bursting to share them with Toby, his throat joined in as an ally in earnest!

On his return from Germany, Toby looked grey and haggard and as we had long ago given up the pleasure of eating out owing to his problem, I put my foot down with a heavy hand. By chance I had to go with my youngest daughter to see our GP and I took the opportunity to explain Toby's symptoms. Boy did I get a shock: not only did our doctor want to see him, he wanted to see him now!! Now we all know the system: you make your appointment and are ill in six weeks' time. I had to phone Toby and get him over to the surgery straight away. We passed on the road, me taking my daughter back home and him to see the GP!

Our GP referred me, with what I felt was indecent haste, to a specialist at the Royal Bournemouth Hospital. This individual maintained the momentum by getting me an appointment within a week for a barium swallow and an X-ray. All of this was faintly alarming, and I pressed for an explanation. The possibilities were, I was told, two-fold: first, but less likely, was cancer; the second was *pharyngeal* pouches – a sort of 'Hamster Syndrome' – in the side of the throat, a not-too-uncommon phenomenon, I was told, especially for singers, and one which could often lead to problems of the kind I was experiencing. It was the cancer possibility which was causing the alarm.

The spectre of cancer definitely focuses the mind, so while we were waiting for my X-ray appointment we sat down to review what we were doing and actually try to define where we wanted to go with the rest of our lives. We had met ten years earlier as fellow distributors for an American network marketing company, when I had been divorced for four years and Susan was on her way out of her second marriage. By then my children were grown-up and living elsewhere, as were Susan's eldest, but her youngest were respectively eight and nine and very much with her; and while my children were independent of me I did have an aunt in her eighties who, although cared for in a physical sense in a rest home, had no other relative beside myself who took an interest in her, let alone visited her. So we were neither of us in a position to do anything radical.

After we had decided that we would quite like to go through the rest of our lives with each other rather than without, we had to resolve whether to remain in network marketing or to try something new by way of generating an income. The latter won by a short head and we set up in business for ourselves in a service industry franchise. Unfortunately this was at the end of the 1980s, a time when the economy of the United Kingdom went into deep recession, and our business mirrored it precisely; we were lucky to salvage anything from the wreckage.

Our next venture took us to Bournemouth where, with the help of our friendly high street bank, we bought an ex-guest house, with the aim of using it both as our home and as a source of income. Here Fate relented. Unbeknown to us, Bournemouth has an abundance of English Language schools, and when we approached them with offers of accommodation for their students, we were overwhelmed. So for two years we had a procession of guests from places as far apart as Siberia, Argentina, Okinawa and Quebec, and great fun they were too.

It took me a while of observing this tapestry of cultures passing through the house to make the elementary deduction that if our guests were in England to learn English, then someone must be teaching them. And if someone, why not me, an idea made more pressing by the fact that our income from simply boarding students was not quite enough to live on and meet the demands of the bank. So, at the ripe old age of sixty, I set out to obtain the necessary qualifications (quite the hardest work I had done for years) and, having done so, spent the next three years teaching at a number of language schools in and around Bournemouth, and at home.

This was fun, and I enjoyed it immensely, but it was also extremely hard work, and although it generated the necessary income it wasn't actually going anywhere. I had entered the profession too late and was too old to have any future beyond being simply a class-room teacher and this, while thoroughly satisfying, was a job more suited to a younger person, so when the throat problem crystallised as it did, the idea that a change of direction and perhaps even a change of pace might be beneficial now fell onto rather more receptive soil.

Had it been cancer there would have been, of course, limited choices. But if not, then we felt that, given our respective ages, we had perhaps reached our last chance to do what we wanted, instead of being driven by circumstances, and that if we didn't make the right choice now, we would be condemned for evermore to 'second best'. We were helped by the fact that by now the last of Susan's offspring had just left home to pursue her own version of fame and fortune (mercifully totally unaware of the turmoil we were in following my GP's pronouncement), and my aunt had moved on to another dimension, so we were blessed with a rare opportunity to reconsider our options while time was still on our side.

I know it must seem selfish to some for a mother to desert her children for other shores but I had been looking after children –

helping my own mother with foster children, then as a mother's help and finally my own – for more years than I cared to think about. It felt as though all I had ever done was care for children, and that life – and the world – had passed me by. Now, it seemed I was free at last, with a man I loved and who loved me. Suddenly a veil was lifted and there was more to life than child-rearing, so why not go for it and see what was out there!

So, what *did* we want to do? Well, we still had to generate an income, so figuratively lying on the beach was out, and besides, the Puritan Ethic was too deeply ingrained for that – temperamentally, we would have to remain 'productive', whatever that might mean in a new context. Equally, we wanted to escape, if we could, the treadmill of everlastingly owing the bank, which seemed to have governed our lives since we had met, and actually have time to enjoy each other's company. So, putting these two together, we needed to go on working, preferably together and probably for ourselves since we had both been self-employed for longer than we had been together and we were by now likely to be temperamentally unemployable by anyone else, irrespective of considerations of age, but to try to achieve a certain quality of life, before it became too late.

One thing we had in common from our respective backgrounds was that, as children, we had both been brought up on farms. As a result of my childhood experiences, I had always said that the last thing I would ever want to be would be a farmer, but time has a habit of making one eat one's earlier words, and as we discussed the options open to us, the notion of going back to a farming way of life began to gather momentum.

My father had been a wheelwright carpenter when alive, so dolls and girlish things were not for me in my early years: I had enjoyed the fun of learning to sharpen what are now considered antique tools and watch my father make things out of wood by hand. By the age of ten I was quite a good chippy according to Dad . . . but then he was biased. As a child I had rabbits, chickens, ducks and white and harlequin mice along with a dog and cat. The farm he worked on was my playground (when I could evade looking after a foster baby or some other task Mother might try giving me to keep me out of harm's way), miles of it.

10

I have never forgotten getting up before school to walk over to the old stables to bottle-feed the orphan lambs and or to take the weaker ones into Mum to live by our Rayburn. I can remember getting wet, cold and generally miserable owing to the English weather, so this held me back, too, from the idea of going into 'farming'.

If we did turn to farming, it was clear that it couldn't be large-scale commercial farming as understood in Britain today; we had neither the resources nor the energy to undertake that, and it definitely wouldn't be an escape from the treadmill. What we began to realise we wanted was a smallholding, somewhere where we could be partly self-sufficient yet also where we could produce enough on top for a little 'jam' when we wanted it.

Looking back on it now, it amazes us that two reasonably intelligent, relatively mature people could seriously consider this to be a realistic possibility in Britain today. It's everyone's dream, isn't it: out of the rat race, out of debt, back to nature, doing your own thing? The BBC made one of its most successful sitcoms ever out of the idea; attracting some of the best acting talent around, and proved beyond doubt that everyone harbours the dream of being like 'Tom' and 'Barbara'. But that's all it is: a dream. It isn't something you seriously consider doing. It's just as well we never realised that, or we might never have started!

However 'where ignorance is bliss, 'Tis folly to be wise' as Thomas Gray so shrewdly observed, and we set about researching the possibilities of smallholdings both in Susan's native Dorset and further afield – and came up all-standing on the matter of cost. There was no way we could begin to afford what we had in mind, unless the place were so remote and run-down and lacking in facilities that it would require a fortune spent on it to bring it up to 'acceptable' standards – which brought us back full circle to money.

There was also the matter of climate. All the smallholdings which we might have been able to afford were in bleak and desolate areas. Now, while we have the deepest admiration for that redoubtable lady, Hannah Hauxwell, we couldn't see ourselves following her footsteps: we were altogether too soft for that! So with no possibility of affording a smallholding in the UK, Susan tentatively suggested we turn our attention abroad, and if we had to leave England then, as she succinctly put it, *'better to be hot and dry than cold and wet'*, as this would involve less expenditure on heating and clothes, as well as generally being more agreeable.

I had been worrying about how to 'sell' Toby on the idea on living abroad. Although I had done my homework and was convinced that it was the best option for us, I knew that I would have to broach the subject with extreme caution: when Toby is presented with a radical idea too suddenly, he tends to react like a startled rhino; one can easily find oneself being trampled underfoot! The risk had to be taken, though; left any later, it was likely that neither of us would have the energy to undertake such an enterprise and, worse, we could even face the spectre of age making it impossible, for one reason or another. So I went along with the research into buying a smallholding in Britain less in the expectation of success than in the hope that the answer would be a lemon - and, Bingo, it was!

For me at least, the notion of living abroad took a bit of getting used to, and at first I balked at it. Although I had spent many years working abroad England, for all its faults, had always been 'home', and the idea of forsaking its shores for somewhere else was deeply unsettling. However as the days passed and the numbers simply didn't add up I found myself having to give it serious consideration. So now the question was, if we did leave Britain, precisely where would we go? We both agreed that wherever we settled should be within sufficiently easy reach of England for our children to visit us, and for us to be able to get back to see them, so going seriously far afield was 'out'. Equally, with the European Union having virtually removed the frontiers between its member States, there were significant attractions to staying in Europe. And here Susan, who should have been a chess player, used her knowledge of my past to take me on to the next stage of her stratagem.

Shortly after the end of the Second World War I had been sent as a boy to stay with two wonderful French families in Normandy and the Gironde respectively, when, despite my extreme immaturity and inhibition at speaking French, I had absorbed certain indelible and highly favourable impressions about France and the French. Later I had become a Military

Interpreter in French, so France had clear attractions, if only that language would be less of a problem there than elsewhere. And besides, the French play rugby football, a game deeply imbedded in my psyche from the thirty-odd years I played and refereed it, and anyway they are splendidly cussed and xenophobic - just like the English - so much so that I am a committed Francophile.

So France was an obvious first choice as a future home. We got magazines and brochures, attended property exhibitions and bought books, and otherwise did vast amounts of homework, and found any number of wonderful properties at amazing prices. However among the 'small print' in our researches we stumbled upon a major snag so far as we were concerned, one which was carefully not emphasised by those engaged in the sale of properties in France: this was the total inflexibility of French laws where inheritance is concerned. These, as they were interpreted to us, give absolute priority to the interests of children over those of the surviving spouse when it comes to the disposal of property after a death.

It may seem strange that inheritance considerations should have formed an over-riding factor in disqualifying France for us, bearing in mind that we had virtually nothing to leave to anyone, but our circumstances were peculiar, albeit not unusual these days. Between us, we have seven children, all from previous marriages. Given the provisions of the French laws, this was likely to have serious consequences for the survivor from whichever one of us died first, should any of those offspring decide to exercise their perfectly legitimate legal rights: it was not inconceivable that whoever was left behind could find him or herself homeless. Besides, from past experience we knew that there is nothing like the possibility of financial benefit following a death in the family to cause acrimony which can last for generations, and this we were determined to avoid at all costs, and in any event we would certainly have difficulty in disposing our meagre estate in the way which we wished, which was something we felt very keenly we wanted to do.

Try as we might - and we consulted at length three expatriate British families living in France and two British solicitors experienced in French law - we could find no way round this barrier, so reluctantly we abandoned our researches and turned our attention to Spain instead, it being the next nearest, largely hot European country, to see what its inheritance laws had to say. Here we found, to our great relief, that while they have similar provisions to those of France, the Spanish authorities make one major concession: if you are a foreign national living in Spain, then you may, at their absolute discretion, dispose of your estate there in accordance with the laws of your country of origin, provided that you make a Will in Spain to this effect.

This was altogether a more attractive proposition, and since Spain also appeared to have the edge over most of the rest of Europe in the matter of cost of living, we began to focus our researches there (which had been Susan's intention all along).

At this point, readers may be forgiven for asking themselves, why hadn't we considered Spain in the first place? Well, for one thing, neither of us spoke a word of Spanish, and learning a new language at an advanced age does present its challenges. For another, the hot part of Spain is a lot further away from the UK than the hot part of France, making it a little less easy for relatives to visit us and for us to return to see them. But most of all, I was 'sales-resistant' to Spain thanks to certain television programmes in the UK. These had relentlessly portrayed Spain to mean all-night 'rave' bars and wet T-shirt competitions, swank hotels and 'boozeramas', crowded beaches and high-rise blocks in tourist resorts like Benidorm and Marbella, which might have their appeal in certain circumstances but were definitely not what we had in mind for somewhere to live.

Now, of course, Spain is all of this, plus *tapas* bars, flamenco, bullfights and sherry, just as England is fish and chips, Morris dancing, fox-hunting (until Mr Blair outlaws this piece of English culture), beer from the wood (and the European Union outlaws this one), Brighton and Blackpool. But like England, Spain is also over a thousand years of history. It is the might of the Spanish empire in the sixteenth century, when Spain was the premier Catholic power in the world and England a third-rate Protestant one, and the *tercio* was the most feared military formation in Christendom. It is the *conquistadors* and the spread of the Spanish language to most of the New World. It is artists like Velásquez and Picasso, writers like Cervantes, musicians like Segovia and Carrerras, and sportsmen like Ballesteros.

But somehow, while we all know a bit about and acknowledge the validity of French history and culture, probably because France is so inextricably linked historically to Britain, we seem to know relatively little of Spain's (and what we do know we generally denigrate) possibly because, throughout history, Catholic Spain and Protestant Britain have been on opposite sides, and there is nothing like rivalry or enmity or religious prejudice to cloud historical judgement. Look at our respective views on Sir Francis Drake.

However at this stage all this was academic. What mattered first was, what exactly was wrong with me, since if it was cancer, all this planning could be so much wasted effort. The day for my x-ray duly came, and with considerable trepidation I set off for the hospital. After waiting what seemed an eternity, my turn finally came. I had my barium swallow, and stood in front of the x-ray machine (ironically manufactured by the same engineering company whose engineers I was teaching when I had my last public manifestation of the problem). There was then an agonising few minutes wait, until the specialist called me over.

'The problem lies here,' he said, pointing to the screen, 'in these pouches on either side of your throat. They will need to be dealt with in due course, but they are not life-threatening in themselves, and you will no doubt be glad to know,' he added, looking me straight in the face 'that THAT IS ALL THAT IS WRONG.' Well, yes, you could say that; you could also say that I virtually leapt in the air with relief.

Oh the relief: to know it was something not life-threatening was well beyond me for words! No big C hiding in the corner any more waiting to grab us. What to do, what to do? Well, one thing for sure was do something; I wasn't going to wait for the vacuum to be filled by other things, so I started the ball rolling by letting my children know that all was under control but that changes were in the air and that we might be selling up and going to live abroad.

I was reassured with their respective reactions. They have never been overly surprised at their mum's various enterprises, and they seemed to regard this as just another one to be watched with interest – at least I hope that's what it was! However with the relief also came the knowledge that now Toby didn't have the worry of 'have I, haven't

15

*I?'; he would be worrying instead about 'should I, shouldn't I?'
I knew I couldn't win either way but at least life wasn't going to be
dull!*

Back at home, after a suitably joyous celebration, we now had to resolve the question, what were we going to do next? *(What did I say!)* We had talked about it long enough, but were we now going to take action, which was a very different matter? Were we really serious about our decision to go to Spain? If so, how would we go about it? Would we first take a holiday, see if we liked it there, and then make a decision? If so, how long would we take, and what would we do with our home in Bournemouth in the meantime, where we still had a mortgage to pay? Would we let it, if the bank would allow us to, to generate the necessary income, or would we burn our bridges, and go as if we were never coming back?

This was all a bit heavy, and as we churned the matter round, Susan enthusiastically, me dragging my heels, it became irrefutably clear that we had reached 'make up your mind' time: a 'decision gate' in computer-speak. Now, when most of us are faced with a decision which will have far-reaching, possibly permanent unknown consequences, there is often a 'let-out' clause that allows us to slide away from the moment of truth: a 'what about granny' syndrome. Unfortunately for me, we had none.

We had no inescapable commitments or responsibilities to others, and no compelling social life or membership of clubs or societies to anchor us down. So far as our children were concerned, we had always taken the view that the purpose of a fledgling is to fledge, and that of its parents is to help it do so (you don't see too many parent birds pulling their offspring back into the nest), and since none of our children was now physically dependent on us, we could, if we chose, take this route. It was then that Susan looked me in the eye, took a deep breath and said, *'Why don't we sell up and bugger off?'*

The look on Toby's face when I said this was one of total panic, and his immediate response was, 'What will I do if we do?' Although this was, on the face of it, just a little self-centred, it was entirely understandable, given his background: if the shoe was on the other foot, I would probably have said the same. In fact, I am sure I would because, looking back, I knew it was coming. 'What do you want to do?' I countered. 'What do you mean, what do I want to do?' he replied. I could see this going on all evening, so I tried to force the issue. Toby has a splendid lapel button which someone once gave him, which says, 'Enjoy life, this is not a rehearsal,' so I said, 'You've spent all your life doing things because of other people, some of them enjoyable, many not; isn't it time you did things which you enjoy, for yourself?'

That threw me. I hadn't actually thought of doing, for a living, things which I thought I might enjoy ever since I gave up the idea of being an engine driver at the age of twelve. When I was at school - well, certainly the boarding school I was at - there was no such thing as 'Career Counselling'; you were just supposed to know what you intended to do, by a sort of osmosis. My parents were absolutely no help having, between them, an entire library of prejudices about what one should or should not do to earn one's daily crust. Besides, in those days there was National Service to be done which, for me, meant I could postpone any decision until after that. So, having spent the first few months after leaving school bumming round London with my trombone in the respectful wake of a certain Mr Chris Barber I marched, to my parents' absolute horror - all that expensive education gone to waste - into an Army recruiting office and signed on for three years as a regular Gunner, on the simple philosophy that if I had to do two years' National Service, I might as well commit to a third year and get paid more for doing so; I had nothing better to do, and it would postpone the need for a decision for a bit longer.

Luckily for my parents I was plucked from Basic Training fairly early on and sent on my way for officer training whence, two years later, I was commissioned into Her Majesty's Royal Artillery. On finding to my surprise that I really quite liked the life and that I was moderately good at it, there I stayed for twenty-five years. This wasn't quite as directionless as it sounds. It was simply that my temperament dictates that I should settle down and do what I have to do as well as I can do it until either a more attractive alternative presents itself or my present employment proves unendurable, on the basis that, having made a commitment, then the least I can do is to give it my best shot, and this seemed to satisfy my employers enough to continue to promote me.

Because what I had to do at first was work directly with the soldiers and NCOs I was privileged to command, I enjoyed Army life enormously, but inevitably, as the years went by and I advanced up the promotion ladder, politics, in their broadest sense, entered the equation, and some of these I found difficult to accommodate. So, twenty-five years to the day after I had joined I left, with a wealth of totally irrelevant experience behind me and still no nearer discovering what I actually wanted to do with my life, but now with the added factors of a wife, two children and a mortgage which meant there was no time to give any thought to it at that moment; what I had to do, immediately, was to earn a living, and this was what I was still doing, ten years, a divorce and an awful lot of mental and emotional 'luggage' later, when I met Susan.

By this time I had tried a whole raft-full of ways to put bread, and sometimes even jam, on the table. Some had been dismal failures, some remarkably successful, considering they never fully matched either my temperament or my goals. It was in one of the more successful enterprises that I had met Susan, when I was still no nearer knowing where I should be headed. So Susan's suggestion that I should do things which I enjoyed doing, for myself, wasn't too helpful.

By now I had developed the philosophy that I had better ensure that I enjoyed whatever I was doing until or unless this proved impossible. This is not quite the same thing as doing what you enjoy, and is the exact opposite of George Bernard Shaw's exhortation - an exhortation which is all very well if you have relevant talents, as were possessed by the great man, which can be developed to a sufficient extent to permit you to earn a living from them. It is not much help when your talents for the things which you enjoy are modest in the extreme, and when the things themselves do not, or did not then, lend themselves to commercial exploitation.

There were, to be sure, things I had enjoyed doing in the past for their own sake, but these were either connected with the 'luggage' which I was trying to lose, or were unrealistic as a means of earning a living for any number of reasons. In any event I had at last come to realise that what I enjoyed doing was more related to the person or people I was doing it with than with the activity itself, and first among these now was the person who had suggested we 'sell up and bugger off'. So, having no better idea myself, and with our lives together stagnating largely due to financial circumstances which were entirely of my making, and with our lack of meaningful prospects and the dread spectre of 'retirement' relentlessly looming ever nearer I took a deep breath and agreed to go.

I could understand some of Toby's reluctance to come to a decision but couldn't see any reason not to 'do a runner'. He was nearing bus-pass age and already had a work-related pension that we could live on adequately if not exactly luxuriously until we found our home in Spain. Was it just nerves or was it the workaholic in him that refused to lie down which was holding him back?

When Toby first joined the Army I, being nearly fifteen years younger than him, wasn't even in Primary School! After that, while he was enjoying himself in Germany and elsewhere, I was enjoying the delights of Secondary Modern school and a premature marriage. My mother suffered from a dislike of me, to put it mildly, probably due to losing her sons, eight boys in all, either through miscarriages or at full term, so it was hardly surprising, with me being the only surviving child and a girl to boot, that we did not get on. I wanted to be a hairdresser on leaving school but in 1966 you had to pay a premium to be trained to become one and Mum wanted money coming in to pay for my keep, so Woolworths got the greenhorn, on the make-up counter.

After that it was on to be a mother's help and nanny until at the stupid age of eighteen I married my first husband, which seemed to be the best way out of a bad situation. Looking back, it really was a good idea at the time but now with hindsight, nuts. Unsurprisingly this marriage failed and I married someone else on the rebound, so for twenty-five years I was involved pretty much full-time in baby production and child-rearing, and the need to work the other hours of the day to supplement our income(s). Now, after five children and two failed marriages, having found the right man and with a happy marriage for the very first time in my life, I could be a rebel at last and as my husband was coming round to the idea of revolting with me, it was the chance of a lifetime to capitalise on it.

Chapter 2

Live the journey.
(Eternian motto, *Masters of the Universe*)

We made the ferry with just ten minutes to spare. We had decided, after much debate and many sleepless nights, that we would, indeed, sell up and bugger off; that we would sell the house, put the proceeds in the bank to earn a little interest, put our belongings into store for an indefinite period and simply drive south, trusting in fate and the Duchess to get us to wherever we were going more or less in one piece.

This plan – or rather, lack of one – appalled a delightful Yorkshirewoman we met in the hotel we stayed in when we first arrived in Andalucía. 'What if something had gone wrong?' she asked in horrified tones. Well, it hadn't, had it and besides, what actually could go wrong – apart from breaking down, highway robbery, having an accident or one or even both of us being taken to hospital with unwashed underwear, all things which she then flung at us in the manner fluently described by Ms Maureen Lipmann in her books as being characteristic of her mother.

'But what about the risk?' she persisted.

'What risk?' I countered.

'Well,' she specified, 'what if you don't like it here?'

'We have a car, we can go somewhere else,' I replied.

She sat back, temporarily stumped but still far from convinced and I suppose, to be fair, she had a right to be. Here we were, two apparently sane, middle-aged and middle-class people, who had suddenly up-sticks and left hearth, home, job(s) and loved-ones to seek some will-o-the-wisp dream of a new home in a country where we couldn't even talk to people!

'Doesn't it worry you at all?' she finally challenged me.

Well, yes, it did, but I certainly wasn't going to admit that to her, so 'No,' I replied, 'not a bit. It's an adventure.'

And then it struck me. It really was an adventure, an adventure of our own making, not a very great adventure but an adventure all the same, something which had been there when we had started our lives together but which had become overlaid as the years had passed and drudgery of making a living had taken over.

Now, this is the lot of most of us and why, you may reasonably ask, should we expect anything different? Doesn't life begin as a time of infinite possibility? Don't all relationships start as an adventure, and don't both life and relationships flicker, dim and sometimes snuff out altogether as the dead hand of reality extinguishes the dream with the passing of the years? Why should anyone, especially when middle-aged and with parental responsibilities, presume to buck the system? Well, anyone who is an incurable romantic, that's who.

'There's got to be something better than this for me,' sang Kevin Bishop as Jim Hawkins in the movie 'Muppet Treasure Island' (and it should tell you something about us both that we, as adults, still even watch this movie, let alone quote from it!). One of the things which attracted us to each other was an innate, perhaps foolish, optimism, the conviction that if you fire enough buckshot, you are bound to hit the right target some day and that this target is right around the corner. We both expected life to be an adventure, and so it had proved to be after we had got together and started up in business for ourselves, until the accumulating challenges finally overwhelmed us and circumstances forced us to settle for something, anything, to take us through each day and keep our heads financially above water.

And here was the crux: for whatever reason, we had gradually abandoned the entrepreneurial approach to earning a living which had brought us together and, although we remained technically self-employed, we had slowly but surely mentally become 'employed'. Worse, for me at least, was a vigorously suppressed, escalating panic: the realisation that I had conspicuously failed to achieve anything significant with my life, something I had been brought up to believe I ought to do. That I had not done so was undoubtedly due in part – besides a mediocrity of talents – to my singular lack of direction: the movers and shakers of this world know exactly where they are going and what they want to achieve, and pursue them both with single-minded determination. I had none of this, and I was now beginning to suspect that I never would. The ambitions I had assumed in my military career had been insufficient to take me to high office, and the goals which had supplanted them in my business life had largely been imposed by those in control of the parent companies which I served.

Now all too many years had passed, and I was still no nearer the expectations with which I had been brought up, nor to the vague dreams which had accompanied them. More to the point, I was beginning to realise that, at a ridiculously advanced age, I would have to totally redefine my goals if I was to achieve any lasting satisfaction from life, and time was not on my side. At the same time, the adolescent optimism with which we are both cursed was clearly still alive. Unconsciously I, as well as Susan, had been seeking a way to restart the engine and 'do our own thing' again and this, without my realising it until I was confronted with it, was what we had now achieved. The stagnation of recent years was gone. We had burnt our bridges and were off again. Life was once more an adventure.

Mind you, the experiences of the previous three months nearly had us crashing on take-off. We had had the usual yes-you've-sold-it-no-you-haven't routine which seems to be an inescapable feature of buying and selling houses in England and Wales (how is it that the Scots seem to be able to organise conveyancing so much better from the point of view of the actual participants?), and when the contract was finally signed it gave us less than a fortnight in which to vacate the premises. This is little enough time under normal circumstances, but our circumstances were far from normal. We weren't buying another house in Britain. We weren't buying another house at all. We were putting everything we owned into store with our removal company, Union Jack and were setting off to find a new home in Spain, which meant that getting out of our house was a good deal more complicated than usual.

For one thing, everything had to be packed on the presumption that it would be shipped abroad in due course. This in turn meant that we, personally, couldn't pack any of it, no matter how experienced as packers we might be (and which I was); it had to be packed by the Union Jack, to comply with the requirements of their insurers. In our case they needed four days for this, with a week's notice beforehand!

For another, it meant that we had to have a crystal ball about what we would need to withhold from store and take with us to sustain us for an indefinite period of reconnaissance, living in unforeseeable conditions and with unpredictable weather. The result was that, on the day for the completion of the sale of our house, we were to be found still trying to load the Duchess with everything we felt we might need to meet any situation which fate might fling at us over the next few months, while the packers tried to jam the last of our belongings into a Tardis-like removals lorry, watched with increasing astonishment by the new owner who was vainly trying to get her belongings in!

Well, crunch time. My children couldn't quite believe Mum was about to bugger off. Teenagers with no commitments take a year off but mothers? That appears to be a whole different ball game. Toby and I had watched with great interest a TV programme about the 'Grey Nomads' in Australia: sane couples and even single ladies in their early sixties selling up, buying a motor home and leaving family to go 'Walk about' (or in their cases, 'Drive About'). If it was really that simple we should at least have fun even if at the end of it all we find ourselves creeping back to the UK. Think what we will have seen.

We were over an hour late leaving, and having stopped of necessity to fill the Duchess's tanks - she was a very thirsty lady* - were the last car onto the Portsmouth ferry. We were booked for the night at a B&B owned by a British couple at a village near Falaise, but with an eight hour crossing behind us, it was nearly 11 p.m. by the time we arrived. This fazed our hosts not at all; they made us incredibly welcome, and it was well into the early hours of the morning by the time we made our way to bed. There, because it was extremely cold, we filled a hot water bottle from a tap in the bathroom. This promptly burst, necessitating the rapid deployment of sundry towels before we could settle down on some exceedingly damp sheets. Luckily we were so tired it really didn't make much difference, and it was all dry by the morning.

We had intended to leave promptly at 9 the following morning, but in fact it was 9 o'clock before we staggered down to breakfast. This put our hosts out a bit, as they had hoped to go early to the market, but they were very good about it, and they cheerily waved us farewell (at least, I think that's what they were doing) at just gone 10.00 a.m. After that, with both the Duchess and ourselves fully refreshed, we made excellent time on a cold but bright sunny day along the outstanding French roads, wonderfully empty after England, past Alençon, Le Mans, Tours and Poitiers to Angoulême and on to Barbezieux, where we decided to spend the night.

We checked into the only hotel which appeared to be open, despite the fact that Barbezieux is the principle town on the N 10/E 606 between Angoulême and the outskirts of Bordeaux, and went for a walk in rapidly dropping temperature to stretch our limbs before enjoying a taste of southern French cuisine for dinner. Or so we hoped. We were out of luck. Barbezieux was shut for Christmas. When I asked in the hotel where it would be possible to eat - it was clear from the lack of activity in the *salle à*

* Our decision to use the Duchess as an extremely comfortable, if somewhat unusual, removals lorry had been forced upon us, yet again, by our impeccable timing. We had bought her only two years previously for her then market value, but a year later the European Union, aided and abetted by Mr John Prescott, the Deputy Prime Minister of Great Britain (who has two modern cars of the same marque), outlawed leaded petrol, which the Duchess was designed to use. As a result, despite her unquestionable quality and intrinsic class, we couldn't even give her away, much less sell her, so a removals lorry she became, and outstandingly successful she proved to be.

manger that we could wait for eternity there before being fed – the duty manager gave a magnificent Gallic shrug and pointing down the street along with the verbal equivalent of a sneer, replied *'Lundi soir? Peut-être là.'*

'Là' was a Mexican restaurant, which did indeed prove to be open, and we pushed our way thankfully into the warmth past a friendly dog which greeted us hospitably at the door. It was only after we had sat down, and were studying the menu written, as always, on a black-board in totally indecipherable handwriting, that I noticed the sign, *'Attention au chien!'* By way of exercising my French I said to the *patron*, who was hovering to take our order, *'Il est dangereux, votre chien?'* 'Non,' he replied, *'il fait le pi-pi.'* There's not much you can say after that except to order dinner, or leave. We ordered dinner.

The *patron* also distinguished himself by conforming absolutely to stereotype: he cooked our excellent meal wearing a black woolly hat and smoking throughout. So Barbezieux redeemed itself after all, especially when three women came in, *chic* by French provincial standards, obviously either regular *habituées* or connected in some way with the establishment, and proceeded to look us over as though we had crawled out from under a stone. It is good that some things never change; it would have been so disappointing if they had actually been polite. As it was, Barbezieux reassured us that while *service* originated as a French word, its practice remains something of a rarity in its country of origin.

The next day we pressed on through the seemingly endless miles of pine forests of the *Parc Régional des Landes de Gascogne*, past the rugby football 'meccas' of Dax, Bayonne and Biarritz and across the border into Spain. After lunch in a motorway service area, where we tried vainly to get our tongues round the complexities of Basque nouns, we pressed on to Burgos, a Spanish equivalent of Coventry, where we decided to spend the night. This was an experience that will remain with us forever.

The hotel we (Susan) chose, at the end of a long, dry, dusty afternoon, was a mock castle on the southern outskirts of the town. I knew we had made a mistake when a man uniformed like a banana republic general came to park the car. However we were committed by then and besides, we had driven enough for one day. The hotel was dark, brooding and Hollywood-baronial, and our room was no different. In fact our room was not a room, it was a suite, with a small sitting room with French windows leading out onto a lawn, as well as the usual other facilities. However even the latter were slightly surprising; I mean, it's not every suite that has a full-sized clear window between the bedroom and the bathroom, nor where the bathroom contains a white, towelling-covered corner settee, too large to sit on and too small to lie on. Naturally, being British, we had no idea what it was for!

After we had bathed, changed, and experimented with the settee, we went down to explore the bar and the dining room. The former was unexceptional, being full of Solihull-businessmen clones complete with their 'secretaries', but it did have one feature which redeemed the hotel in our eyes: this was a small, terrified mouse, which appeared from under a radiator. We pointed it out to the children of a Spanish couple sitting at the next table, and their cries of '*un ratón, un ratón*' at the tops of their voices were most satisfying . . . and we learnt our first new Spanish word.

Dinner was great and, considering the pretensions of the hotel, not over-priced, but the rest of the night was a disaster. The air-conditioning system in our room moaned rhythmically like the Beachy Head foghorn and, as we discovered when a couple occupied the room above ours at 1.30 a.m., the ceiling was wafer-thin. We could hear everything – and I do mean everything – they did, from then until they finally settled down at around 3.00 a.m.

The reason for the stop at the only hotel we had seen or were about to pass was quite simple: before leaving England the Duchess had gone into the local garage which had cared for her for most of her life for a complete service and any necessary work to meet the rigours of the journey, including crossing the Pyrenees in December. The problem was that the garage had taken the heater to pieces to fix a fan and forgotten to put the lower air tubes back on, something we did not discover until we were well on our way. On a long drive we were warm from the hips up but below that, Siberia. We stopped because I could no longer feel my feet! The memories of the hotel are with me still. Toby sat in the bath and I took a photo of him through the picture window from the bedroom; now that's something you don't see every day.

We left before breakfast, much to the dismay of the girls on reception, paying off with our bill a large slice of the Spanish national debt, and made our way south. Getting round Madrid on the orbital motor-way was just like the M25, only hotter. However when we eventually got through the continuous traffic jams and found our way onto the ruler-straight *Autovia del Andalucía* we knew that we were definitely on the last leg of the journey.

We drove past Toledo, across the vast and still brown plains of *La Mancha*, through Jaén Province, on to Granada and down through the foothills of the *Sierra Nevada*. The scenery was spectacular, the driving rewarding and the Duchess loved it, treating the gradients as if they simply weren't there and eating up the miles effortlessly. We made such good time that we were into Málaga Province by late afternoon, and having turned south on the N331 before Antequera, arrived at our hotel outside Colmenar as darkness began to fall, one day earlier than planned.

Drivers beware, not of the traffic, nor of road works, nor of the weather; beware of roads that aren't on the map! We had been given directions to find our hotel but they failed to tell us that there were two other exits from the motorway directing us to Colmenar before the one we should have taken. We took the first turning – naturally – onto the 'old' A-356. This seemed logical, especially as it conformed to our map. We didn't know of the existence of the 'new' A-356, which leaves the autovia *two junctions further on. We didn't know of its existence because it didn't appear on our touring map, despite having been built a good five years earlier.*

In any event we paid for our mistake. As we turned onto this road, two things became immediately apparent: first, that the road was extremely narrow and had a singular lack of passing places; and secondly, that the surface presented a gloriously tapestry of diverse textures and colours in the repairs which had been done to it over the years, a wonderful assortment of unmarked potholes of varying depths and a surface of gravel, rock and even bare earth where the tarmac had worn through altogether.

The road was so bad the car bonnet popped up several times, which meant having to stop in the gathering gloom for me to leap out and bang it shut. It was as well, coming at the end of 1,500 miles of driving, that the Duchess's headlights were as good as they were, otherwise we could easily have become a semi-permanent feature of the local landscape. It took us nearly half an hour to cover the five miles to Colmenar. It also meant we came into the town from the wrong direction, but with the help of the local and very friendly farmacia we found the hotel after the second attempt.

We had chosen Colmenar as the base for our search because of its location. Once we had finally decided that we would come to Spain, we had debated endlessly about where to start looking. Spain is a huge country, with a very varied climate. Although predominately a Mediterranean country, its sheer size means that central Spain, which lies well above sea level and is largely separated from the coastal regions by mountains, is blisteringly hot in summer and can be bitterly cold in winter, while in the extreme north-west Galicia is not unlike Norway but with a Cornish climate and Asturias is positively Swiss, and in the south-east Murcia is a semi-desert. Even the various *Costas* have considerable differences. How would we know where to begin? We could spend literally years looking, if we weren't careful.

As with France, we had sent for all the literature we could get – surprisingly little, by comparison – and finally settled on the Málaga and Granada Provinces of Andalucía as the area most likely to suit us, a decision based largely on their topography and reputed climate. There was also the small matter of language. With my Spanish confined to *'buenas dias'* and *'gracias'*, and Susan's even less, we realised that we would need English-speaking assistance for all sorts of situations in the early stages of our lives in Spain (assuming that we stayed there), of which finding and buying a home was likely to be the most immediate, and this assistance we knew would certainly be available on the *Costa del Sol*. So we wrote to all the agencies we could find in the available literature, and it was one of them which had suggested we come to Colmenar.

Of course, arriving when we did meant that, instead of looking at properties, our first experience of Spain would be an Andalucían Christmas. This, we discovered, is quite a different affair from the commercial bean-feast we have become accustomed to in Britain.

As a party, it is a non-event; as a religious festival, commemorating the birth of Jesus of Nazareth, it is entirely appropriate. There is no Santa Claus, no stockings are hung on Christmas Eve and there is no Christmas tree. With consummate logic, present-giving is kept until Epiphany or Twelfth Night - 'Three Kings Day' - when the Wise Men reputedly arrived in Bethlehem with gifts for the infant Jesus. Although Christmas Day is a public holiday, this is largely devoted by Spaniards to attending mass and to celebrating the birth of Jesus of Nazareth with a feast at home, or by families eating out together.

We learned this when we were told by the hotel's proprietor that the dining room had been fully booked for lunchtime, and that while we would of course be looked after, we might feel a bit 'left out'. This nod being as good to us as the proverbial wink to a blind horse, we decided we would use the day to find out about the *Costa del Sol* - the area west of Málaga - and its immediate hinterland. So we set off to visit Coin, Mijas, Marbella, the Alhaurins, and all the resorts along the coast road back to Málaga. What we found confirmed our instinct: that although the attraction of these places was obvious, and evidenced by the huge number of expatriates who lived in them, they were unlikely to offer what we were looking for. However now that we were on the brink of beginning our search, we felt that the time had come to identify exactly why we felt this was so.

We had received a clue to this from our reaction to the advice given to us by the male half of an English couple we had spoken to briefly after dinner in *that* hotel in Burgos. 'Make sure,' he had said earnestly, 'that the infrastructure is in place.' We pondered this wisdom while listening to our air conditioning and the activities of the couple overhead and came to the conclusion that what he meant was that wherever we chose to live we should look for good roads with pavements, mains services, street lighting, postal delivery to the door, a lending library down the road, doctor's and dentist's surgeries close at hand and our favourite supermarket nearby. In other words, what we would expect in England.

Now these things are, of course, important, but the extent of that importance depends on your perspective. In England, they could be regarded as essential by many people - including us. But this was not England, it was Spain, and not just Spain, it was

Andalucía, and our gut feeling was that if we clung to our British priorities we could miss something vital from the experience of living in a foreign country. And that was the crux of it: we were about to *live* in a foreign country, not simply go there on holiday.

To us this meant facing the challenge of learning a new language if necessary, and of embracing the opportunity to learn about and share in the culture and way of life of the locals, so far as we were able. This was not in any sense to denigrate the priorities of those expatriates living in Spain who feel differently, and we were certainly not adopting a 'holier-than-thou' attitude. It was simply how we felt, and still feel, and we were reassured to find we were not alone when we later read an article in one of the English-language coastal newspapers, which referred to an amazing letter written to the paper by an expatriate Englishman who was extremely aggrieved that his French neighbour of fifteen years in an *urbanización* on the *Costa del Sol* still couldn't speak *English*! The idea that he and the Frenchman should properly communicate with each other in Spanish clearly hadn't occurred to him.

The writer of the article commented on the wonderful insularity of this outlook: that only the English could take a beautiful part of Spain, full of friendly Spanish-speaking people and turn it into that 'corner of a foreign field that is forever England', and where only the English could classify a native Spaniard living in their *urbanización* as a foreigner! Later we were to find this attitude reinforced in what, to my mind, was an astonishingly-worded advertisement in the same newspaper by the Gibraltar branch of a supermarket well-known in Britain. It read, 'Labels you can read...food you can eat.' To us, the implications in these words were truly disgraceful, so far as British expatriate residents in Spain were concerned.

We were extremely relieved to read the article, because it confirmed what we concluded on our drive back to Colmenar: that if we were to achieve what to us would be the true satisfaction of living in this superb country, never mind combining it with finding our dream property, we would almost certainly have to relinquish those priorities which our adviser had urged us to retain, and move beyond living in an expatriate community where the only differences from living in Britain would be the weather and the cost of living, and try to become part of the local Spanish community, so far as they would allow and our grasp of Spanish would permit.

Travelling the settled ex-pat areas was an experience. 'Bijou' villas with pools, gardens and garages, all fenced and padlocked. Country properties close to all amenities yet within only a short distance of the sea or with stupendous views of the mountains or the ocean or both. They were wonderful, they were glorious, they were all you could possibly wish for. They could also have been equally in Palm Beach, Florida, Amalfi in Italy or the Côte d'Azur and they weren't remotely what we were looking for.

Arriving back at the hotel in the late afternoon we found that the lunch guests had departed and the dining room set with a long table in the centre and a small one off to one side, near the fire. As we contemplated this arrangement, the *dueño* led in the hotel staff to enjoy their Christmas lunch together at the long table, and seated us and the other few residents at the side one. Seeing that this was clearly going to be a family affair, we wondered if we might be ignored. Not a bit of it. The *dueño* swept us all into the festivities, announcing 'lunch on the house' and pressing free glasses of *cava* onto us until it poured out of our ears (we could just see that happening to complete strangers at a hotel in England on Christmas Day!). After we had eaten ourselves to a standstill we exchanged toasts and mutual good wishes (without a word of English being spoken) and it would have been hard to find a better omen to reinforce our feelings about where and how we wanted to live.

Chapter 3

Without change, something sleeps inside us and never wakes.

(*Dune*)

With Christmas behind us, we embarked on house-hunting in earnest. We made appointments with those agencies which were prepared to see us, and with them we drove hundreds of kilometres each week, often re-negotiating tracks we had gone down a few days earlier, viewing an average of four properties a day. We saw houses that were like railway carriages, with connecting corridors between all the rooms; we saw 'bijoux' cottages, crumbling ruins, modern villas and splendid farms. But none were quite right, for one reason or another, and as the days went by and so did the number of disillusioned agents to whom we had entrusted ourselves and our dream, we began to wonder if we weren't asking altogether too much, and whether we were doomed to be a human *Marie Celeste*, endlessly roaming the 'seas' of Andalucía, or to be like some modern-day Arthurian knights seeking an increasingly unrealistic Grail, while our belongings rotted expensively in store.

However our forays in search of our dream, besides showing us an awful lot of Andalucía, brought a benefit for which there is often no substitute: 'time in the saddle'; they started us on a long learning curve about what was available in the *campo*, and a bewildering choice it was too, far beyond the range of possibilities available in the UK. Certainly, in the UK there are detached, semi-detached and terraced houses, bungalows and cottages, former vicarages and converted barns. All with or without garages, central heating and double-glazing. But generally speaking, it is rare nowadays to be offered a house there, even when euphemistically described as 'ripe for conversion', which has no mains electricity, water or drainage, let alone be in a condition which would have it instantly condemned by the authorities as unfit for livestock, never mind human habitation. This is far from the case in rural Spain.

We learned that we could, if we wished, simply buy a tract of land (a *parcela*) and take on the whole business of getting planning permission, arranging for the provision of mains water and electricity and sorting out the drains, matters which, in the UK at any rate, are nowadays generally undertaken by a developer, rather than by a prospective house owner him/herself. This idea is great as, of course, you can build your dream house from the ground up, without having to alter or renovate an existing structure, but there is a hidden trap: this is that each local authority has its own policy on what constitutes a sufficiently large plot of land on which to grant planning permission to build a house. In the *campo* this can be as high as six acres. So it is vital to have this piece of information to hand before you buy that idyllic *parcela*, or you could possibly be left with just that: an idyllic *parcela*. Of course, you can always picnic on it, but it could be an expensive way to secure your own barbecue site in southern Spain!

An alternative is to buy a ruin. This has a distinct advantage over a 'bare lot', since where there has been a ruin, you can generally build another house to your own design, without the need for planning permission. You do have to get a 'renovating building licence' before you can start, for which you have to submit the plans for your new house to the local authorities, and of course you still have to lay on water and electricity and sort out the drains, since it is highly unlikely that a ruin will have these facilities, so it is not all sweetness and light, but at least you can start rebuilding once you have secured title to the property and got the licence, which does save a lot of time.

From buying a ruin you can progress by infinitely variable stages via a small *casita* which has only been used by almond pickers as a temporary shelter from the heat of the Andalucían sun, and while possibly in good-ish repair will have no services connected, right the way up to a fully modernised working *finca* with umpteen hectares of productive land, a country villa with a swimming pool and satellite TV installed, or even your very own castle in Spain.

One of the last houses we looked at before we found our dream stood about a third of a way up this range, and since it encapsulated all of the characteristics which had been shared among the other houses we had seen, I recorded our impressions in detail.

'We'll park here and walk down,' said the agent, 'here' being a lay-by on an 's'-bend on the mountain road to Competa. This announcement intrigued us, since up to that point no track, however unpromising, seemed to have been too daunting for the agent. We were even more intrigued when the English vendor appeared at that moment, and parked her car in the lay-by too, announcing, brightly 'I always park here,' especially as we could see no sign of any track or driveway in the vicinity.

The agent and the vendor then walked to the rear of the lay-by, where the verge appeared to border a sheer drop to the valley below, and vanished. As we followed, in almost total silence and disbelief, we found ourselves at the top of an unmade track with a 1:4 gradient down to a house perched on a ledge at the bottom, about 100 metres away. We picked our way down this 'drive' with extreme care and arrived at the front door of a building which was, certainly to me, depressingly familiar.

When my father retired from the Navy at the end of World War II, he and my mother bought a farm in North Cornwall. The farm had a huge Dutch barn, a grain store and mill, a 'shippen', an implement shed and a cow shed, the last built on a slope, with thick, whitewashed walls, no electricity, doors tall enough for a cow but a bit of a challenge to my 6'5", an earth floor and a superfluity of ventilation. From the outside, the house we were now looking at was a dead ringer for that cowshed!

As we entered it I was struck forcibly, and literally, by the eucalyptus branch lintel over the front door. Once inside, and sufficiently recovered to look around me, I realised that what I had taken to be the hall was, in fact, the kitchen, the evidence being a two-ring electric hob perched on a ledge. But that was the only clue. There was no oven, sink, work surface or refrigerator, and no storage facilities unless you counted a few jars placed in recesses in the walls. Washing-up, we were told, was done at the cold tap outside, and the clean glass, cutlery and crockery was kept on a shelf in another recess in the wall, behind a curtain.

However if there was little to catch the eye on a horizontal plane, there was plenty above and below. The floor was of tiles, laid straight onto the earth. Over the years this had risen into great ridges and waves which flowed away like a petrified sea, and were an absolute death-trap to walk on. Above it there was no ceiling, just the underside of the roof: a row of roughly parallel, more or less evenly spaced, extremely bent eucalyptus tree trunks, mostly untrimmed, running from the top of the walls to the ridge pole above. These supported a mat of canes onto which the tiles had been directly laid using a mud-based mortar. In days gone by this was a widely adopted, cheap and simple way to roof a dwelling, using locally-available materials, and is extremely effective at keeping out the ferocious Andalucían sun. It is, however, less effective, as we were later to discover for ourselves, at keeping out an Andalucían rain storm, even when the mud-based mortar is replaced with cement.

Beyond the kitchen was the 'living room', an open space containing a sagging settee and little else. Beyond that again was a small bedroom, from the rafters of which the owner's clothes were suspended on hangers. Beyond, up a flight of 'interesting' steps was the main bedroom, containing an equally sagging double bed and a wardrobe. This bedroom was over a storeroom. When we subsequently inspected the storeroom, we noticed that three of the eucalyptus beams forming its ceiling were cracked, and recently, too, judging by the colour of the exposed wood; we imagined that this might have had something to do with the recent arrival of the vendor's partner from England, and we hoped that they would not find themselves deposited into the storeroom in the next forty-eight hours!

There was mains water, generally reliable we were told, but since in Andalucía water can sometimes become an extremely rare commodity, it came by way of a *deposito*, a large storage tank on the hillside above the house. This was fine, except that the *deposito* had no lid, and in consequence was full of mosquito larvae and other unmentionables. Electricity, on the other hand, did not come via the mains. Instead there was an antiquated solar generating system, whose output was changed into DC electricity by way of a converter, and was used to charge a wondrous assortment of batteries. Current was then taken from the batteries and transformed into 220-volt AC by way of a regulator. 'The regulator's broken,' the vendor announced, cheerfully!

These revelations were a bit much for us. Although we were prepared to accept some of these deficiencies in whatever property we bought, to have them all at once was rather too daunting, and while this was clearly a property which would be eminently suited to a couple with slightly more stamina and years ahead of them than we had, it wasn't quite what we had in mind, despite the view and the almost eleven (precipitous) acres of olive trees which came with it, and the very reasonable price. So we thanked the vendor profusely for showing us round her 'utterly charming home', climbed wearily back up the slope to the car, and added yet another entry to our list of the types of properties we didn't want!

This list was becoming ominously long. We now had a fair idea of what we didn't want. We knew that we didn't want a bare lot where we would have to start from scratch, nor a ruin, nor even somewhere where we would be faced with a major rebuilding project to make it habitable.

Equally, we didn't want to 'go native' and pretend to be Andalucían peasants. Although we certainly wanted to integrate with our Spanish neighbours, that didn't have to include copying some of the more basic living conditions we had encountered during our reconnaissance; we had both had quite enough of outdoor sanitation, no electricity and primitive cooking arrangements as children to consider anything similar to be remotely attractive now as a permanent *mode de vie*.

At the same time we didn't want - at least not yet - a terraced house in a village, a villa in an expatriate enclave in an *urbanización* nor, for us the ultimate horror, an apartment in a tower block on the coast. What we wanted was to live in the country, relatively isolated but not remote, reasonably close to but not in a town or village, in a house which was basically sound, probably needing renovation but which we could live in and do or have done as we went along, with a bit of land where we could maybe keep chickens and perhaps a pig, and adopt a stray dog or two. Surely that wasn't too much to ask? Well, apparently it was, at a price we could afford.

Pricing was another matter on which we were getting a good grounding, though it took a lot of thought and analysis to reach it. It was clear that prices set by Spanish *campesiño* vendors were not determined by the size of the house, nor even on its condition; nor was the value equated to the number of square metres or hectares. In fact, many Spanish landowners in the *campo* didn't know the precise area of their land, only that it ran from this olive tree here to that white painted stone there and then up along this side of that ditch. 'None of my metres is square,' as one landowner is said to have put it.

No, what established the value of a piece of land, certainly with the *campesiños* we met, was its productivity in terms of the number of fruit trees, especially olive trees, their yield and the quality of the crop, and whether the land was irrigated. Their asking price was based on the size, quantity and quality of their olives or almonds, pears or peaches, regardless of the fact that a prospective expatriate purchaser may have quite different priorities in mind.

One property we were shown exemplified this. It stood on a sort of mound, about half a mile outside a sizeable village. The house had water and electricity - just - but no drainage. It had no view to speak of, and the agent warned that the wind blew through the valley in which it lay almost 365 days a year. It was certainly blowing fiercely when we were looking at the property, accompanied by driving rain, much of it coming through the considerable gap between the roof and the kitchen wall, which itself was parting company from the rest of the house.

But it had thirty good olive trees, so the asking price was 13 million *pesetas* - about £55,000. We calculated that it would take another 8 million *pesetas* - £34,000 - to bring it up to standards acceptable to us as a year-round dwelling, making the minimum outlay nearly £90,000 - and this without a swimming pool or any refinements of that kind, let alone providing some sort of shelter from the perpetual wind. To us this made it a non-starter, and we thanked the vendor kindly (and her somewhat odd teen-aged son, who insisted on letting off fireworks around our feet while we were talking, unchecked by his mother) and departed - leaving her totally perplexed at our failure to appreciate the value of what it was she was offering us.

At the same time as we came to this realisation about pricing, we also began to get the measure of agents offering properties for sale in the *campo*. All the books we had read before we came out warned of the perils of buying a house in Spain without proper legal assistance, and they gave many sad instances where those who have ignored this advice have come unstuck, but none had talked about agents. As a result, we had blithely assumed that all English-speaking agents in Spain would work to the same standards of integrity and efficiency, and follow similar codes of practice, as their British counterparts. That this was not the case became evident all too soon, with the agents we met after parting company from Kevin.

Like others, they had sent us in November a very attractive brochure of prospective properties, and we had exchanged several faxes and telephone calls with them (at our expense, which should perhaps have served as an 'amber', if not a 'red' light). Their representative had arranged to meet us at 10.00 a.m. on 28 December, but eventually turned up at 10.45, and further endeared himself to us by immediately settling down to talk to another couple, whom we had met the night before and who we knew weren't looking to buy for another twelve months.

After 10 minutes talking to them, he finally deigned to come over and talk to us. He then gave us a book of photographs and descriptions to look at and asked, as it were in passing, 'Can we go in your car, our only 4 x 4 is in the garage?' While Susan began to look through the album, I took the representative gently by the elbow, and led him to the window. 'That's our car,' I said, pointing to the Duchess. 'If you are happy to take her somewhere where you need a 4 x 4, I'm game - so long as your agency covers the insurance.' I don't know why, but he turned quite pale, and went off to make a phone call, after which an ordinary car, not a 4 x 4, unaccountably became available.

It was perhaps this, and the revelation made by Susan as we were getting ready to leave that she had represented a Florida realtor in the UK, and had made herself familiar with US real estate legislation and practices in order to do this, that put him off us: there is nothing so discouraging to persons of doubtful integrity as to find themselves dealing with someone who already knows something about buying and selling property outside the UK, and so may be alive to the possibilities for skulduggery. In any event, he became strangely reticent in his dealings with us, and it wasn't long before he returned us to the hotel in favour of easier prey.

After this experience we were told of one British agency, awash with letters indicating membership of this and that organisation, which had succeeded in obtaining £2,000, to which they were not entitled, from a British purchaser of a property bought through them. This came about, we were told, through the common practice in Spain for transactions involving cheques to have the cheques made out to *portador* (bearer). This is preferred by many people because there is no record of who cashes the cheque. In the case of the British purchaser, our source told us, the time had come for a number of payments to be made, and she was busily writing cheques, made out to *portador*, and passing them to the agent who had undertaken to ensure that they reached the appropriate payees.

Because she was preoccupied with what she was doing and trusted the agent, we gathered she unwisely, and perhaps naïvely, didn't cross-check the purpose of each cheque before she handed it over. The agent, presumably noticing this and being extremely quick on the uptake, asked her to make out an extra cheque for £2,000, again made out to *portador*, which he then pocketed. When she realised later that there was £2,000 unaccounted for, she queried this with the agent and, we understand, received the reply, 'It's gone into my pension fund.' We were told that, to her credit, she took the matter to court and recovered £1,000, but we understand she couldn't afford - nor did she have the energy - to take it further.

That same agency, we were also told, on being asked by a British property owner to let a property for her in her absence, charged a Japanese tenant double the rent agreed with the owner while taking their commission from the owner as well. This only came to light when the owner, on her return, went round to see her tenant to enquire if all was well. 'Oh yes,' said the tenant, 'the house is wonderful, but I am having a little difficulty in meeting the £600 a week rent.' 'You mean £300, don't you?' queried the owner. 'No, £600.' Since the owner was only getting £250 herself she was so appalled at this exploitation that she offered the tenant the use of the property rent-free for the next month. But by this time the tenant had also learned that the agency had been 'kindly' replenishing her gas bottles when necessary, charging her double the going rate and pocketing the difference and she declined the offer and left as soon as her tenancy agreement had expired.

We realised that these cautionary tales were not meant to imply that all agents offering properties for sale in the *campo* were crooked and inefficient, and our own experiences confirmed this. But they did serve to underline a third rule of buying a property in the *campo*:

The principle of 'buyer beware' applies to dealings with an agent no less than with anyone else.

So how do you find a reputable agent? That's easy: as David Searle advises on how to choose a legal adviser in his admirable book *You and the Law in Spain*: ask! We took this advice, and found that, in fact, we hardly had to ask at all: when we casually mentioned the subject, people virtually fell over themselves to tell us their experiences. Although, as often as not, they ended up telling us which agents *not* to use (and lawyers, dentists, builders, plumbers, electricians, garages, etc.) we gradually compiled a highly valuable list of just about anyone we might need, both then and in the future.

Chapter 4

Si nous ne trouverons pas des choses agréables,
nous trouverons du moins des choses nouvelles.
If we do not find anything pleasant,
at least we shall find something new.
(Voltaire, *Candide*)

In January our searches were rewarded when we were shown a house which, though not exactly what we had in mind, would have done us very well as a starting place from which to ease ourselves into living in Spain. It was within the boundaries of a sizeable village near Lója, in Granada Province, so all the local infrastructure was in place. It was realistically priced, and required almost no work to make it habitable. It had virtually no land, so the idea of a smallholding would have to be put on hold, and it did have the possible drawback of being sandwiched between two local families, but we met them both - in fact, one apparently owned the house and had initiated the sale - and found them agreeable and friendly. So we said 'yes' and asked the agent to go ahead with the next stage.

We were now to discover a characteristic of sales of this nature, which took us by surprise as former house-owners in the UK. There, when a property is put up for sale, the vendor generally asks the highest price he or she hopes to get while being willing to negotiate a lower price once a potential purchaser has shown an interest. In the *campo*, where sales by Spanish nationals to foreign purchasers are concerned, the vendors often set a price which they hope will attract a potential buyer and then, when they think they have got them hooked, increase it. (It is not unknown for unscrupulous agents to do this, too, if they think the prospective purchasers are sufficiently gullible, desperate, short of time, or affected by any other factors which could influence their decision.)

In this particular instance, within a day of our agent making a formal offer, the vendor increased the price by 30 per cent. This was clearly ludicrous; it isn't possible to negotiate anything from that kind of price hike. We presumed that the vendor no longer wanted to sell and felt that, tactically, this was the best way to get out of things. The question was: why? Over the next few days we were fed story and counter-story, each replacing the other with bewildering speed (including the suggestion that the vendor, who reputedly had a history of mental instability, had had a nervous breakdown), until, weeks later, we finally learned the truth.

The vendor, who was indeed one of the possible neighbours we had met, a delightful lady who certainly hadn't appeared to us to be suffering from any kind of mental disorder, was one of four siblings who had inherited the property from their uncle, who had died in the summer leaving neither spouse nor issue of his own. Thus all four siblings owned the property. The neighbour was the only woman among the siblings. She had nursed the said uncle in his dying moments, and now wanted to sell the property because of the memory of this episode (the uncle's death had been particularly traumatic). She had obtained the agreement of her brothers for the sale to go ahead, and they had all agreed to sell her their share of the property, so that she would be the sole owner when it came to the sale.

However, when she put the property up for sale through the agency, because the agency dealt with foreigners, the price they suggested she should ask was more than double the price she and her siblings had agreed would be the basis for their buy-out. The others hadn't remarked on this at the time, but now that a possible buyer had actually made an offer, they had woken up to the situation, and greed had entered the equation.

The brothers, understandably, wanted the increased share to which they felt they were entitled from this increase in price. Their sister, equally reasonably, felt that an agreement was an agreement, and that as she was the one who was taking the risk and the burden of handling the sale, the provisions of the agreement should stand. Neither side would give way, resulting in complete stalemate, and so the sister had said, fine, if that's how you want it, then I will put the price up so high that no-one will buy the place, and you can all sing for your share. And so far as we know, that's how the situation remains.

However we didn't know this at the time, and we had a frustrating and frantic forty-eight hours of sitting by the phone garnering endlessly conflicting reports, and being told firmly that we couldn't, as our instinct dictated, simply cut through everything and go direct to the sister. In the end we came reluctantly to the conclusion that we might be wise to resume our searches, as otherwise we could wait till Doomsday. In other words,

Hope for the best in situations like this, but plan for the worst.

At this point a truism which we have long accepted manifested itself. This is that

when one door closes, another often opens.

The same day that we made our offer on this house, we had left the hotel in Colmenar and moved into a B&B in the same village as our prospective purchase, run by a delightful English couple who normally only catered for guests in the summer, but who kindly agreed to have us so that we could be on hand during the course of the sale (poor them: they weren't to know when they were persuaded to have us that I would go down with 'flu within a few days, and they would be stuck with us for weeks; nor that, after we had left, the wife herself would go down with the same bug, which I had generously shared with her). While sympathising with us in the collapse of our purchase, the husband casually mentioned the agent who had sold their previous house for them, and who had found them the house they were in now. He suggested we could do worse than go to see her, and we arranged to see her the moment we suspected that our purchase might not be going through.

With the husband as guide and introducer we made the voyage to the agent's office in Torre del Mar, a seaside resort near Velez Málaga. As we gazed at the details displayed in her window and selected three properties to see, Susan said that one of them seemed to 'glow' at her from the page, even though all that was visible was a window and part of the roof – the rest was totally obscured by foliage and a palm tree! She said would be quite content just to see that one. However, it had to take its turn with the rest, and the next day Judy, the agent, showed us a nice little house up a short drive with raising-drying racks and some good olive trees on the inevitably steep, though reasonably-sized piece of land in front of it, but sadly this house was too small.

Next came a magnificently-situated, original-condition house perched on a ledge above a hamlet near Periana, about twenty-five miles inland, with spectacular views over Lake Viñuela. The only trouble was that the house could only be reached on two feet or four hooves – even Judy's husband's Mitsubishi Pajero couldn't get near it – and we had a moment of sheer delight, picturing our removals firm trying to get the deep-freeze and a glass-fronted corner cupboard up this precipice.

Then it was the turn of the one that had 'glowed' at Susan. We drove down from the eyrie, following a former railway track which now makes a wonderfully scenic route between Periana and Zafaria (if you ignore the vast, unofficial rubbish dump at one end), on the way learning another aspect of life in the *campo*. This was when Judy suddenly yelled out, 'There's one,' and when Bill braked to a halt, leaped out and, opening the back of the car, removed a number of plastic bags which she dumped into a wheelie-bin parked outside someone's house.

Knowing how householders would react to this kind of behaviour in England we expressed our astonishment and asked her to explain. She told us that there isn't any refuse collection from houses in the *campo*, not even in the towns. Instead the local authority places communal wheelie-bins at strategic spots, to which you take your rubbish. Even though these may be sited directly outside someone's house and look as though they are private, they aren't: they are for use by every and anybody. When these wheelie-bins were emptied remained a mystery until we stayed in Torre del Mar, since we never saw it being done (rather like the work on the motorways in Britain, which as everyone knows, is done by the orange cones), but that was for the future.

After this interlude, and the undoubted relief for us all at the absence of the pungent aroma from the back of the car, and about which we had felt unable to comment until then, we drove down, down, down into a hidden, fertile valley, over a hair-raising little bridge with no parapet and along a rutted, dark, unpaved lane overhung with the branches of quince and pomegranate trees to a *finca* - a smallholding - with a date palm in front of the house. We stopped the car and got out and stood, letting the atmosphere wash over us.

Thank goodness my husband knows me well and trusts most of my instincts. This house not only glowed on its paper, it said to me, 'I'm the one!' Although I had helped to pick a few more for viewing beside it (being cautious and not wanting to have too much egg on my face if I had got it wrong) I didn't think any other would be right. None held that magic 'here's home' feeling.

We couldn't go into the house, as the owners were out, but we all walked round the 8000 square metres of gently sloping land, all the time with this silent crescendo of sound ringing in Susan's and my ears, 'This is IT.' However, having learned from our own, and other people's previous experiences that it is extremely unwise ever to make a decision about any property on a single viewing, and in any event because we hadn't seen inside the house, we were back again two days later, this time with the owners present.

We went into the house (a *cortijo*, we were told, not a *casa*, because it was part of a *finca*) and found that it had mains water and electricity, and a telephone, all far from common benefits in a property of this kind. Its two-storey walls also appeared to be reasonably vertical (though the back wall had an interesting bulge inwards on the first floor), and had no significant cracks. It had a recently renovated roof, done with concrete beams and special internal roof tiles called *bovadillas*, not the old eucalyptus beams and cane matting technique, and a total of seven large rooms, plus a huge, newly built storage room running the entire length of the house on the first floor above the rear downstairs rooms, all at a price which was reasonable and, better still, which we could afford. It was almost too good to be true.

Outside it got even better. There was a terrace at the front of the house, shaded from the summer heat by a mature, overhanging vine. There was a magnificent date palm, and there were a lean-to mule shed, currently occupied by chickens, and a lean-lean-to outhouse attached to that, part of which had once been a piggery. The 8000m^2 of land was irrigated, and it was covered in fruit trees: peach, pomegranate, pear, persimmon, quince and some venerable olives, making it a true *finca*, the smallholding of our dreams. And, miracle of miracles, the land sloped steadily down to a river - a river with water in it, not so remarkable in rain-swept, flood-prone Britain, but extremely rare in arid, mountainous Andalucía - which formed the eastern boundary to the property.

One of the things Susan and I had always dreamed about was to live by a river. The nearest we had got to this was when we nearly bought a house in Devizes, on the Kennet and Avon Canal. Otherwise we had been within walking distance and sight but not sound of the sea when we had lived in Bournemouth, but this was not the same thing at all as living by a river. It was the last thing we had on our minds when coming to Andalucía, yet here, it seemed, we had found one. It was definitely too good to be true.

There were, to be sure, one or two small problems to be overcome. Like that 'cowshed' we had seen earlier, the downstairs floor tiles had been laid direct onto the earth, with identical results. Although the house had mains water, it didn't have hot water - there was no boiler - and the only water inside the house was in the 'bathroom', and this was only connected over a basin, not to the toilet. There was no kitchen; again like that cowshed there was just a two-ring electric plate on a counter in the hall: *la señora* washed the clothes and the dishes in a stone sink outside under a single cold-water tap. Furthermore, besides having no water to it, the drain under the only toilet didn't appear to be connected to anything; evidence of where 'it' had been going for over forty years was a magnificent stand of prickly pears a few metres from the back of the house!

The electricity supply was only rated for 1.9 Kw, with wiring to match; there was nothing approaching a British Standards 13 amp ring main. The telephone system was the UHF one favoured by *Telefonica* in the *campo*, and prohibited thoughts of getting back onto the Internet. The two lean-to's were verminous and distinctly shaky and would have to go, and the vine over the patio was supported on a string and bamboo structure which was definitely on its last legs. Still, these things were all correctable, and there was nothing so fundamentally unsafe or unacceptable that it could not be remedied so far as we could see, so we now began the delicate process of indicating our interest in the property.

Readers who can think back fifty years may remember, depending on their upbringing, cold water being the only water in the house, outside toilets and washing coppers, electrics that flickered or no electricity at all, and solid fuel or paraffin heating. Well, this is what we were cheerfully preparing to get ourselves into, for the time being at any rate.

With Judy and her husband Bill acting as interpreters, we sat on the terrace and talked with the owners, two shrewd, stocky, currant-eyed Andalucían country folk. We heard that Pedro, the husband, had lived there for forty-five years, and that he had inherited the *finca* from his father. He and Luisa didn't really want to sell (we could believe that, all too easily) but they were getting on (not so far as we were concerned, they weren't; they looked far too robust and healthy for people contemplating retirement), and their daughters in Granada wanted them to go and live near them.

This was the only reason they were selling, they said. They had had an offer the previous autumn from some Germans, but that had come to nothing. Did we like the place? Did we like it! It was all we could do to restrain ourselves from making an offer there and then. But sanity prevailed, while we listened in case there were any 'nasties' lurking under stones which could prejudice the sale, like siblings or other relatives who might have a beneficial interest in the property. We were extremely relieved to hear – though this of course still had to be confirmed officially – that only the daughters had a beneficial interest, and as they were the ones pressing for the sale, they were unlikely to cause any difficulties.

After a suitable interval, we all took our leave and drove away, Susan and I scarcely able to contain our suppressed excitement. 'What should we do now?' we asked Judy. 'Wait a few days,' was the wise, but very hard-to-accept advice. 'If you show too much interest right away, they will immediately put the price up.' So away we went, back to our B&B lodgings, to wait until Judy judged the time to be right to make an offer.

It was three days later, on Sunday evening, that she telephoned us. 'There's good news, and there's bad news,' she said. 'The good news is that they still want to sell. The bad news is that they won't accept less than 250,000 *pesetas* [about £1,000] above the price I quoted you. What do you want to do?' Now as it happened, in the meantime Susan and I had discussed this very eventuality, and we reckoned that, if push came to shove, we could possibly go to another half million *pesetas*, so 250,000 was definitely within the budget, even allowing for the resulting increase in the taxes and fees we would have to find on top of the agreed purchase price.

'Well,' I replied, not wishing to appear to bite Judy's hand off, 'it's a bit much, increasing the asking price after we have been to view the place.'

'I know,' she answered, 'but they do have the house with another agent, and he is asking half a million more than I listed it for.' (A fact which we subsequently checked, and found to be correct).

'Hmmm,' I said. 'Well, in that case, I daresay we could just go another quarter of a million. Will you now get back to them with this final offer, and let us know whether they will accept it?'

'Of course,' she said, and rang off.

Another nail-biting day came and went before she telephoned to say that the sale was now on, at this revised increased price. The matter wasn't yet over by a long way, though. The next essential step was for the vendors and ourselves to sign a preliminary private contract, the *Contracto Privado de Compraventa* and for us to pay a 10 per cent deposit. Although this would not be the final document for the sale, it would at least secure the sale of the property to us.

Now we encountered our next problem. Preparing such a contract is specialist work and all the books we had read very rightly stressed the need to retain a lawyer for such a purpose. Among major considerations, all the documentation must be written in Spanish yet we, of course, wouldn't be able to read it, so someone bilingual was clearly essential, and while it was a great relief to us when Judy made it quite clear that, for this purpose, we should use someone independent from herself – we were still haunted by the tales of the agents who had offered to 'take care of it all' – finding a suitable lawyer presented a major challenge.

For openers, the Notary in front of whom the final sale documents for our house would be signed and witnessed was in Torre del Mar, so it was clearly desirable for us to retain a lawyer there or thereabouts, since they would be in daily contact with the appropriate people in the various agencies with which it would be necessary to deal, something which is much more advantageous in transactions of this kind in Spain than it is in England.

Where we were staying was nearly two hours' drive from Torre del Mar. Not only that, it was in a different province. Finding a good lawyer in the area to which you are moving is difficult enough in England if you live two hours away; finding one in Spain in similar circumstances if you don't speak Spanish is nearly impossible. And this was the nub. Although there are any number of English-speaking lawyers on the coast in Andalucía, in Torre del Mar they are (or were then) a rarity. So we were faced with a choice: either we spent a day (or days) in Torre del Mar, physically walking into every lawyers' office and asking if they spoke English, or we forewent the advantages of having a local lawyer, and went for someone from (much) further afield with whom we knew we could communicate.

And here came the second problem: we had very little time. With a growing interest in properties in the area in which we had found our *finca*, added to the overall boom in property sales in Andalucía, we knew it would be sooner rather than later that someone else stumbled upon our dream house and bought it from under our noses. So spending time swanning round Torre del Mar, or even nearby Velez Málaga, to look for an English-speaking lawyer was out, as was briefing someone elsewhere whom we would still have to locate and visit. We needed to appoint someone that week.

It was then that we found an office which seemed to offer a way out of the dilemma: English-speaking staff who, though not legally qualified, nevertheless purported to offer a representative service of the kind we required. We had certain misgivings in approaching them, since we had experience of quasi-legal organisations of this kind in the UK and knew their limitations. Still, it was a case of 'any port in a storm', so we asked them to prepare the private contract for our purchase and to try to arrange a meeting with the vendors that week.

At the same time that we did this we asked them to confirm the fees and taxes we would have to pay on completion of the sale. We understood from David Searle's book that the major sum would be the transfer tax, the *Impuesto de Transmisiones Patrimoniales,* or *ITP* for short, which would be 6 per cent of the price declared in the private contract. What came as a bit of a surprise was the query, by the office, whether the price to go in the contract was the one which we had agreed with Pedro and Luisa. When we asked for an explanation we were told that, in the past, people had often declared a much lower amount for the value of a property being sold than the price actually agreed, so as to keep the *ITP* to a minimum. We could still do this but if we did, then we might face a problem with regard to capital gains tax as and when we wanted to sell the property again since, if we declared a low value now, we would be liable for a much bigger tax if we sold for a much higher price.

There was also the possibility that, if we declared too low a figure, tax inspectors might come round and make their own assessment. If they found that the transfer had been significantly under-declared, they could apply heavy penalties to both us and Pedro and Luisa. So, we were again asked, what did we want to put in the contract? Without any discussion, we said to go ahead on the price we had agreed with Pedro and Luisa.

Beside the *ITP,* the office told us, we would have to pay their fees and that of the Notary, the latter being on a fixed scale of between 50,000 and 70,000 *pesetas,* depending on the amount of land, the size of the house and its price, and for the registration of title with the *Registro de la Propriedad,* once the property was ours, and which would be for a similar amount.

The only other tax of concern was the *Arbito Sobre el Incremento del Valor de los Terrenos,* or *'Plus Valía'* for short, a municipal capital gains tax on the increase in value of the land. This was based on the increase in value of the land since its last sale. The percentage levied would depend on the time which had elapsed since then. Over the years it had become the custom for the buyer to pay the *Plus Valía,* but recent legislation had restored the original practice for the seller to pay it, and our adviser undertook to ensure that our final contract would also stipulate this.

There was otherwise one final warning: this was that we would be liable for any undisclosed debts on the property once the sale went through, since in Spain these remain with the property, not with the previous owners. The office would do its best to uncover any such debts, if they existed, but we should be aware of the situation: the process of discovery was not nearly so encompassing as that of the Searches and Enquiries which accompany the sale of a house in England.

Fortunately none of this came as a terrible shock: it had all come to light while we were doing our homework, but it was reassuring to know that there was nothing we had missed in our calculation that we would have to find roughly 10 per cent on top of the purchase price by the time it was all over. So with this settled, we left the office to get on with preparing the private contract, and to try to get the vendors to agree a day and time when they would come in for the signing ceremony.

The benefit of the private contract cannot be overemphasised. It identifies the vendors and the prospective purchasers, the title and address of the property, the declared purchase price, the amount to be paid as deposit and the date on which the balance is to be paid and the sale completed. Once it has been signed and the deposit paid it is binding on all parties, who cannot back out or change what has been agreed without substantial financial penalty. Thus, unlike England and Wales, the vendors know they have got a sale, and the purchasers know that they cannot be 'gazumped'.

Conventional wisdom dictates that it is crazy to sign this contract before all the searches on the property have been carried out, but these were not conventional circumstances. We knew from Judy that there were other interested parties in the pipeline (indeed, we learned from her later that only forty-eight hours after we had signed the contract, she was contacted by three other prospective purchasers with requests to view), so there was considerable urgency to button down the sale before some rival purchaser put in a better offer. This faced us with the choice either of signing the contract, knowing that there was a risk that something untoward might emerge from the woodwork which could, at the very least, involve further costs and, as the ultimate horror, prejudice the sale altogether leaving us with a serious amount of egg on our faces, or of waiting an unknown period of time while the searches were carried out and risk losing the sale to some other purchaser who was less cautious about the risks. For us there was, in fact, no choice: waiting simply didn't enter into it.

So far as we were concerned, there then followed an ex-cruciating few days before the office contacted us with a date to come back. We drove down to the coast with butterflies in our stomachs - it was always possible that the vendors wouldn't show up or had changed their minds - and were mightily relieved to find Pedro and Luisa sitting in the waiting room, Pedro with a stinking cold which he generously shared with us. With due ceremony the contract was read out in both English and Spanish. This was fine, until the final paragraph, the one stating when the balance of the purchase price was to be paid and the sale completed.

Unbeknown to us, Pedro and Luisa had told our adviser they were in no hurry to complete the sale, and had asked that the date for completion be set for four months hence, the maximum time permissible, to allow them time to find a flat in Granada which suited them. Susan and I looked at each other in horror. Four months! That was a third of a year. Were they serious about selling, or what? However we were immediately brought back to reality with the warning that every day of those four months would be needed to prepare the final contract. This would be explained once we had got the immediate proceedings out of the way.

So we reluctantly agreed to the four months, provided the vendors signed the private contract. This they duly did, but not before I had handed them an envelope containing one million *pesetas* in cash (around £4,255 at the then prevailing rate of exchange), which we had collected from the bank that morning. This was the deposit we were able to put down immediately, and was also a nice, round sum, even though it wasn't a particular percentage of the agreed price, but it was more than enough, according to our advisor. However the expression on the vendors' faces when they opened the envelope and saw this pile of money was, though gratifying, not quite as enthusiastic as we had expected; we were to discover the reason for this a couple of months later.

We were also intrigued - and slightly alarmed - with the fact that we paid the deposit direct to the vendors, albeit in our advisor's presence. In Florida, as Susan knew from her previous experience, the deposit is paid into an 'escrow account'. This account is required by law. It is opened by the realtor handling the sale specifically to hold the purchaser's deposit, and any other monies involved in the purchase, and the money in it cannot be touched by anyone until the final transaction for which the monies have been paid has been concluded. The Spanish system, while nice for the vendors (it meant they could use the same money as a deposit for their own house purchase) meant that for us, should anything go wrong in the meantime, *e.g.* should a Search reveal that Pedro and Luisa didn't actually own the property, we would have to institute legal proceedings in order to recover our money from them, instead of being repaid from the escrow account. Still, if that was how it was, so be it; at least it meant that, if they <u>did</u> use it as the deposit for their own house purchase, it would be highly unlikely that they would pull out, or do anything else likely to prejudice the sale.

With the sale of the property now contracted to us, and with severe financial penalties in place should either side pull out of the sale, then short of a catastrophe the property would be ours, once the necessary paperwork had been completed. So Pedro and Luisa departed, and we waited to be told why it would take four months to do this. There were, we were told, a number of reasons. First, because the house was a 'rustic' property in the *campo*, it was highly unlikely that it had ever been registered or that it had an *Escritura*, a conveyance of title. This was not, in itself, necessarily a problem. Pedro had said that the *finca* had been left to him by his father, and that he and Luisa had lived there all their married lives, so it was improbable that there was a dispute as to ownership, nor that there was any skulduggery about the land on which the *cortijo* stood. However we had to be certain, as otherwise we could find that we had parted company with our hard-earned cash with nothing to show for it at the end, and with the current boom of property sales, this could easily take four months to resolve without any other considerations.

As a first step to establishing whether the property was legally Pedro's and Luisa's to sell, the office would check on whether they had paid the annual municipal real estate tax, the *Impuesto sobre Bienes Immeubles*, or *IBI* for short, up to date <u>in their own names</u>. This tax is not unlike the old British rates, and their payment of it would provide *prima facie* evidence that the property was theirs to sell, and indeed they would have to produce the receipt to the Notary when we came to sign the final contract to confirm this. The receipt would also show the number given to the property by the *Referencia Catastral*, the other authority concerned with property registration. This number would be needed when the property was finally registered in our names with the *Registro de la Propriedad*. The receipt would also show the official assessed value of the property, the *valor catastral*, upon which the *IBI* was based. And finally, it would also confirm that we would not be faced with a demand for back-taxes, since the receipt implies that all payments are up-to-date.

In addition to this documentation, we stipulated that we wanted a further safeguard when we came to sign the final contract: that Pedro and Luisa should swear on oath before the Notary and in front of witnesses who must have known them for some time not only that they were, in fact, the owners, and entitled to sell the property and that there was no mortgage, lien or other outstanding charge on it, but also that no-one else had right of access to or over the land or the house. This information would normally be held by the *Registro de la Propriedad*, but if the property was not registered, this would be the only practical way to obtain it.

Some care would be needed in the framing of this oath. We had heard of one case where a single room in a terraced house actually belonged to the next-door neighbour ... and that this room was used by him to stable his mule! Fortunately this came to light before the sale was concluded, but in another case, a year after the completion of the sale of a country property similar to ours, a property with land and olive trees, the new owners had woken up one morning to find a man standing in their orchard, gathering the fruit from one of their trees.

'What are you doing on our land?' they asked. 'Tending my tree,' he replied, 'and it's not your land, it's mine!' It was, too – just the bit round the tree, together with right of access, and of course the tree itself. It had been his for years, and he could prove it, in writing. No-one had thought to check with the vendors whether anyone besides themselves had rights to any part of the property, and now it was too late: either the new owners had to accept it, or they had to come to an arrangement with the man to buy him out. So it would require particular care on our part to ensure that there was no possibility of a similar situation existing with our *finca*.

There was another aspect to right of access which we were glad was unlikely to concern us. Two English friends of ours had bought and restored a ruin part of the way down a track. The ruin came with a small plot of land and, at the time that they bought it, the only other dwelling there belonged to the Spanish vendor, who lived next door. As part of their restoration plan, our friends re-routed, with the assistance of the former owner, the path from the track onto the property so that it fitted in with their new terrace layout.

Unfortunately neither our friends nor the former owner thought it necessary to record the change on paper, still less have it registered or Notarised. In due course our friends sold the property to another English couple. Because they hadn't made an official record of the change to the access path, the new owners were unaware that any change had been made, and our friends didn't tell them, not through any duplicity but because they simply didn't think it mattered.

Shortly after this, the former Spanish owner sold his house, too, to a German couple. This house shared part of the access track. The Germans checked the route of the track with the *Catastral* and found that an unofficial change had been made. They asked for the original route to be restored. Unfortunately this now lay slap across the terrace in front of the English couple's house, and they declined. The Germans remained adamant, the English un-repentant, the litigation continues and international relations have been destroyed forever. Luckily for us our *finca* had direct access from a council-owned cart-road, so no-one else could be involved.

There would also be the need to check the boundaries to the property, and this would present a different problem. Although the boundaries would be shown on the *Catastral* records and, of course, with the *Registro de la Propriedad* if the property was registered, matching them with the actual situation on the ground would be less straightforward than it generally is in England. There are very few fences in the Andalucían *campo*, partly because the fields do not have to constrain livestock and trees aren't known for straying on their own, partly because the terrain is so unforgiving that erecting a fence is a vastly more difficult job than it is in England, and partly because a fence would be an inappropriate way to indicate the boundary round a single tree isolated in the middle of a field. As a result, the delineation of boundaries has to be done by some other means, usually by smearing dollops of white paint on conveniently placed rocks. This system works well enough, and where the stones run along a feature such as a terrace, watercourse or track there is seldom a problem. However where they do not, it does have its drawbacks.

Stones can move, either during a rain storm or through some human agency, and unless they are restored to their original position by the person adversely affected, the new position has a habit of becoming permanent. We met one English couple who bought from an absentee owner a water mill with a surrounding plot of land. The vendor had not checked the position of the stones around the plot and the buyers didn't think to ask. While the sale was in progress, their neighbour quietly annexed a piece of the land by moving the stones and had planted vegetables on it. He then claimed that the annexed piece of land had been his all along and, adding insult to injury, he tried to sell it back to the new English owners! Luckily the previous owner discovered what was going on and stepped in to rectify matters, otherwise the situation could have become quite ugly. Equally luckily, the boundaries to our *finca* ran along well-defined features, and there were no outlying *parcelas* to contend with, so there wasn't likely to be a problem.

We visited newly-made friends to see the property they had bought the year before and the land they now owned. 'Our land goes to about there and ends about here,' said Vic as we took a walk on it. At first we thought he was joking but no, he knew he owned a certain amount of land but because the other owners were either old, dead, lived in another part of the country or world or didn't care to speak with the foreigner, no one including Vic was quite certain about his boundaries. His lawyer was following it up, he told us brightly!

There was a valuable lesson to be learned from both these experiences:

Check and double-check boundaries and access routes before you buy - knives are drawn between neighbours and countries go to war over such things!

Having ensured that we were actually negotiating the purchase with the right people, then the final contract to be signed before the Notary, the *escritura de compraventa*, could be prepared. This would require a certificate from the *Referencia Catastral* and to provide this certificate, the *Catastral* would have to search its records to find the exact location, physical description and boundaries of the property. With the present explosion of house sales and purchases this could easily take three months, and the *escritura de compraventa* couldn't be prepared without it. 'So,' we were told, 'that's another reason why it's going to take four months. Any questions?'

No, there weren't, but it did present us with another question: what were we to do and where were we going to live for up to four months, while the due process of Spanish property legislation ground its remorseless way forward and the vendors found themselves a new home? Of course, we could have gone back to England and stayed with one or other of our luckless offspring but that, we felt, would be defeatist. Besides, we were having far too much fun soaking up our first impressions of Spain. So we needed to find somewhere local and cheap to wait out the four months, and try to devise some intelligent but expenditure-free way of passing the time, an activity which would have to include giving our new home a name.

We had noticed the absence of any kind of identification during the course of our negotiations. This, we learned, was in no way unusual in the valley. Most houses were simply known by the people who lived there, and ours was no exception: it had been *La Casa de Pedro* for as long as anyone could remember. This would hardly be appropriate for us and besides, we wanted to give it an identity of its own, but with minimal Spanish at our command and absolutely no idea where to start, this posed a slight challenge.

It was now that Judy showed her true worth. 'You could always call it *"Casa la Palmera"*,' she offered, 'on account of the palm. But there are quite a few variations on *Las Palmas* around. Why not focus on the thing that makes it perfect from your point of view? Why not call it *"Cortijo del Rio"*, the Farmhouse by the River?'

We mulled this over, savouring the words on our tongues. They definitely had a ring to them. 'OK,' we said, after a minute or two, 'let's do it. *Cortijo del Rio* it is. All we now have to do is to get the locals to accept it!'

Chapter 5

There is the coast ... and there is the interior −
which might as well be another planet.
(Clare Francis, *Wolf Winter*)

Our search for accommodation was shortened by our meeting
a locally resident English couple while we were staying in
Colmenar. When we said we might be looking for self-catering
accommodation if and when we found ourselves a property, they
revealed that they owned a converted olive mill next to their
house five miles outside Colmenar which they rented out and
which was empty at this time of year. So now that we did have a
purchase under way we went to see them, looked at the mill, and
agreed to rent it for a couple of months.

Having settled that immediate problem, there were two other
matters which we needed to deal with urgently before any more
time elapsed. The first was for each of us to obtain a *Numero
Identificación de Extranjero*, or *NIE* for short. This number is issued
by the local police on behalf of the Ministry of the Interior to all
foreigners other than short-stay tourists, and identifies them to
the Spanish tax authorities. It is necessary for almost everything
financial done by resident or long-stay *extranjeros*, such as opening
a bank account or buying a Spanish registered car, so it was
essential for us to get this under way without delay. In the event, it
took six weeks for us to get this number, so it was as well that we
started the process when we did.

The second thing was for us to open an account with a bank in
Spain. This was clearly necessary for us as future residents, since we
needed a local account to which my pension and any other
income could be credited in due course and from which regular
bills such as those for the telephone and the electricity could be
debited automatically, as is now standard practice in Spain. It was
also desirable immediately from a practical point of view, both as
somewhere to hold the balance of the purchase price when we

transferred it from England, and as a repository for such income as we had from England because, although places like restaurants and filling-stations on the coast take credit cards, many others, including some supermarkets, only take cash (as we were to discover to our embarrassment on one occasion, when I had to go and find a bank to draw some cash while Susan patrolled round the aisles finding even more unnecessary things to buy—watched by an increasingly suspicious security guard), and it made every kind of sense to have an account in Spain to deal with this kind of situation sooner rather than later.

We briefly considered opening an account with the nearest branch to the *finca* of a British bank, to facilitate communication, but realised that this would scarcely be in keeping with our views on taking up residence and besides, it was over two hours' drive away. So we went to the Colmenar branch of a major Andalucían bank, where the Deputy Manager not only spoke some English, she also understood the problem of the issuing of *NIEs*. She kindly arranged for us to open an account there and then, on the understanding that we would bring her copies of our *NIE* certificates when they were issued, and we left the bank with those ultimate symbols of commitment to residence, a Spanish cheque book and a cashpoint card!

Having opened our account with the bank in Colmenar we have used this and other branches on many occasions over the ensuing months, and we have found them to be as efficient and modern as anywhere else in the EU. However in the *campo* their clients frequently aren't, and it has not been uncommon, especially on market days, for us to find ourselves at the back of a queue of twenty, each member of which has a pressing need to share his or her current family news with the cashier. It is one of the high spots of their week: a captive audience - literally - which is obliged to listen to their laboured tale, since otherwise it runs the risk of losing the client to a more sympathetic ear in a rival bank, but for us at the back, the result has sometimes been a wait of up to two hours before we have been served.

There is also the small matter of knowing <u>when</u> you are at the back of the queue. Spanish banks kindly provide seats for their clients which, in the *campo*, are invariably occupied by ladies 'of a certain age' together with the occasional man of even greater antiquity or infirmity. These good citizens line the walls, chatting animatedly to each other (though generally not knitting, like the infamous spectators at the *guillotine*), apparently paying no attention to the proceedings in front of them. This is deceptive. These clients are very definitely in the queue, and the fact that they are not stood in line makes no difference whatsoever. It took me a while to notice that Spanish clients entering a bank often murmured *'¿Qui e l'último?',* and from the reply noted where they were in relation to those ahead of them, possibly calculating roughly how long it would be before they could be attended to and thus making a decision whether or not to wait, or come back at another time (or day!).

Having settled the immediate priorities, we were faced with the challenge of usefully filling the four months which stretched ahead like a prison sentence, a term made all the more real by the conditions at the mill, which had seemed wonderfully picturesque when we first saw the place, but which now revealed a number of snags. Although there were to be times when we wished fervently that we could have avoided them, they were, unwittingly, to form a valuable foundation for our learning curve about actually living in the *campo*.

The first step on that curve came on our first night. With the fall of darkness came a familiar sound to citizens of the United Kingdom: the fall of rain. Within minutes this had turned from a gentle pitter-patter to a roar like a waterfall. The roof of the mill was of traditional design, with eucalyptus trunks and cane mat 'ceiling' supporting tiles. Although the tiles in this case had been relaid using a cement-based mortar to replace the original mud, it was still totally ineffective at keeping out the monsoon-like deluge. Within minutes there were ominous drips and even a small stream descending from the canes, and by the end we had five saucepans and several towels strategically placed to cope with the flood. Luckily this storm didn't last long, but it served as a useful warning of what to expect in winter in the form of rain, and about the possible problems which might be encountered with roofs, especially as we learned later of an occurrence which seemed to us to be incredible.

An expatriate couple had had a new house built, complete with tiled roof. With the onset of their first winter the rains came and their roof leaked. When they remonstrated with the builder, the latter replied with the remarkable riposte, 'You never said you wanted it to be waterproof!' 'What do you mean, "we never said"? All roofs are supposed to be waterproof.' 'Not here they aren't,' was the astonishing reply.

Seeing their amazement, the builder explained. 'The principal problem here, unlike your country, is heat, and roofs are built with that in mind, using tiles. These are inherently porous. During the summer any protective coating can be adversely affected by the heat, and the material used to fix the tiles can crack. Making a roof permanently waterproof is possible, but it costs more money than you were prepared to pay. A lot more. The alternative is to treat the roof each autumn. This I can do, but not within the price I originally quoted you.'

Whether this received wisdom is generally true or whether the builder was simply 'trying it on' we have yet to discover, although we have heard it from more than one source since we have been here, and certainly our own roof at the *cortijo* has lived up to his words, so the lesson we learned from it and from our experience was:

Rain is often encountered during the winter months and is frequently violent; this can be overlooked during the balmy days of summer. Be warned!

On our second night came the wind. It was not like the winds of Wellington, New Zealand, or Chicago, Illinois, which are in a class of their own, but it was windy enough and it went on for days, at around Force 5 or 6. There was a stand of eucalyptus trees just outside the door of the mill. The noise these trees make in a high wind is more than enough to keep you awake at night, since amongst other things, you live in a constant though unjustified fear that they are going to fall on you (unlike the inhabitants of a certain Gaulish village, whose only fear was that the sky was going to fall on their heads) and was very trying indeed. Luckily, so far as we could see, this wasn't likely to be a problem at the *cortijo*, but our experience of this wind taught us another vital lesson in the siting of a prospective home in the *campo*.

The absence of a 'wind shadow' or the failure to allow for wind in the positioning of a house can make a vital difference to the comfort of a home in winter.

These two episodes gave us a good deal to ponder during our troglodyte existence at the mill (it had only one, unglazed window, a metre square, to illuminate an interior measuring six metres by five, with a pitched roof rising to five metres at its ridge!), and fate hadn't finished with us yet. In our second week it snowed!

I can honestly say the place could have made a saint depressed. I need light, and the electrics not being up to much except for the neon tube over the stove it was very depressing. Once the novelty of living in an old mill (complete with grinding stone and circle which made the sitting area very cold most of the time) had worn off (about twenty-four hours), I couldn't wait to leave it. Great for a two week holiday but for months, I don't think so!

It didn't actually snow at the mill, but the hills around us were dusted overnight, and the tops of the distant mountains were covered. This brought us up all standing. This wasn't in the guide books. They all eulogised about the dazzling white, jewel-like Moorish villages, not the dazzling white, snow-covered *sierras*. They waxed lyrical about golden beaches washed by the azure sea and hillsides covered with almond and olive trees, not hillsides looking like Christmas cake. The only thing which remotely matched what they said was the sun, which blazed down from a cloudless sky with the ferocity of a blow-lamp.

It was our own fault; we had forgotten that the *Sierra Nevada* is in Andalucía, and *nevada* means 'snow-covered'. People ski in the *Sierra Nevada*, for heaven's sake - it's famous for it. And when the wind blows from the north-east, across the *Sierra Nevada* snowcap, as it often does, then the rest of Andalucía gets the benefit, especially if you are at altitude, as we were at the mill.

Snow, of course, is cold, and since traditional Andalucían houses are built to repel heat, not contain it, they can be very cold indeed. The mill was no exception. Noel Coward once famously wrote, 'The English, though effete, are quite impervious to heat.' Well, Andalucían country-folk, who are clearly not effete at all, appear to be impervious to both heat and cold, since most of their traditional houses have no heating of any kind.

For most people other than the very rich, the only concession made in the past to the desirability of heating was the *brasero*. This is a pan of hot ash, in concept not unlike the warming pan used in eighteenth century Britain to air the beds. But the *brasero* has a more general use. It is placed in a circular hole cut on a shelf joining together the legs of a table. A tablecloth which reaches the floor all the way round is then placed on the table, and those seated round the table can toast their legs in the heat emanating from the *brasero* under the tablecloth.

Nowadays you can buy a thermostatically controlled, electric *brasero*, which at least doesn't smoke, flare up or go out, but even so, traditional *braseros* still abound in the *campo*. However, while they provide an economical and eminently sensible way to heat the lower half of the body when seated at a table, and they do, indirectly, assist in heating the small living rooms found in the average Andalucían home, they aren't the most practical system for heating a large room, let alone a whole house or a converted olive-oil mill. We spent more nights in our mill than we cared to think about, getting undressed in front of a portable gas fire and going to bed with two hot water bottles, six blankets and three layers of clothing and still we shivered in our bed, from which we learned two further lessons:

For year-round living in the *campo*, some kind of general heating is essential; and secondly, we wished we had brought more warm clothes!

We also came to understand why the campasiños *buy large plastic storage boxes, and pretty cardboard ones as well. They keep their winter clothes in them during the summer and summer clothes during the winter, an eminently sensible arrangement. Mothballs are still for sale here in great quantities and other clothes protection products I have never seen before. Bedding and blankets are treated the same way, stored in summer in protective boxes or bags.* Campasiños *store away anything they are not using now so as to have more room for daily life in what is sometimes a very confined space.*

These lessons brought sharply into focus a fact of life in Andalucía which we had simply not anticipated: that for the greater part of the year, Andalucía has weather - like the stuff we have in Britain, when we get all four seasons in one day, twice, and which we talk about endlessly. That sort of weather. While Andalucía is predominately hot and is usually so sometime each month, it can be guaranteed as a daily occurrence for less than half the year. So if rain, wind, snow and cold also play a significant part in the scheme of things, then clearly it is prudent to take them into account when considering whether to settle here and whereabouts to do so if you decide to go ahead. Although in our case it was a bit late for that, and we certainly weren't having second thoughts, it caused us to review with concern the possible effect that prolonged rain might have on our ability to use the access track to our *finca*, and the fact that the *cortijo* was unlikely to have foundations and stood on a fairly steep slope!

However this was being a bit alarmist - so we thought - and in any event, of course, the sun does shine most of the time in Andalucía, even if in winter it doesn't heat the air much when you are 900 metres up a mountain, as we were at the mill. We found that, when the sun disappeared below the horizon in the late afternoons, the temperature dropped like a stone, but it was sufficiently hot at mid-day to burn us if we weren't careful, and it certainly gave us enough of a tan to make friends and relatives at back in England extremely jealous. And of course, from late spring to early autumn, and occasionally at other times, the sun can be very, very hot indeed.

The attitude to this heat is generally different for those who intend to live here from those who come on holiday. Of course we all want to enjoy it - after all, it is one of the reasons why we come here - but enjoyment can become punishment if there is no escape. In Spain, for five months of the year, those who live here tend to avoid the mid-day heat and for two months shun it altogether. Holidaymakers, on the other hand, lie broiling on the beach throughout the day, vigorously acquiring sun-tans in the fourteen days allotted to them. Those who live here are grateful for small windows, high walls and narrow streets, which always provide a degree of shade. Tourists prefer panoramic views and open balconies, so that they can capture the full benefit of their fortnight's sun. This can lead to spectacular errors of judgement when former tourists buy houses here.

We visited friends who had bought a house the previous winter in which the picture windows in the main reception room and their bedroom faced west, giving a wonderful evening view towards the sea. Unfortunately the consequence was that the rooms caught the full strength of the afternoon sun. Unshaded and without air-conditioning, in summer they became untenable and our friends had found it necessary to take substantial – and expensive – remedial measures in order to use them at all between May and October. Some of these almost entirely obscured the view, thus defeating the original object of the exercise!

What can seem idyllic as a home in the sun from the perspective of a British winter can be a nightmare in the reality of the Andalucían summer - be warned!

In tandem with our learning curve about the climate in the *campo* came the revelation about its roads – not the *autovia* (motorways) or the major trunk roads, which are generally similar to their counterparts right across Europe, but the regional roads, the C-roads and the roads with two-letter prefixes, the nearest equivalent to which in Britain are the three-figure A-roads and B-roads. And beyond these, figuratively and literally without number, are the 'country' and 'cart roads', all of which are official roads allegedly maintained by their local council, and which are the equivalent of the roads which lead to and between villages and hamlets in the UK; these are just a little different from their British counterparts!

Susan has written about our first encounter with these roads, on the 'old' A-356, and this was to form the yardstick against which we measured our subsequent experiences. G.K. Chesterton wrote:

> Before the Roman came to Rye or out to Severn strode,
> The rolling English drunkard made the rolling English road.

That's as may be, but today all but the very rural roads and lanes in England have been straightened out as far as possible long since, and their gradients have been smoothed out by engineering them through, rather than over, features such as hills. And there are few, if any, public roads which do not have a metalled, 'tarmac' surface. This, we discovered, was far from the case in Andalucía.

There are good reasons for this. Unlike most of Britain, inland Andalucía is mountainous, and the time, cost and upheaval of blasting through these mountains, and of spanning the intervening valleys with bridges for the hundreds of little roads which criss-cross the *campo*, are major undertakings which, until comparatively recently, simply weren't justified – there wasn't the vehicle-owning public to warrant it. Now, with Spain's membership of the European Union and the massive influx of foreign settlers, together with an almost exponential explosion of business in the area, the task is being addressed, but it isn't one which can be completed quickly.

Think of the walkers' paths and bridleways in England. Now put them to use as roads. In wet weather the cars, tractors and lorries which use them churn them up and make them all but impassable and leave vast holes in their wake. They can become awash with water, either because part of the track may actually be a river bed, or simply because of the amount of drainage coming off the hillside. It is an abiding experience to watch cars of all shapes and sizes navigating these roads. It is like something out of another era. If their owners have been accustomed to taking a mule or horse there they see no reason why a car cannot do it. To see a Fiat Panda venture up a muddy, winding track to a casita *half way up a hill in the middle of nowhere and return full of vegetables grown on the car owner's land, or a small van full of huge sacks of olives slithering down a sodden track on its way to the mill is a wonder to behold.*

In the days which followed we learned a good deal more about *campo* roads, a process which began on Boxing Day at the hotel in Colmenar courtesy of Paul, a retired accountant whom we had first seen on the day we arrived, trying to make a call to his wife in England on the hotel's coin-operated telephone, a nerve-racking experience at the best of times, not helped by his simultaneously endeavouring to control an eight-stone, two-year-old St Bernard with which he was sharing a single room at the hotel. For some unaccountable reason he looked a trifle harassed!

Paul had shared the table with us on Christmas Day, when he had diffidently asked if we would like to see the house he and his wife had bought and were renovating 'up a hill, just a few miles from here. We'll go in my car if you like [a Cherokee Jeep],' he added, 'only I think the track up to the house might be a bit much for your Daimler. We'll go by "Slaughter-house Hill", though, so that you will know the best way to get through Colmenar with a car like yours.' *Slaughterhouse Hill?* 'They keep the goats for slaughter there. Sometimes you see them killing them on the side of the road.' *Oh, great. Welcome to Spain!*

We set off, with Mack, the St Bernard, breathing wetly in our ears and trying hard to show his affection through the dog-guard fitted behind the rear seat (we have news for the manufacturers, by the way: their guard was totally inadequate for a dog like Mack. We had to brace ourselves against it all the way to prevent us from being squashed flat!). We swung right-handed round the town, down past a disused warehouse, round a 120 degree bend and up this 15% gradient hill and there it was ... a goat being skinned by the side of the road, watched not at all impassively by several dozen others!

From the edge of the town we took what we now know to be a good country road: that is to say, it was surfaced with tarmac. Otherwise it had totally unguarded bends, with a drop on one side so steep that all we could see of the almond trees which bordered the road on that side were the tips of the topmost branches. It had no verge on either side: the tarmac simply came to an abrupt stop in a lethal, tyre-ripping serrated edge. And of course there were the pot-holes of varying size and depth, unmarked, unguarded, and wonderful traps for the unwary. Susan and I clung to each other for mutual support for every yard of the journey like the survivors of a shipwreck.

After about five miles, Paul pointed up a track off to the left of the road. 'The house is up there,' he said. The track was almost vertical, only just wide enough for the Jeep, and to us seemed impossible (and impassable). *Up there?? Good grief, a goat couldn't get up there (memo: I must get my mind off goats).* Oh yes it could, and apparently so could a Cherokee Jeep, without even using 4-wheel drive. And this, as we were to discover, was very much 'the norm' for access roads and tracks in this part of the Andalucían *campo*. Unsurprisingly this led us to decide, sadly, to part company with the Duchess and exchange her for something less glamorous but a little more suited to our needs.

To while away our time at the mill, and to make our shopping forays to the coast more interesting once we had changed the car, we often tried to find different ways of getting back there on the return journey. By now we were fully accustomed to the idea that a 'road' – at least, the kind of roads we were using – would often be unsurfaced, would generally follow the contours of the terrain, would usually have minimal or no signs indicating where it was leading (although it would scrupulously display a 'Stop' sign at the point where it joined a major road) and would, in short, be far removed from what we had come to accept as a road suitable for motor cars in the UK.

Following these roads we had a number of experiences which remain indelibly carved on our memories. On one occasion, coming back from Málaga on the magnificent C-345, a road which rivals both in its scenery and in the need for total concentration on the part of the driver the *Grande Corniche* and the Amalfi drive south of Naples, we decided, when in sight of Colmenar, to turn off onto a 'cart road' which looked promising: it ran in roughly the right direction and it had a speed limit sign just beyond where it joined the C-345, which we presumed meant that it must lead somewhere, mustn't it? Well, yes it did, but not quite where we thought.

After nearly three kilometres of downhill driving, along a road which steadily deteriorated from being merely unsurfaced to being unsurfaced with mammoth potholes and being far too narrow to attempt a three-point turn, we came to a stop outside a *cortijo* which someone was clearly renovating. Here the road ended, on a spur running out from the side of the hill, with nothing in front of it except a drop of a few hundred feet. That was it: no village, no junction, nothing but a small house with a cat wearing an amused smile. So we carefully turned round, conscious of the echoing silence around us, and retraced our steps up the same three kilometres of unsurfaced road.

On another, coming back from Torre del Mar up the 'Arc Road', we decided to turn off and follow the sign to the village of Los Romanes. For the first two kilometres this was as good a metalled road you could wish to find anywhere, largely because of a major development of fairly exclusive houses with a view over Lake Viñuela. After that, the surface changed to concrete, and took us through the village itself. Beyond the village, the concrete stopped, and the now familiar dirt road branched in two directions. We took the left-hand branch, principally because it looked as if it was heading in more or less the right direction and had marginally the less horrendous surface, aware as we did so that we were being followed at a discreet distance by a little white van. Such vans are ubiquitous in Spain, but nevertheless we were slightly apprehensive at its limpet-like shadowing.

The next kilometre was hair-raising. Not only did the 'road' pass along the side of a precipitous cliff, with a vertical rock face on one side and a sheer, totally unguarded drop of about two hundred metres on the other, it also narrowed to barely the width of our car, and not even that in two places. When we reached a small plateau, we stopped to draw breath. The little white van stopped, too, and a large, hairy man got out and advanced towards us. We became extremely apprehensive, as we were miles from anywhere and totally out of contact with the rest of humanity.

We needn't have worried. The Neanderthal stopped several yards from our car and asked courteously, in the unmistakable accent of North Island, New Zealand, whether we had been down this road before. No, we replied, we hadn't. 'In that case,' he said, 'I would advise against going any further. The road gets very steep just round the corner, so steep that for most of the year, you can't get up it. And there is this right-angled bend, too, and you have a fairly long car...' His voice tailed away. We thanked him, and in view of the fact that he made no comment at all about the width of the road ahead, presumably because he found nothing out of the ordinary concerning the width of the road we had just negotiated, we decided to take his advice!

The successful completion of a voyage along roads like these made us feel as Marco Polo must have done, but negotiating our way through *campo* towns and villages faced us with a completely different set of challenges to keep us on our toes (or wheels). These towns and villages almost all stem from the Moorish occupation of Spain, and have more in common with their cousins in North Africa and southern Italy than they do with those in Northern Europe. The streets are often extremely steep usually because, for strategic reasons, many of these towns were built on dominant geographical features, and because they were built to keep the heat away from the buildings, the streets are usually exceedingly narrow, even in the larger towns. Such streets can be faintly nerve-wracking at first encounter.

Casabermeja is a major town near Colmenar, and provides the locale for the schools which serve the area. It has its own exit from the *Autovía del Andalucía*, and the road from this exit not only gives access to the town, it is also the feeder road for Villanueva de la Conception and Colmenar. The town also lies on the old main road from Antiquera to Málaga. Until the *autovía* was built, this was the only route between the two cities. We were therefore fooled into thinking that it would be a well-signposted main road. We were wrong.

Turning left instead of right at a critical junction we made our way into the town centre, and up behind the schools. Having successfully negotiated a number of extremely narrow, right-angled turnings, we found ourselves facing a long, familiarly 15% uphill street, paved with cobble-stones and still with the original centre gutter to wash away the mule and goat droppings. This street was unusual in that it ran dead straight; it was not unusual in that it was wide enough only for two (small) cars to pass abreast. However, not only was this street open to two-way traffic, there were also cars parked along its entire length. These left room for only one car at a time to drive on the remaining available space. Inevitably we met two cars coming down while we were going up, for one of which I had to back down the street into a side turning – and of course then found that this car wanted to turn into the same side turning – while the other had to back fifty metres up the street to let us pass.

We left Casabermeja at the end of the tarmac road along a newly scraped out, brick-red earth road. Following our noses we came to the road we were trying to find in the first place. The old Casabermaja to Málaga road is narrow and winding with wonderful views out over the countryside. It was marvellous, if occasionally slightly hairy, to glimpse the motorway far below and we were glad we had come this way. While it needed more care to navigate, owing to a noticeable scarcity of any kind of wall or fence along the verge, we did not pass one car nor were passed by a car until we were close to Málaga.

Colmenar has no such by-pass, and its 'through' streets - roads would not be the right word to describe them - all have gradients of around 15%. On the steepest of these roads is a popular supermarket. Outside the supermarket the road is around 18%, where it is also at its narrowest. There are no pavements and, like that back street in Casabermeja, the street is two-way and can barely accommodate two small cars abreast. One morning I came up behind two men, with a mule and a dog, walking sedately up the middle of the street, oblivious to the bus coming the other way. It proved an interesting experience.

Elsewhere it is often the width of the streets, not the gradient, which presents the challenge. In Periana, a substantial town, the nearest to our future home and again one where all the schools for the area are centralised, most of the streets are wide enough for only one vehicle. At the same time, the corners are near right-angles, and many have no pavements - the walls of the houses form the edge of the road.

Recognising that these conditions present problems for tourists, which the town is trying to encourage, the local authority has introduced a one-way system. Locals who have lived there all their lives find this restriction unnecessary. One market day I found myself confronted, as I scrupulously followed the white arrow on its circular blue traffic sign directing me around a totally blind corner, by a Land Rover and another vehicle coming the other way. Since two against one are no odds I stopped, intending to back up, only to find that I now had another vehicle directly behind me. How the Land Rover in front of me got past without taking off my car's bumper I shall never know. And now they have installed traffic lights which the locals don't obey either!

All this sounds very negative, which it certainly isn't. It simply requires an expansion of one's preconceived notions about what is suitable for a modern wheeled vehicle, and the willingness to adapt one's driving attitudes accordingly. The beauty of it all is that because you are obliged to accept these conditions, your own driving attitudes have to change; the alternative is acute frustration and possibly a coronary. Although you need the skills and reactions of a rally driver and you cannot relax your concentration for a second, it is a totally different pressure from the stress and nervous tension from which we certainly suffered, coping with the aggressive, noisome and congested traffic in southern England. But, if wide metalled roads, pavements and adherence to traffic regulations are essential to your peace of mind, then the advice must be:

Choose the site of your future home with care ... or avoid the *campo* altogether!

Associated with roads and driving is, of course, traffic. The lack of vehicular traffic in the *campo* remains a source of wonder to us. A man riding a mule is often a more common sight on the roads than a lorry, and a herd of goats going to and from pasture is a great deal more common than a bus. In the early mornings and late evenings these animals amble along the streets in the towns and villages and the country roads nearby, going to or returning from work or grazing, and we have learned to expect this. In many cases they actually live in the villages and towns in the same

dwellings as their owners, the evidence for which is readily apparent down the middle of the streets! One evening, when I was driving through Colmenar, I found myself brought to a halt and obliged to wait while two mules were unhurriedly unharnessed in the middle of the road and were then led straight into one of the terraced houses that formed the street. From this, and other experiences, we learned that

Mules often take priority over cars in country towns...

That this was not so remarkable as it sounds was born out by the experience of an English couple we met, who were invited to dinner in a village house. They had sat down as dusk was falling outside. As their hostess was bringing the first course to the table she stopped in mid-stride and rolled back the carpet inside the front door. Within seconds later the door opened and in walked her husband leading their mule, which he took straight through the house to its stable at the back. His wife then repositioned the carpet and resumed her conversation, while her husband cleaned both the mule and himself before joining his wife and their guests at the table (leaving the mule in its stable).

This is also a land where, until comparatively recently, not only was the mule the principal form of transport, it was also one which invariably gave way to human beings. This, we suspect, is the root of the wide-spread practice for people here to stand in the middle of the street to talk to friends and pass the time of day, since it was all too easy to get out of the way of a mule, and in any event a mule would stop. It is also reflected in the reaction of pedestrians in country towns and villages to on-coming cars which we have learned to anticipate, having had one or two heart-stopping moments when swinging round one or two blind corners only to find local citizens walking down the middle of the road, blithely indifferent to the possible consequences of being struck by something large, heavy and fast moving!

So do pedestrians!

Perhaps as a result of this, driving standards we have found on the whole to be remarkably good in the *campo*, although there are, of course, exceptions. There is little of the aggression commonplace in Great Britain and many other north European countries; drivers are far more patient, and more inclined to wait or give way as appropriate at intersections than their northern counterparts.

We have also found that lorry drivers, so often vilified in other countries, are far more considerate in the *campo* of the needs of faster vehicles behind them than any others we have met. The reason for this is perhaps historic. Years ago, when Pegaso, the Spanish lorry manufacturer, occupied a similar position to that once held in the United Kingdom by British Leyland, their lorries had a green light mounted on the rear beside the tail lights. This was to enable the driver to signal to anyone behind that it was safe to pass, a necessary courtesy on the roads which prevailed at the time. Sadly this green light is now history - Brussels again, no doubt - but the attitude appears to remain.

Driving is once more a joy. Out in the campo *they have an unhurried approach, with minimal traffic and beautiful views. On the coast is a different story as is Málaga itself but no worse than driving in a busy town anywhere. Everyone is so polite even if you get it wrong; road courtesy is not dead here. There are accident black spots and people who drive too fast, of course, but every paradise has its serpent.*

There is also the convention on narrow, mountain roads, with which the *campo* abounds, that vehicles coming down should give way to those coming up, everything else being equal. This perhaps stems once more from the early days of lorries, and certainly from the days of bullock-carts; either of these, if stopped while climbing a steep gradient, might quite literally be unable to start again. Although bullock-carts are now a rarity and lorries are generally sufficiently powerful for this courtesy to be redundant it is still practised, and we have found the overall awareness by Spanish lorry drivers of the needs of other road users to be exceptionally high.

Chapter 6

In great affairs we ought to apply ourselves less to
creating chances than to profiting from those that offer.

(*La Rochefoucauld*, Maxim)

Apart from this sleuthing, our daily routine at the mill was boring in the extreme: we got up when it got light (around 8.00 a.m.), lit the gas fires and the water heater in the cavernous main room, had a shower if we could bear the thought of standing in the freezing cold shower stall until the water heated up, had breakfast, did the washing if necessary, read books on the patio once the temperature had risen sufficiently, tried to learn Spanish from our cassette course, had lunch, went for a walk, back indoors when the sun went down and early to bed, as the lighting in the mill was so poor it made reading difficult, and anyway by then we had read enough.

This time-filling tedium was forced on us by the need to save all the money we possessed for the renovations we knew we would have to undertake on the *cortijo*, the cost of which we knew from the hard-earned experience of corresponding activities in the UK would be at least 50 per cent higher than any builder's estimate and, from the experience of others here, would probably be the same again as the price we had actually paid for the property. So culturally improving trips to Seville, Jerez de la Frontera, Córdoba, or the Alhambra Palace in Granada were simply not on, which was particularly frustrating as we had more than a sneaking suspicion that once we started work on the *cortijo* it would be many a long month before we could take time off for diversions such as these.

However it was while we were at the mill that the idea for a business, other than simply administering the *finca*, was conceived. The catalyst was our experience from staying at the B&B near Loja. Although that establishment was run by charming people from a charming house in a pleasant village, with a small swimming-pool and magnificent views of the nearby mountains (mountains up which most of their guests chose to walk as their holiday activity), it had no land at all and was well over an hour's drive from Málaga Airport. Yet it thrived, had repeat bookings, and was in all respects a success. Couldn't we do something similar? We would have an equally magnificent view and would have land for guests to stroll round and room for a much larger pool. We would be near an equally pleasant village and a much nicer small town, and only forty-five minutes by car from the same international airport. More importantly, we would have time in which to prepare our plans for the renovation of the *cortijo* with this new enterprise in mind. It also wasn't as though we would be going into such an activity totally 'blind'; our experience with foreign students, many of whom had been adults holding down highly responsible jobs, had proved that in principle we could do it and make a success of it, albeit with a little 'fine tuning' to adjust ourselves to purely holiday guests. So why not add the cultivation of paying guests to the already settled idea of cultivating the *finca*?

This thought was beginning to gestate, but had not evolved into anything concrete, when our lives were suddenly, and permanently, altered when Eloïse (not the name she started with) was thrust upon us. We had gone into Colmenar early, partly to buy bread (we had run out at the week-end, and weren't able to store a reserve, as locally-made bread went stale in a day unless frozen, and we didn't have a deep-freeze) and partly to go to the bank and the post office. Once we had completed these chores and had filled up with petrol, we had then gone to the hotel to show the *dueño* our photos of the *cortijo*. However, before we got to see him we encountered an English couple, Helen and John, who were also house-hunting, and who were sitting on the veranda having coffee, Helen looking more than slightly shattered.

We could see immediately one possible reason for this: a beautiful young pointer, clearly a new acquisition, sitting beside them as still as a Staffordshire stone dog. 'Where did he come from?' we asked. 'The roadside,' came the reply. 'He had just been dumped, and when we spoke to him he came up to the car and simply got in.' This is not uncommon in this part of Spain, or even England in the post-Christmas period, so we were not surprised at this. What did surprise us was the dog's calm, his incredible good nature and his obedience, which weren't consistent at all with the fairly horrendous scars on this head and hindquarters, and his status as a stray.

We were also surprised when, having finished telling us about Jason, Helen opened her anorak to reveal a kitten, which Susan estimated couldn't have been more than three or four days old, clinging to her sweater and mewing continuously. 'We found it dumped too,' she said, 'yesterday. In Seville. In a cardboard box. I just couldn't leave it there, but it kept me up for most of last night. I did my best to feed it - I used a thin makeup brush to let it suck some milk from - but it wasn't easy in a hotel bedroom at 3 o'clock in the morning, and I'm really not sure what to do with it now.'

Susan looked at the kitten with an expression I know only too well. 'Can I hold it?' she asked, managing to make it sound more like an instruction than a request. Helen handed it over. It fitted almost exactly into Susan's not very large hand. Susan proceeded to stroke its tummy and rear end with a tissue, and was immediately rewarded with a flood of urine, all over her jeans. 'That was part of the problem,' she said. 'It hasn't been able to wee.'

I could see her Machiavellian mind turning over as she continued to stroke the kitten with a (different) damp tissue. 'You've done a fantastic job, keeping it alive this long,' she said, 'and the makeup brush idea was inspired. But look; we've got a stove and some milk at the mill. Would you let me take it back and feed it? You could come and get it later; you know how to find us. Any time is OK, but around 4 o'clock would be best for us.'

Helen's look said it all. She handed over the kitten without a word - and I held my peace. A few minutes later, Susan said, 'Well, if we're going to get some food into it, we really ought to be going.' Talk about obvious! Feeling the need to nip this particular idea in the bud, I said, 'We're absolutely not going to keep it, are we?'

No reply.

'Are we!' I repeated.

'No dear,' said Susan. We walked down to the car in silence - apart from the kitten mewing, that is. We got into the car and drove off. The silence, and the kitten's mews, became deafening.

A three-day-old kitten doesn't have the strongest grip on life without its natural mum, and one which has been left in a cardboard box in the sun and then had to survive its next night on earth in a hotel bedroom with a year-old pointer for company and a surrogate mum who had neither the experience nor the resources to deal with its needs was defying the statistical odds, and Susan acknowledged this. Still, if it was going to have a fighting chance, she was as well equipped as anyone to give it, as this would by no means be the first foundling she had reared.

Before I met her she had, in her time, incubated, hatched and hand-reared African grey parrots and cockatiels as a hobby; incubated, hatched and reared a silver pheasant chick, no mean feat since a solo chick can't be left alone. She had rescued and helped to fledge wild bird chicks which had fallen out of nests, and hand-reared any number of kittens and lambs, ducklings, chicks and calves from her days as a farm worker. So she certainly had the knowledge to deal with this situation.

What was less easy was equipment. Hand-rearing a kitten of this age presents a number of problems which would be much less critical with a kitten even a couple of weeks older. The first, and so obvious it can easily get overlooked, is the importance of mum and mum's tongue. The latter not only cleans hygienically; it also stimulates the digestive system and the evacuation process, provides comfort and reassurance, and teaches the kitten how to clean itself. And, of course, mum herself provides warmth and a living, breathing presence for the kitten's security.

More technical problems include gastro-enteritis, which can be fatal for nursing infants of any species; hygiene, with regard to the means of feeding and cleaning the animal; and the absence, locally, of the kind of pet shop resources available in England, where kitten 'feeders' and kitten milk formulae are available to cope with situations such as this. Possibly the local veterinary clinic could have provided some, but it was shut.

I had a fair understanding of some of this, having been brought up on a farm myself, so when we were half way home, I asked, 'What are you going to feed it with?', wondering if I was going to get a reply.

'A mixture of milk and some of that cream we've got,' Susan said smartly.

'And how are you going to replicate "mum"?', I persisted, feeling I was getting further and further out of control of the situation.

'Well, you know that sterile medical pack which we kept in the car and never used? The one which expired in 1996. It's got three 5 ml syringes in it. I'm going to try using one of those – without a needle, of course.'

Of course. Why couldn't I think of that?

When we got back to the mill I found the spare hot-water-bottle and boiled a kettle while Susan, holding the kitten to herself with one hand, found an egg-cup and put in a little cream and twice that amount of milk with the other. She also had some sterilising tablets in a toiletry bag which we had bought as a precautionary measure before we left England since she tends to suffer with IBS, and felt that they might 'come in handy'. I don't think even she imagined they would be used to sterilise a syringe after it had been used to feed a kitten!

When the water was reasonably warm, we decanted some into a cup and put the milk-filled syringe into it to bring it up to blood temperature; the rest I used, once it had got to nearly boiling, to fill the hot-water-bottle which would lie in the bottom of the kitten's bed, and to fill the thermos flask which my son had thoughtfully given us as a Christmas present, to serve as a back-up syringe-warming system. (I don't think Simon had quite visualised this use for his present, but then, he doesn't know Susan quite as well as I do now.)

With the syringe filled with the blood-temperature mix, it was crunch time; would the kitten drink the mix? Would it ever! Susan had modified the syringe by reducing the rubber gasket in the cylinder to a narrow ring. This allowed the cylinder to act almost as a 'demand valve'. When Susan gently pressed the plunger and allowed some of the mixture to flow into the kitten's mouth, not only did it start to drink as though its life depended on it (which I suppose it did, come to think of it), it also quickly learned that if it sucked, it achieved the same result. Within minutes, and with the kitten making a noise not unlike a drain emptying, 5 ml of mix disappeared from sight.

Over the next four hours, a further 20 ml of mix disappeared the same way! At feeding time Susan took the opportunity to wash the kitten's eyes with a damp cotton bud and, using a piece of toilet paper moistened with warm water to imitate as best as possible a mother cat's tongue, encouraged it to pass urine and faeces. With the kitten's incredible rate of ingestion, we were slightly worried about the possibility of colic, but the kitten seemed to regulate its intake to a manageable rate, and anyway, it seemed an acceptable risk to take at this stage, as the kitten clearly needed to make up for lost time.

After the kitten's fifth feed, at 3.40 p.m., we put it to bed, where it slept for three hours, Susan and I taking turns to check on it every ten minutes to make sure it was actually sleeping, and not doing something rather more permanent. At 6.45 p.m. we woke it up for its sixth feed, and when this passed in the same way as the other five, we began to hope that we were over the first hurdle, and although we weren't out of the woods by a long way, at least death by starvation had been avoided.

In between our visits to the sleeping kitten, Susan and I sat outside in the bright February sunshine. Although it was cold in the shade, it was pleasantly hot by the pool, and as we sat gazing over the sparkling water, wishing it was heated so that we could go for a swim - in fact it was arctic! - we idly discussed words which we liked, both manufactured and real, by way of passing the time.

'I like "thrunging",' said Susan. 'I can't think of a better word to describe what Baggy's doing right now.' (Bagshawe was one of our landlords' two dogs which we were "dog-sitting" while their owners were on an impromptu visit to England. He was at this moment down the hill, busy in the undergrowth.)

'I like "rootling",' I offered. 'It describes perfectly what you do when you search through a kitchen drawer for a bottle opener you know is in there somewhere.' Then, to add an international flavour to the conversation, and to claw back a bit of pride, I added, 'Then there's "*bricolage*", a wonderful word that the French (and the Spanish) use to talk about DIY. And "*oggi*", [pronounced "odgy" as in "dodgy", not "oggi" as in "moggy"],' I went on. 'It means "today" in Italian.'

I should have quit when I was ahead. 'What a good name that would make for the kitten,' Susan mused, 'sexless, and it sums up perfectly how we are going to have to treat it: day by day, with every day being like today.'

'Just a minute,' I thought, bells ringing loudly, *'just what does that mean - "day by day, with every day being like today"? I thought the kitten was going back to Julia. This afternoon. We agreed that. Didn't we?'*

Aloud I said, 'Very true, dear.' I then added, realising that it would be gracious to bow to the inevitable, 'Could it be that you would like to keep it? If so, I could possibly change my mind.'

Susan sat bolt upright on her poolside lounger. 'Would you really?' she asked, sounding just as though she hadn't known all along it would end this way, 'After all, I do think I can give it a chance, and I really don't have anything else to do at the moment.'

Well, that was certainly true, and not only for her. And, as I suddenly realised, looking after the kitten would relieve the boredom for us both, and perhaps reduce the growing tendancy to snipe at one another to an acceptable minimum.

I had been slowly climbing the walls of the mill. I am not and never have been good at doing nothing. To have a purpose is to me a focus. There was nothing to do in the mill once the housework, which was minimal, was done and as we had to watch the pennies outings were restricted though necessity. Sitting in the sun was OK for a while but for months, not me I'm afraid. To have the kitten to take care of even if it went back to Helen at a later date was great. What else did I have to do? So life started to revolve around the kitten.

There was, however, the small matter of taking it to the *cortijo* in due course, where the five cats already in residence might react just a little at the arrival of this infant which didn't belong to any of them. As if reading my thoughts, Susan continued, 'None of the cats at the *cortijo* are house cats, so if Oggi is brought up to regard the house as his domain, we shouldn't have too much difficulty there.' *'No,'* I thought, *'and pigs might fly.'*

But I didn't say it. Neither did I mention the five dogs we were also going to inherit with the *cortijo*, let alone the problems we would face, keeping Oggi out of the way of the builders. Time enough for that.

'I think he's a boy,' I said, bringing the subject back to the present. 'He's so strong, and has such a will to live.'

'I agree,' said Susan, immediately. 'He eats so much, makes such a racket, and complains so much when he has his face washed, he's got to be a boy!'

So much for the modern, emancipated thinking in which Susan and I take so much pride. At the first sniff of controversy, we drop our guards and revert to classic, stereotypical sexism!

Around us as we sat, the early signs of spring were in the air. Bees hummed busily in the almond blossom (Colmenar is famous for its honey). Great flying beetles with iridescent, royal blue carapaces coupled vigorously on our chair legs, then flew away like oversized bumble bees. And down in the almond groves, clouds of Wood White butterflies, looking in the distance like blown petals from the trees, performed an early courtship quadrille.

That evening Helen and John arrived, bearing a bottle. When they hadn't appeared at 4 o'clock, we had wondered whether they had thankfully turned their backs on the kitten, and us. We did them an injustice. They arrived at 7.00 p.m., just after we had settled Oggi down following his sixth meal, and when we were turning our thoughts to our own supper. The bottle they had brought had a two-fold purpose: first, to thank Susan for looking after Oggi for the day and secondly, by way of a lubrication to help persuade us to keep him. When I announced that, if they didn't want him back, we were both happy for him to stay (well, I had to save face somehow), the sigh of relief was audible across the room!

This having been settled, the way was now clear for us to 'wet the baby's head', which we proceeded to do with a dedication which would have done a certain well-known charismatic English footballer proud. First we despatched the bottle of *rosado* they had brought. Then we despatched a litre bottle of red from our supplies. Then John went out to the car and brought in a wicker-covered flagon of the local aperitif wine - a heady, Madeira-like libation with a wonderful tawny colour and a texture of fine velvet.

When a good deal of this had gone the way of the preceding bottles, Helen very fortuitously remembered that she had phone calls to make to England, which she would have to make from back at the hotel as we had no phone. After a further glass or two for the road, we escorted them out into the cold, starlit night . . . and had to restrain John from backing their car straight over the precipitous verge and down into the almond grove below!

Back indoors, we turned our thoughts to food, which now seemed strangely unattractive. However, while we were considering our options Winny (Winston), our landlords' other dog, ensured that these were relegated to their rightful place by having two fits in quick succession. The older of the two dogs, he looked like a cross between Basil Brush and a miniature jackal – with a temperament strongly favouring the jackal. He was also a hyper-intelligent little dog who, like Baggy, had been dumped at the mill one day when a puppy. This resulted in his case in a neurotic personality bordering on the paranoid. Add to this a tendency to take all the world's problems on his shoulders, and also to be highly protective of those whom he was prepared to trust, his reaction to too many new situations at once could be dramatic.

When we had first come to the mill, it had taken him three weeks to be prepared to speak to us – outdoors. Indoors took several more days. Now we were not merely accepted, we had been cast by him in the roles of pack leaders. And when, in one day, we presented him with a potential prey from which he also felt compelled to protect us plus, in the forms of Helen and John, two new people whom he was obliged to face within the confines of the mill, a couple of fits were, on reflection, quite a mild reaction. We telephoned our landlords in England to tell them of this occurrence (using their phone for the purpose), and luckily they were fairly relaxed about it; evidently he had had this problem before.

The reaction of the dogs to the kitten was interesting. Winston's was easy, and conformed to his attitude to all other small creatures: kill! Bagshawe, who looked exactly like a descendant of the Phaeros' hunting dogs portrayed in Egyptian wall-paintings, simply wanted to play with it. Unfortunately, he was not the brightest of dogs, and his idea of play erred a trifle on the over-vigorous. As a result, most small creatures he played with ended up dead. When this happened, his confusion was almost painful. 'I didn't do that, did I?' you could see him thinking. 'Come on, wake up. I know you're only pretending.' And when there was no response he walked disconsolately away, periodically scampering back, if he was allowed to, to give the object a nudge to see if it had changed its mind.

After Winston's fits, the rest of the evening was a bit of an anticlimax. By now we were well past wanting to eat anything, so we decided to bring the evening to an end and go to bed. Because of the need to feed Oggi in isolation, Susan took him into the bedroom, while I bedded down on the bed-settee in the main part of the mill with the dogs. We felt that, if I hadn't, they would have caused even more pandemonium, the moment they heard Oggi 'give tongue' for his next meal. This happened twice during the night, and when it did they both rushed to the bedroom door at the first 'mew', and stood quivering like pointers until silence was restored. What it would have been like if they had been out in the main room on their own didn't bear thinking about!

The result of all this was a more-than-slightly disturbed night for us both; none of this 'it's your turn to feed the baby' routine. We were both up with a vengeance, Susan feeding Oggi and me cursing the dogs. Add to this the highly potent effects of the alcohol we had consumed on empty stomachs, what little sleep we did have was filled with lurid and highly confused dreams. We were both very glad to see the dawn, though unaccountably found facing breakfast a bit of a trial!

Our main problem now was Oggi's diet. The milk and cream mix was certainly providing some nourishment, but we could tell it wasn't enough by the crying which continued long after he had been fed. Although he was full, he wasn't satisfied. Luckily the following day we knew we had to go to Fuengirola, down on the coast, where we hoped we could resolve this dilemma. We had bought our Spanish-registered car from a garage there and, as it was under warranty, when it developed an oil leak in its automatic transmission, we took it back there to get it fixed. When we mentioned our other problem the very glamorous receptionist kindly drew us a map of how to find a veterinary clinic in the town centre from which, in due course, we emerged with a large canister of something called '1st age milk'. Although this was strictly speaking a lactation mix for puppies, we knew it would be perfectly suitable for Oggi, and a lot better than what we had been able to give him up to then. The instructions for the mix were written in eight different languages. We liked the description in

Dutch best: '*Instant melkpoeder voor pups.*' Seemed to catch the spirit perfectly. Even better, the canister contained a feeding bottle and a selection of teats, which we knew would also be far more suitable than the modified syringe.

We had taken Oggi with us to Fuengirola in a cardboard box placed inside an overnight bag (he was much too little to risk leaving at the mill all day, and besides, Winny and Baggy were there!), and having bought the milk mix we walked on towards the sea front, looking for somewhere to feed him. We found a café which suited perfectly – and which, incidentally, also sold us the largest cooked 'English' breakfast imaginable for just under £3 each (British motorway cafés, please note) – and the milk mix clearly did the trick as, after the inevitable 5 ml-worth and a cuddle, Oggi fell asleep for the next three hours without a murmur, though not before Susan had had to go through her usual procedure with a tissue at his rear end, which brought a mixed response from the passers by – British, Spanish and others – who witnessed it . . . especially when she was successful!

Over the next few days, Oggi's intake increased to anything up to 10 ml per meal, and since he was still consuming six meals a day he took on the appearance, after each meal, of Baloo the Bear in the Disney cartoon film of the Rudyard Kipling's *Jungle Book*. We expected him to break into 'The Bear Necessities', like a miniature Phil Harris, and do a portly tap-dance. Oggi? More like Podgy!

Outside the confines of the mill, spring was now in full flood. The second variety of almond tree, the one with the pink blossom, was now in bloom, and the hillsides were covered with a patchwork of what, from a distance, looked like a blanket of pink and white old man's beard. One morning, when I let the dogs out at ten past seven, I went out onto the terrace still in my dressing-gown to watch the dawn. Although it was chilly, it certainly wasn't cold, and while it would be another forty minutes before the sun broke my particular horizon, it was clearly already up for those on the coast.

From where I stood the slopes of the still snow-capped *Sierra de Tejeda* changed, as I watched, from deepest slate where they remained in shadow to an opalescent pearl where the sun was beginning to strike, while beyond, the distant *Sierra de Almijara* marched in a haze-covered procession of mountain peaks, like an illustration from *The Lord of the Rings*, all bathed in the rosy gold of the still invisible rising sun. And this on 20 February, a date when, in more northern climes, you probably couldn't even see distant mountains for the clouds, or the rain, or the snow, let alone stand outside to look at them in your dressing-gown.

An hour later, as we were getting ready to go into Colmenar to buy some groceries, I watched a *peon* ride by on one mule while leading two others, and listened as he sang the high, quavering cadences of an Andalucían *canción*. We caught up with him later, a surprisingly young man, who gave us a cheerful wave as we passed him, and we couldn't help wondering which of us was more in tune with the landscape, he with his mules or us in our car? A few minutes later, we passed an almond grove where a man was ploughing with two mules on an almost vertical slope, and we were left in no doubt that it was we who were out of step.

By the way, mules used for ploughing are left- or right-handed, and neither can change even if they wanted to. For a ploughing mule to die is disaster for the owner. He will have a hard time finding a replacement. Not a lot of people know that!

After shopping and the inevitable pit-stop for petrol, where we had the embarrassment of having our Spanish bank's cash card refuse to pay through lack of funds, we called in at the hotel to show Oggi to Helen and John and to have a restorative *café con leche*. What we hadn't expected was an even more restorative *café grande con lec y coñac*, the *coñac* courtesy of the *dueño*. And this at ten o'clock in the morning!

The days now passed by in ponderous procession, each one a copy of the last, like elephants holding each others' tails, while we contained ourselves with fiercely controlled impatience for the slow Spanish system to spew out the paperwork for the *cortijo*. This was extremely frustrating; we were acutely aware that the year was advancing, and unless the owners of the *cortijo* were remarkably untypical, human nature dictated that they would be less conscientious now with the thousand-and-one things that always need doing around a farm than they had been when they were the beneficiaries of their labours. This meant that with every passing day we knew we would be faced with an increasing

number of remedial things to do to the land and the trees, as well as all the things we wanted with the house. And beside the land and the trees there were the five resident dogs, five cats and five chickens, all of which we were inheriting, a 'dead' Fiat 500 parked under a tree, sundry crates of empty beer bottles secreted in the hedges, and any number of strange, anonymous things buried in the grass which needed removing. (As I typed this list, I realised more and more just how like my parents' farm in Cornwall this one was when they bought it - talk about history repeating itself!)

The countryside was coming to life but all we could do was watch, looking wistfully over the intervening valleys towards our intended home, and make plans. One day we tried to find our way to the finca on our own (we had been driven there previously by Judy and her husband), to take measurements and have another look. The first time out we ended up on the other side of the river with no way across and no idea of how to reach the house. The second time was better but we had to turn back as the track from the village to the river was being tarmaced by the various owner of fincas beside it. The third time we made it but became totally confused as the bridge over the river had been moved - a new bridge had been built and the old one dismantled and all in less than a month since our visit!

Our daily life with Oggi also slid slowly by. By now we had developed a routine. At 6.40 a.m. we would get up, me to put the kettle on for tea, Susan to get Oggi's breakfast ready. Susan would then go back to bed and extract a by now highly vociferous kitten from the grey, overnight bag in which he slept in his cardboard box, and give him his feed. This Oggi would take on his back, holding the bottle with his paws, the way a sea-otter holds a clam prior to smashing it on the stone balanced on its chest. Luckily Oggi never learned this trick with his bottle!

I would watch this process, and the descent of the level of the fluid in the bottle like bath water running out, while the tea was brewing, since living in the mill was very like living in a caravan, with everything on one level and within easy reach of everything else. The tea I would then bring back to bed with me, first putting the kettle on again for Oggi's hot water bottle, which of course had grown cold during the night. Peace would then reign until Oggi drew breath from drinking to complain that his TUMMY HURT and he needed a WEE (or worse)! His tummy hurt, of course, because of the speed at which he had been drinking, and he needed a wee (or worse) because he hadn't got round to it during the night.

There is, I am sure, something intensely bonding about lying in bed beside one's wife, tearing off strips of toilet paper and folding them into three, while she operates the other end of the production line, wiping a kitten's rear end with a moistened tissue, trying to encourage it to wee (or worse) a few inches from one's face ... and then trying to cope with the ensuing flood when 'let down' finally occurs, while one simultaneously tries to drink one's own tea before it gets stone cold, but it escapes me for the moment. Suffice it to say that it was a relief when, regular to the minute, there would be a thunderous crash on the mill house door at 7.30 as the dogs, who were let out by their owners (they were back from England by now) at that time, came to bid us good morning and find out whether anything had changed about THAT THING during the night.

Baggy would invariably tire of this after a minute or two, and would slope off to find something more rewarding to do, like barking at a muleteer passing a quarter of a mile away, but Winny would bounce onto the bed, give us both a passing lick by way of greeting, and then settle down with his eyes glued on the kitten, his head turning at every move like a miniature Wimbledon spectator. Nothing would deflect him from this especially when Oggi, after he had completed his breakfast and his toilet, would have his first period of play with us.

This play period was important. Already we had noticed that, because he was being fed from a bottle and not by his real mum, Oggi had not developed the knack of 'kneading', an essential skill to encourage the milk to flow under normal feline nursing conditions. What the psychological results of this deprivation would be in later life, if any, we couldn't begin to guess. Additionally, in the absence of mum and any feline siblings, there was none of the rough and tumble of nursery life which would be the normal lot of a growing kitten. This we had to replicate as best we could, not only for the psychological benefits but also for the physical ones, since this type of exercise is essential in helping a kitten develop the necessary strength of limb, speed of reaction and simple aggression appropriate for a hunting animal.

We tried to give as much time as possible to this first play period of the day, so it was usually around 8 o'clock when we came to put Oggi back to bed in his overnight bag, on his by now replenished hot water bottle covered with a towel, and we evicted a strongly protesting Winny into the outside world (his owners insisted that he and Baggy were '*campo* dogs', not domestic pets, despite the fact that they themselves let the dogs into the house in the evenings and overnight, and shouldn't be encouraged into the mill - not the first nor the only inconsistency we encountered during our stay there). After this we could actually consider getting our own breakfasts. Whoever was it said that having animals is restful?

A few nights later the weather broke. The clouds had been building up ominously for some time, and as darkness fell, so did the rain. Only a little at first, but accompanied by tumultuous rolls of thunder and great flashes of lightning, cracking and roaring and lighting up the sky as the mountain gods played their games of bowls. Then came the rain, in torrents, and with the rain the clouds fell upon the mountains and sank into the valleys, so that soon nothing could be seen from the windows of the mill but a grey-white wall of mist.

When I went outside, all I could see was the swimming pool on one side of the house and the track leading down into the valley on the other. Of the valley itself, and the groves of almonds and olives, and the road to Colmenar, nothing. It was as if we were suspended in the clouds themselves, and since, prudently, no-one was driving at this time, the silence was absolute. Later, when the rain stopped, the mist remained and the silence was broken by the steady drip, drip, drip of water from the eaves of the mill, from the branches of the eucalyptus and the invisible olive and almond trees... and from the washing which I had hung out earlier in the day when we got back from shopping and before Susan had taken to her bed with the 'Colmenar Lurgy', and which I had forgotten to bring in!

It was at about this time that Oggi acquired his ultimate name, Eloïse. It came about first because, one day, we realised, embarrassingly, that 'he' was actually 'she'. With this realisation, and in the light of our experiences with her, we decided that a name change was appropriate, and we chose Eloïse because her behaviour reminded us totally of the heroine of a wonderful series of French children's books, a child of that name of about eight years of age, who lives in a hotel with her extremely wealthy parents, is looked after by a nanny, and populates her private world with imaginary scenarios which are wondrous in their inventiveness. It seemed to us, watching her, that our kitten mirrored this precisely!

Shortly after this we began to wean her onto cat food. In fact, 'wean' isn't quite the right word, since from the moment she started, Eloïse took to solid food in much the same way as she had taken to the milk and cream mix six weeks earlier. We didn't feed her kitten food directly from the tin straight off, of course, nor was it simply put onto a dish in the hope that she would eat it. Her initial intake was diluted with a little boiled water and, since she had no 'mum' to copy in the difficult skills of eating or lapping, we fed it to her on a plastic tea-spoon.

This conjures up a scene of cottage-like cosiness: little kitten serenely swallowing small mouthfuls as they are offered to her, while doting surrogate parents look on. In fact, from the word 'go', Eloïse would try to hook the spoon towards her and cram the entire contents into her mouth in one gulp. There was nothing cosy about this at all. A flashing right hook would scythe out from under her chin, razor-sharp little claws fully extended, and Eloïse would fight for every last scrap. After that, she would turn her attention to her bottle, and if that wasn't immediately ready, it would receive the same treatment, in a blur of 'left-and-rights to the head and body'. It was a miracle she didn't puncture it, and her work-rate was of an intensity of which Barry McGuigan at his best would have been proud. To this day the bottle bears the evidence of these sparring sessions.

Travelling by car was just like taking a baby out. Bottle, hot water in a vacuum flask, tissues and milk powder. The café we frequented in Torre del Mar got used to the request for hot water and the owner, Antonio, would watch fascinated as Eloïse tucked into her bottle. It was good for his business too as people stopped to chat and stayed for coffee. She really became a star attraction.

The teat incident happened shortly after this, and Eloïse moved irrevocably away from kittenhood. Because of the problem of getting the teat which came with the bottle far enough into Eloïse's throat, Susan had gone back to using the syringe, but now fitted it with a long, thin teat which she had been sent from England by her daughter as part of a Mothering Kit. This teat worked a treat, only what we hadn't realised was that, being designed for the pipette with which it came, it was a fraction too loose a fit around the end of the syringe; only a fraction, but it was enough. With a slurp like someone untidily eating spaghetti, the teat was whipped from the end of the syringe, and before Susan could react, it was gone.

Susan looked at me in horror. 'She's swallowed the teat,' she said.

'What's the answer?' I asked, flinging responsibility smartly back where it belonged.

'I don't know,' she replied. 'it wouldn't show up on an X-ray and besides, she's far too little to operate on. I suppose I'll have to give her some olive oil with her food, and see if it comes out gift-wrapped!'

So that was what we did. And although Eloïse suffered a few days of tummy-ache, it soon passed (in a manner of speaking), but we never did see that teat again.

Chapter 7

Dimidium facti qui coepit habet.
To have begun is half the job.
(Horace)

In the first week in February we made our third visit to the house, this time as potential owners, to take photographs and detailed measurements of everything we could think of – including the thickness of the outer walls, which averaged half a metre – from which to prepare scale drawings of the house 'as was', so that we could then have 'meaningful' discussions about how we hoped not only to improve it, but also how to enlarge and adapt the useable accommodation with our B&B enterprise in mind.

Equally crucial was who we were going to get to do the work. The accumulated effects of *anno domini* and sundry injuries acquired over my sixty-plus years ruled out my doing any significant lifting, and Susan, while a great deal more of a handy-person than I (as she should be, being the daughter of a man who could build a horse-drawn carriage from the ground up, including the wheels) suffers the consequences of bearing five children, so doing the work ourselves was out; we would have to find someone else to take on the whole project, with our role confined to design and supervision.

Unfortunately with so much development going on in Andalucía there was no lack of work for builders, to the extent that tradesmen from all over Spain had congregated on the *Costa del Sol* to take advantage of this bonanza. This meant that builders could pick and chose what to do and, not unnaturally, most preferred to stick with the simpler scenario of constructing new flats and houses according to predetermined plans, rather than taking on the uncertainties of renovating an old property.

Our second problem was, how would we communicate with whoever we were fortunate enough to interest in our project? We were still at the '*¿Cómo se llama?* - what is your name? /*¿Habla* *usted inglés?* – do you speak English?' stage of Spanish, hardly the perfect platform from which to attempt to discuss, let alone agree, the details for transforming our ideas into the realities of renovation and extension. It was here that Judy turned up trumps again in the form of Michael, a Dutch builder whom she felt might be ideal for our purposes. Michael, she said, not only spoke both English and 'Andaluz', he had done work for her which had been entirely satisfactory and he actually preferred the kind of work we required. We met him at the *cortijo* with Judy, walked him round the building and discussed our plans, decided we could probably get on with each other well enough, shook hands and departed, we to the mill and he to whatever project he was engaged upon at the time.

After Michael had left we were offered a glass of coffee each and some very crumbly cakes – a mark of great favour, according to Judy – over which Pedro and Luisa tried to persuade us to agree to part with rather more than the 1 million pesetas which we had put forward as the down-payment. Through Judy they explained that they had found an apartment in Granada and were now keen to move as soon as possible so as not to lose it. What was conveniently omitted, and on which we failed to get unequivocal clarification, was whether their moving to Granada meant that we could gain access to the *cortijo*. However I did take the opportunity during our visit to check the boundaries to the property, as reindicated to me by Pedro, and paint with new white paint stones strategically placed along the perimeter. I felt it was desirable to do this to pre-empt any attempt by Pedro and Luisa to cede any of it to their neighbours, who were relatives – as you see, I was learning!

Back at the mill we telephoned our legal representatives to try to get some indication of progress. Unfortunately no-one could help us, so we left a list of queries to try and hasten things along, together with a note about Pedro and Luisa's request. I also set to with ruler, pencil and eraser, and after much rubbing-out and redrawing of possibilities, I prepared a final set of drawings of how we hoped the *cortijo* would look once everything had been done. As with so many of our renovation projects in the past, we had begun with relatively modest ideas but had then seen the full potential, and as the drawings evolved, we had expanded them accordingly. It was these 'improved' plans which we passed to Michael, and from which we asked him to give us an estimate.

Before the B&B idea had surfaced, our original plans had simply envisaged creating a breakfast/living-room with an American-style kitchen and a separate pantry on the space currently occupied by the lean-to sheds, with a flat sun terrace on the roof, and otherwise upgrading the existing accommodation and converting the first-floor storeroom into an *en-suite* guest bedroom, plus a bathroom for ourselves. However, having seen the building's full potential, we had gone further, putting two further *en-suite* bedrooms over the kitchen/living-room in place of the roof terrace, with a connecting passage into the main house. Michael's estimate brought us down to earth with a bump.

'Nine million *pesetas*,' he said when I phoned him. 'That's for the plans as submitted, plus a septic tank, the relaid and tiled ground floor, the electric wiring and the bathrooms, but without the *deposito* [storage tank] for fresh water, the hard standing for cars or a swimming pool.'

'Nine million!' I almost yelled back at him.

'Well, yes,' he responded. 'After all, you are asking me to build what amounts to a two-bedroomed house, plus do all the remedial work to the existing one.'

'Hmm,' I said, stalling for time. 'Susan isn't with me [this was true, in fact – Susan was in bed with a stinking cold]. Can I call you back in an hour's time?'

'Certainly,' said Michael, sounding not at all surprised, and rang off.

Nine million *pesetas* was nearly £38,500 at the going rate of exchange, give or take £100. It was vastly more than we could afford especially as, from past experience, we knew it wouldn't stop there; inevitably there would be additions, possibly up to one third more, which would take the bill past the £50,000 mark. Although this was far from excessive for the work involved, it was way above our budget and mercifully sanity prevailed for once in our thinking. So an hour later I called Michael back.

'We've thought about your estimate,' I said, 'and honestly it's a bit beyond what we can afford. What we'd like to do now is reconsider the plan for the extension, probably doing away with the upper storey. I will produce a new set of drawings. Can we meet you somewhere later today to discuss them?'

'Sure,' said Michael. 'If you're going to do away with the bedrooms over the kitchen, why not put a sun terrace on the roof!'

We met in the Camping Bar overlooking Lake Viñuela, a place which, like the Beverley Hills Hotel, reeks of deals being done, though undoubtedly on a more modest scale to those struck by movie moguls in days gone by, and after we had taken Michael through our revised drawings, and discussed some ideas which he put forward too (all with Eloïse asleep in her overnight bag on the floor), we parted company once again, with the agreement that I should phone him early next morning to learn the worst.

When I did, the worst was just about what we hoped it would be, and I agreed it on the spot, even though it was *'ungever'* (approximate), as Michael so nicely put it! Now it was down to Michael to get an architect to prepare official drawings for the extension, and to have them lodged with the Planning Authorities in Málaga ... and for us to actually take possession of the *cortijo* so that he could start. So off we went to the coast the next day, to see if anyone had dealt with our message and, if so, what was the advice over Pedro and Luisa's request for more money.

To our surprise, our adviser expressed no misgivings about this, provided it meant that we could gain access to the property. Nothing had arisen so far to suggest that there might be complications with the purchase and, if there were, they were of the resolvable kind; the only problem was the sheer volume of work with which the authorities were now burdened, and it was this that was causing the hold-up. If Pedro and Luisa were prepared for us to move in after they had gone to Granada, there was no significant risk and much to be gained, especially as our tenancy of the mill was due to expire shortly and we had nowhere to go. So we authorised our adviser to offer Pedro and Luisa a further payment and, if they were happy with the sum offered and were willing to allow us to occupy the premises when it was paid, to go ahead and prepare a new private contract to reflect these changes from the current one.

Unfortunately, getting hold of Pedro and Luisa at all, let alone getting the proposal agreed, proved extremely difficult since they were seldom to be found at home. In fact, Susan and I traipsed over to the *cortijo* several times in the hope of catching them there, only to find the house empty and just their dogs there to greet us – which they now did with more and more enthusiasm on each visit. Finally, though, contact was established – and we learned another facet of Anglo/Spanish negotiations, especially where 'officialdom' was concerned.

In days gone by, the custom when conducting the sale and purchase of a property in the *campo* went something like this. A buyer would identify a property which he liked. He would then enquire in the local bar or village store about its ownership. He would then wait, while the 'jungle drums' went to work. Presently, and this was likely to be after an interval of days rather than hours or minutes, the owner would make him or herself known and a meeting would be arranged. This meeting would establish, after much preliminary skirmishing, whether the property could be for sale. If it could, then a negotiating session would follow, generally in the local bar and possibly with the barman acting as intermediary, at the end of which time either an agreement would be struck or the matter would be abandoned. If a deal was ultimately struck, then hands would be shaken, usually in the presence of umpteen witnesses (who couldn't have been prised away from the proceedings with a pick-axe), the full price would

be handed over by the purchaser, and the key would be handed over by the owner. And that would have been that. No paperwork, no officialdom ... and no taxes!

It was now evident that this was how Pedro and Luisa had expected matters to have proceeded with regard to their sale and our purchase of their *finca*, which was why they were not overly impressed with our down-payment of 1 million pesetas, or with us all having to sign the private contract. What, they wanted to know, was the need for all this other paperwork?

Our legal representative had explained to them that this was how things were done now in Spain, especially with sales involving foreigners; if you wanted the higher prices foreigners were prepared to pay, you had to accept the paperwork (in fact, it was pointed out that this paperwork was now required anyway, but there was no point in going too far down that road with vendors who clearly didn't believe - or want to believe - a word of it).

Now, Pedro and Luisa hoped to correct at least the first of the deficiencies (as they saw it) in our arrangement, by getting us to pay them an extra 2 million *pesetas* without any paperwork or 'officialdom' being involved, the way it always had been (the idea that they might do what other people have to do in their situation, and borrow what they needed, using the sale of their house as collateral, simply hadn't crossed their minds). So they were dismayed that we had involved officialdom again in the form of our representative, and doubly so when they were disabused of the propriety of their notion.

A deposit of 1 million *pesetas*, they were told, was more than generous for us to have paid in the first place since we couldn't complete the purchase until the paperwork was ready and we still had to live somewhere in the meantime. If we were to pay a further sum, it could only be against signing another contract, and provided we got some benefit from the payment - like the right to occupy the property, which is what we understood the proposal included; was this what they had in mind? 'Oh, no,' Luisa had apparently replied, 'I never said they could occupy the property. I only said we would move to Granada, so that we didn't lose our flat there. Foreigners are always getting things wrong.' In that case, our adviser had said, we really couldn't be advised to pay any more money at this stage. 'Fine,' retorted Luisa, 'we didn't want to move until the end of the four month period anyway!' Later we were to find out what they really wanted the money for, and it had nothing to do with the purchase of the flat in Granada.

Mulling all this over, as we did that week-end, I was struck by the similarity between all this and the way things were in North Cornwall when my parents had bought their farm there all those years ago. Cornish farmers then were a breed apart. Like the Yorkshire farmers so beautifully characterised by James Herriot, they were steeped in a way of life that has now vanished, and even then had little to do with the rest of the country. However, unlike Yorkshire, which is at least on the way to Northumberland, Cornwall is at the end of the line: next stop, America. This engendered a certain isolationism in their attitudes, best summed up by the words of a farmer who, when told that something would have to be fetched from Exeter, in Devonshire, observed in my presence, 'That's a powerful long way to go to get summat. Why, t'is t'other side of Launceston!'

Many Cornish farmers, too, in those days, were not above trying to 'put one over' a 'foreigner' - that is anyone from 't'other side of Launceston'; and to doing cash deals over everything if they could, with a little bit on the side and never mind the tax man. And so, apparently, it was with Andalucían farmers today, which we would clearly be foolish to agree to. So we sadly reconciled ourselves to waiting the full four months before we could take possession of the *cortijo*, and set about finding somewhere else to live for the next ten weeks, since our two-month tenure of the mill was at an end and neither we nor our landlords felt like extending it - us because the mill had become unbearably claustrophobic as the weeks had passed, and our landlords because they had now put the whole property up for sale, so for all our sakes it was time for us to move on.

Chapter 8

Pray do not imagine that those who make the
noise are the only inhabitants of the field.
(Edmund Burke, *Reflections on the Revolution in France*)

The sound seeped slowly into my subconscious: a hideous clanking, groaning and shrieking, like an Orc-ish foundry in a fantasy world by Tolkein, or a refuse truck emptying wheelie-bins in the real one. 'What on earth's that?' I mumbled to myself. 'It's a refuse truck emptying wheelie-bins,' said Susan's voice from somewhere above me. 'Well, at least we now know when they do it,' I thought, as my brain clung onto the remnants of sleep. 'Hang on a minute though; how does she know? And how did she hear me? And where exactly is she?'

'What time is it?' I asked.

'Ten past twelve,' came the reply. 'And you were mumbling into your beard.'

I gradually opened one eye, took in the drawn curtains, the discarded clothes ... and the fact that Susan was sitting up in bed beside me.

'In the morning!' I squeaked.

'In the morning,' Susan replied, somewhat grimly, 'and if you listen once they've gone away, you'll find they're not the only ones up and about at this time.'

The refuse truck ate its last mouthful (there were four wheelie-bins outside our block of flats, so it took its time), gave a belch of indigestion and trundled off down the street to disturb someone else's slumber, and in the relative quiet I became aware of a whole symphony of sounds which its chomping and grinding had obscured.

The first to emerge, and the main theme as it were, was the buzz of conversation, the clatter of cutlery, the chink of glasses and the bursts of laughter, all indicative of a large number of people eating, drinking and generally enjoying themselves. Running counterpoint to this theme, and filling the few lulls when they occurred, came pulses of music from the record shop directly underneath us; and weaving between them, binding them all together like a clarinet in a New Orleans jazz band, but infinitely less melodiously, was the rasp and roar of motor-scooters, zooming up the street below our balcony, slowing at the cross-roads, and then surging forward to join their fellows outside the bar between the two restaurants.

'Cup of tea?' I asked.

'Might as well,' came the reply. 'It looks as though it's going to be a long night!'

Thus our first night in Torre del Mar, a small seaside town lying about half-way between the Provincial capital, Málaga, and Nerja, the most easterly and best known of Axarquía's resorts. It has a long stretch of gravely beach, a fabulous *paseo* (promenade), a magnificent bay backed by the foothills and peaks of the stupendous *Sierra Tejeda* and a wealth of excellent eateries. It is one of Axarquía's best kept secrets, and we had found a small flat there to tide us over the next eight weeks. Instead of a mass of foreign visitors it is patronised by the Spanish themselves, and by senior German citizens with their traditions of *das Kur*. It has so far avoided the unsightly excesses which have ruined much of the rest of the *Costas* principally because there were, at the time of writing, no large hotels, and the maximum height for apartment blocks, with one exception, appeared to be ten storeys. There was also, for us, a merciful shortage of the sort of establishments which have made many of the resorts on the *Costa del Sol* indistinguishable from Blackpool, and it bore no resemblance at all to Benidorm.

We had visited Torre del Mar several times while we had been at the mill and at that time had found it a quiet, unassuming sort of town built around the old coast road through Axarquía. We did notice a large number of ice-cream parlours, discos and bars which, though boarded up, gave evidence to a lively holiday season, but we had enjoyed sitting in the winter sun, drinking superb coffee at one of the few places open on the *paseo*, and thought to ourselves, 'What a nice place this is.' We were right, though perhaps not in the way we had originally meant.

Our one-bedroomed flat was in the centre of the town, which was convenient (we could walk everywhere), easy to reach and although it was in excellent decorative order and fully equipped in all respects it was, above all, cheap - £50 a week, including electricity. We were soon to find out one possible reason why it was so cheap: it overlooked the two busiest streets in the town, though this wasn't evident at the time that we looked at it. Although by the time we moved there for our eight week stay the summer season was beginning to appear in sight over the horizon, more shops and eateries were open and there were more people about, it was still reassuringly peaceful. Our first week was to put this into perspective.

Our first night was a Monday; Tuesday, Wednesday and Thursday were the same. And the bustle and activity wasn't confined to the nights. The days started quietly enough: apart from some bread shops and the work on the building site fifty yards down the road, which began at around 8.00 a.m. - British builders, take note - almost nothing opened before 10.00 a.m. From then on, however, there was a gradual build-up of activity towards lunchtime between 2.00 p.m. and 4.30 p.m., when everything except the restaurants closed for the afternoon *siesta*. Everything, that is, except the building site, where work continued unabated, work involving a mechanical digger and the removal of the remains of the buildings which had previously stood on the site by joyfully dropping them into the backs of a procession of tipper lorries with a succession of thunderous crashes. By the time this activity had stopped, the shops were reopening, and the town was coming back to life, to repeat the pattern we had experienced on our first night - except that at the week-end, it stepped up a gear.

Our new temporary home was on the fifth floor of an apartment block on a corner of the town's main boulevard to the sea front. It had a balcony which gave a restricted view of the sea, and an unrestricted view into the bedroom of the flat directly opposite. On the ground floor of our block was a '100 *peseta* shop' (something like a market-trader's stall moved indoors), a ladies' hairdresser (which Susan patronised one evening with results from which she took some time to recover), and a record shop where the same tunes (mainly Spanish disco or Cher) were played with mind-numbing repetition. Further down the street were two *marisquería* (sea-food restaurants), one of which was the second most popular restaurant in the whole of the town, a small bar patronised by teenagers largely from the motor-cycle and scooter crowd (of whom more later) and the aforementioned building site.

It was perhaps unwise of me to patronise the hairdresser down at sea level before I understood, and could speak a bit more Spanish! I have fine straight fly-away hair and have a soft perm on it to give it lift and volume. My visit to the hairdresser left me with a fuzz due to her not rinsing out the perming lotion properly or using the neutraliser correctly. Luckily it dropped out after a week but I decided then and there to put up with straight hair!

On our first Friday, after the afternoon *siesta* through which the work on the building site had again continued unabated and the early evening programme had repeated itself, the record shop, the restaurants and the bar showed the real nature of things. The record shop stayed open until midnight, playing its customary counterpoint to all the other noises, the restaurants stayed open until 3.30 a.m. and the bar till 4.30, after which the street remained filled with pedestrians, cars and motor-scooters, all busily occupied with various forms of enjoyment, until around 6.30 a.m., a programme which was repeated on Saturday and Sunday, only slackening off at around 1.00 a.m. on Monday morning. This remained the pattern for the following weeks, steadily escalating in momentum towards the 'high spot' of our stay: *Semana Santa* – Holy Week – the week from Palm Sunday to Easter Day, a week which not only contains two public holidays in Spain, but is also a week when, traditionally, a large number of Spaniards take time off work altogether.

This was our first experience of *Semana Santa*, and we were enthralled. It was like a week from a mediaeval fair, brought up-to-date. At almost every corner colourful ice cream and confectionery kiosks blossomed like exotic flowers, the *paseo* was lined at night with stalls selling everything from 'new age' jewellery to African statuettes, nearly all the bars and discos opened up and stayed open till dawn, the restaurants were packed every night and as virtually the whole of southern Spain seemed to have descended on the town, people thronged the streets from lunchtime until the small hours. Some places only closed between dawn and lunchtime, not just at the two week-ends, but every day of the week - and this in what is recognised as a quiet little resort!

After *Semana Santa*, things relapsed into the earlier pattern. In fact, they almost collapsed, as many places which had been open every day during Holy Week either closed altogether or only reopened at weekends, while the remainder vanished as if they had never been. This was disconcerting, as by now we had become accustomed to the routine and noises, but it did give us the chance to study, in the weeks which remained to us, both Spanish (the language) and the Spanish (the people), and to draw certain conclusions about the latter.

The first concerned noise. Now, towns are generally noisy. We all know that. So we could hardly expect that there wouldn't be noise in Torre del Mar. And all towns have their own characteristic noise. (Have you ever noticed, by the way, that football crowds sound totally different from rugby crowds? Not a lot of people know that, as Mr Michael Caine is over-quoted as having written.) However what we hadn't realised was how much the Spanish love noise, and just <u>how</u> noisy Torre del Mar would be.

Not noise *per se* - in this the Spanish are no different from many other Mediterranean countries, and no aspiring local politician would ever gain office on a 'Noise Abatement' ticket - but particular kinds of noise, and the times of day at which it became most evident. During *Santa Semana* and at week-ends, the continuous susurration was almost soporific with its rhythmic waves of non-threatening sound; but when this died down, individual noises became all the more noticeable and intrusive.

There were many variations which brought us to quivering wakefulness during the nights we were in Torre del Mar - the delightful little boy whose indulgent parents had bought him a cap gun, firing it at midnight in the street below us; the pistol-shots of bottles being dropped into the bottle-bank at 2.00 a.m.; and the roar and crash of the security shutters on the *marisquería* being lowered at 3.30 a.m. - but the two principal, permanent sources of night-time noise were motor-scooters and shouting.

Motor-scooters and small motor cycles are a way of life in Spain and until recently, for those with engines below 50 c.c., riders as young as fourteen were permitted, with no need for a licence. This is now being altered, but the legacy of the old policy is that every other teenager in the towns owns a motor-scooter, and carries the remaining fifty per cent on the pillion. Plus its younger sister. And sometimes its mother as well. With her shopping. And a dog. Noisily. Skilfully. And frequently dangerously.

There are some very potent machines at 49 c.c. They make ideal vehicles with which to engage in races with others of their kind, at all times of the day and night. This is accepted by the indigenous population, but it can be quite a trial to visitors. Susan and I briefly contemplated buying two scooters on the basis of 'if you can't beat 'em, join 'em' (we both have full British motor-cycle licences), but boring common sense prevailed in the end as we knew that, realistically, we had to save every penny we possessed for the alterations to the *cortijo*. Shame, though. It could have been fun.

Spaniards also love to shout. Shouting is endemic to the *campo*, where olive or almond pickers communicate in this way with others working some distance apart up, down or across the steep-sided slopes of the valleys. The towns, lacking almond and olive groves, make no such demands, certainly not in Torre del Mar, which is as flat as a board. But whether it is because the customs and habits of the *campo* are ingrained in the Spanish soul or because they just like to shout anyway, people still shout to one another as a matter of course. This is OK, but when it comes at full volume from children shrilly playing directly underneath one's window at 1.00 a.m. or from citizens who seem unable to part company from their erstwhile companions without protest-ations of friendship or enmity at fifty metres range as they return to their homes in the early hours, it gets a bit much after eight weeks!

And this was the problem. Coming as we did from northern Europe, our biorhythmic 'clocks' had been tuned all our lives to rising at 7-ish, working all day from 9-ish to 6-ish, and going to bed at 11-ish. However, in Mediterranean countries it is necessarily different, especially in summer. As Ted Walker observes in his book *In Spain*, here every day is two days: twice you get up, twice wash and dress to start the day afresh in the cool. If you're accustomed to eight hours' sleep, he says, you take them in two unequal bites: five and a half at night and two and a half in the afternoons. It took us a little while to adapt to this practical routine, and we never really got used to it. Mr Walker attributes this inability to a puritanical (or maybe superstitious) guilt felt by the British about losing daylight time. He suggests that the English in particular have conserved since the days of the Raj a deep-rooted suspicion and contempt for the *siesta* (as Noel Coward wrote, 'Englishmen detest a *siesta*') which, he says, they think is a shame and a waste and that, conversely, when on holiday, they insist on going to bed at 'sensible' times like 11 o'clock, thus missing some of the best things that Spain has to offer.

Whether this is true of us I cannot say: what I can say is that we have still not really accepted the notion that daylight time is not something which needs to be saved here. It is also true that, while we have become quite happy to accept the *siesta* as a *modus vivendi*, we have never become adjusted to staying up half the night. Instead, we get up a lot earlier in summer than we did in England (and a lot earlier than most urban Spaniards do, too), to take advantage of the cool of the dawn. Perhaps it is something to do with age. That and owning a *finca* in the *campo*.

Our last full week in Torre del Mar before we moved out to the *cortijo* provided, were we looking for it, all the evidence we needed to reinforce our decision not to live in a town. On the Monday, at 4.45 a.m., when the night's normal noises had finally ceased, a man called to give a lift to his mate living at a flat down the road. He blew his horn for ten seconds at a time for fifteen solid minutes, shouting as he did so, 'Manolo!' at the top of his voice. This provoked someone else to shout at the top of his voice, 'Stop that * * * * noise' (or Spanish words to that effect). And Manolo's friend repeated this performance every night of the week.

The next night the refuse truck returned (we hadn't seen or heard it for ten days), and at 2.00 a.m. took two sessions, each of ten minutes over a half hour period, to clank, chomp and grind its way through the overflowing contents of the wheelie bins and accumulated rubbish on our corner (which now included a sofa). Then on Wednesday the lorry came to empty the bottle bank, at 1.30 a.m., and on Thursday the refuse truck returned, again at 1.30 a.m.

Wednesday also added a new element, that of the barking dog. Barking dogs are the norm in Spain, but this one was special and particularly maddening, as Wednesday was the one night in the week when the *marisquería* didn't open, and the bar and the record shop shut early. We had made a trip to Málaga, never something to be attempted lightly and always slightly fraught, to look at beds for the *cortijo*, so the prospect of an undisturbed night was particularly welcome. We had gone to bed relatively early, knowing that the refuse lorry wouldn't come two nights in a row (we hadn't anticipated the lorry to empty the bottle bank). It was then that we heard the dog. It was a large-ish dog, judging by its bark, and it had been barking steadily since we had gone to bed, but we just hadn't noticed it among the other noises. However as the late-night noises died away, this bark became increasingly intrusive, until by 1.00 a.m. it filled, as does a dripping tap, our entire consciousness.

The dog had presumably – and I'm afraid there are now going to be quite a lot of 'presumablies' since we weren't able to interrogate the principals – been shut in somewhere to guard something, a task which it found unfamiliar and for which it was unprepared. It was therefore presumably lonely, frightened and possibly hungry, or a combination of all three, and was not afraid to say so, to anyone who would listen. 'I hope it isn't going to do that all night,' said Susan. 'So do I,' I replied with some feeling, 'but I have a nasty feeling that it is.' And it did. 2 o'clock came, then 3 and 4, still with absolutely no break in the tirade, and no possibility of sleep. At 4 a.m. something did happen: a man, probably not the owner, shouted at the dog in exasperation, 'Stop that bow-wow-wow,' or similar Spanish words (bow-wow-wow certainly featured). This was wonderful for the dog: the first reaction it had had for more than six hours. Now it knew that if it barked long enough, someone or something would happen. So of course it redoubled its efforts, and with them departed any possibility of sleep.

Although somebody did complain to the dog's owners, it was still there on Friday night when, of course, the usual weekend programme clicked in, beginning with two adjacent disco bars nearby, which competed with each other until 6.30 a.m. This was repeated on Saturday, which was also enlivened by what appeared to be a fight at 4.00 a.m. By Monday morning Susan and I felt like death and, if the record shop downstairs had had it, would have asked them to play, instead of Cher, who we were still hearing three or four times an hour, the hit song by The Animals back in the 60s, 'We've got to get out of this place'!

With noise endemic to Spain, those who desire tranquillity may have to seek diligently before they find it.

Despite the trial of the noise, a number of highly favour-able impressions about the Spanish were to be etched onto our memories by the time we left Torre del Mar. The first was how little of the merriment we witnessed appeared to depend on alcohol. Certainly there were some who seemed unable to enjoy themselves without getting legless, and there was a tiny minority from the disco crowd who indulged in mindless vandalism, but after England it was a revelation that so many people could enjoy themselves on so little. It confirmed our growing realisation that Spaniards have an in-built exuberance and zest for life which does not depend on any kind of artificial stimulus. Most of those we heard every night from our 5th floor were local citizens of all ages, from babes in arms to grandfathers, for many of whom it would be work as usual in the morning, despite being up till 3.30 a.m. (those going home afterwards were definitely the disco crowd, but even they were remarkably considerate, except for the inevitable few).

Coupled with this came our astonishment at the amazing stamina of the average Spaniard. In Torre del Mar, the only period of comparative inactivity, outside of *siesta*, was between 3.30 and 9.30 a.m.: the rest of the time people were working, eating, drinking, socialising and shopping, and doing the thousand-and-one things which we all have to do every day, besides sleep. Mind you, we had our own theory about why this was so: it was because their neighbours wouldn't let them sleep!

And their work-rate, whether in Torre del Mar or the *campo*, matched this stamina. This drastically altered our preconceived notions about Mediterranean indolence, and we began to understand rather better how the Spanish came to build the empire which they did throughout most of South America, and how close the course of history came to being altered at the time of that famous Armada. It was certainly easier to understand why the Roman army recruited so extensively in Iberia.

It also slowly dawned on us that in Torre del Mar we didn't have that anticipation of possible confrontation and the awareness of potential abuse and even violence which are regrettably the hallmark of life these days in the centres of many towns and cities in Western Europe and the USA, especially at night. The antenna remained furled.

Sadly we know now that this would not be true of everywhere on the *Costa del Sol*, and even in Torre del Mar I tended, just out of prudence, to avoid the dawn 'chucking out' time at certain establishments during *Semana Santa* on those mornings when I went for a walk to enjoy the sunrise, but generally speaking we could not remember when we had felt so at ease in a town, even in the less frequented and less well lit side streets - except, of course, for the need to keep a sharp lookout and honed reflexes against the possibility of being mown down, entirely without malice, by a fourteen-year-old on a motor scooter, riding on the pavement!

It was now, too, that we realised that we would have to come to terms with the differing attitudes between ourselves and the Spanish - or at least, the Andalucians - with regard to animals if we intended to live here. It was no use our ranting and raving at perceived cruelties or neglect; we would either have to accept, if not necessarily share, the attitudes we found around us or take ourselves off somewhere else. This caused a good deal of heart-searching and examination before we finally came to our own conclusions about where these differences lay and whether they were reconcilable.

In his book *The Little Pot Boiler*, Spike Milligan wrote on dogs, 'There was a time when the forebears of our contemporary dog ran free in packs of up to a hundred; short, stocky, yellow-haired fellows, hunting and living as they pleased, enjoying the primitive freedom of a collar-free throat. It's hard to believe that the lump of hairy fat, slobbed out in front of a Belgravia fire, is a direct descendant of these once noble creatures.' This analysis, though intended to amuse, contains, in our view, more than a grain of truth.

Like most other Britons, Susan and I pride ourselves on being fond of animals. Between us, in our former relationships, we owned and cared for a wide variety of creatures, while together we have owned and loved a diversity of dogs, from a trio of French bulldogs to a Great Dane and a bull mastiff. In common, too, with most other Britons, we have always regarded our dogs as companions and, as do many others, we have often bestowed on them totally unjustifiable anthropomorphic qualities, by talking to them as if they were humans - which they aren't. The fact is that dogs are pack animals which, left to themselves, rapidly develop and demonstrate the characteristics of their ancestors; it is only the influence - and interference - of humans which makes them otherwise.

For the most part Spaniards, or at any rate Andalucians, do not appear to regard dogs or cats as companions, let alone friends, on the reasonable grounds that these are roles better performed by people. That is not to say that many Spaniards don't keep dogs and cats as pets; they do, and when they do they are as devoted to them as anyone can be. But the majority of *campesiños* seem to regard dogs and cats as simply being functional, like a car, a cow or a cooker, and to be left alone to get on with it without, to them, inappropriate displays of affection from humans (humans display affection to humans, right, so shouldn't displays of affection to animals be left to others of their own kind?).

And, maddeningly, the animals seem to thrive on it, as we were later to see admirably demonstrated on a farm near our new home. This has a wonderful miscellany of semi-domestic animals, including seven dogs and an uncountable number of cats, all of which roam freely about the property without restraint or human interference, and are casually fed once a day on whatever scraps are going. The result: seven healthy, well-adjusted dogs (it has proved impossible to check on the cats, as these sprint past to avoid being pounced on by the dogs!), which roil around in an established pecking order and remain fiercely loyal and protective to their owners, and remarkably affectionate to us when we call, now that they have got used to us.

This is not to say that we have not also encountered instances of neglect or downright cruelty, which have deeply distressed us, but then Britain is hardly exempt from these, either, as the RSPCA will readily confirm. Of these, in the *campo*, perhaps the most disagreeable, and difficult to understand, is the widespread practice of tying a dog up and leaving it for days on end without adequate food and water, let alone companionship. The dog inevitably howls for most of the day (and night) and there seems to be no logic to this treatment, since the animal is seldom guarding anything – on more than one occasion we have found a dog tied to a tree in the middle of an orchard – and even if that appears to be the purpose, the dog is usually on too short a lead for it to do anything practical, and there is no-one to take action if it is simply acting as an alarm.

Nevertheless we realised that, if we were going to live here, we would have to learn to be non-judgmental about this fundamental difference between our attitudes to animals and those which were manifest around us, and in this we were helped by the vastly tolerant nature of the Spanish character towards everything, including animals. Their view seems to be, 'if what I do with my animal is my concern, I certainly shan't judge you about what you do with yours,' and we have yet to see an owner denied permission to take a dog into a restaurant (presumably on the grounds that a dog should be expected to be at least as well behaved as a child, and no child would ever be turned away) and you don't find this happening too often in supposedly animal-loving Britain.

We were also vastly helped in our adjustment process by the Spanish treatment of their children, which more than made up for any supposed ill-treatment of animals. Children here are adored, which sadly is not always the case in Britain. The incidence of child abuse is so infrequent in Spain that it makes banner headlines when it occurs, and even to hear a child crying in Torre del Mar was so unusual it often caused passers-by to stop in the streets to stop and enquire what was wrong.

The old Victorian maxim that 'children should be seen and not heard' is totally unknown in Spain, nor are children parked in front of the TV simply to occupy them. Unlike many British children, who are frequently merely tolerated, Spanish children are welcomed, and are involved in all aspects of family life. They are treated not as a race apart but as small people entitled from the very beginning of their lives to the same respect and consideration which their elders expect from them.

And this is reciprocated. It is commonplace to see teenagers keeping company with their grandparents, or willingly helping their parents with the shopping and other chores, and entire extended families can be seen - babes-in-arms to grandparents - sitting together in bars, each member receiving equal treatment over what they are given to eat or drink. The children are not fobbed off with something they don't want, or sent to play outside while the adults get on with their chat; they are asked, and given, what they fancy, and are expected to stay and play their part as a member of the group. You don't see too much of that in Britain these days. And you don't find Spanish parents 'buying off' their children with expensive consumer goods, to compensate for their own guilt trip at not spending enough 'quality time' with them. For Spanish parents time with the family will always come first, often at the expense of other priorities favoured by more northern races.

As a result, Spanish children are, well, children. Whether because of cultural background or simply because of lack of money, 'Super Nintendos' and other hand-held computer games are relatively scarce, and children do not spend hours in front of the television, watching cartoons, 'Neighbours' or MTV according to their ages and tastes. Instead they have cap-guns and marbles, and they play with other children, usually out of doors, as children played in Britain fifty years ago. This may be noisy - it usually is - and frequently carried on at times which we might regard as anti-social, but it is seldom malicious (though it can be mischievous, as in the time when we were stalked by a group of twelve-year-olds hoping to ambush us with a balloon filled with water, something I remember doing myself to adults when I was that age if I could get the chance).

These observations and reflections were a great help in under-standing our hosts, but they occupied only a fraction of our time in Torre del Mar. Our main preoccupation was to combat, without spending a fortune, the lassitude and drooping *ennui* caused by our enforced idleness and our cumulative frustration at not knowing for sure when, or even if, our wait would be at an end. It required a major effort to avoid dropping into the attitude summed up in the famous words, 'Sometimes I sits and thinks, other times I just sits', so we walked - oh, how we walked - exploring every street which had anything even remotely interesting to look at.

On our walks we found and bought a wood-burning stove to heat the *cortijo* in the winter; we identified a possible set of fitted cupboards for the kitchen we would have to build; and we found a shop with a vast range of floor and wall tiles which we would definitely need, where an anonymous Spanish businessman passing by stopped to help us communicate with the proprietor, switching effortlessly from 'Andaluz' to faultless English and back again, and wished us 'Welcome to Spain' at the end. We couldn't see this happening in England.

We visited the market every Thursday, where we bought strawberries at 64p a kilo - yes, a kilo! - and the rest of our fruit and vegetables, ceramic egg-cups (the flat had none), T-shirts for the family, a sweater from Peru for Susan, beautiful glass paper-weights as Christmas presents, and on one memorable day, a wonderful blue 'chinoiserie' ceramic elephant, now named Mathilda, with a flat seat where its *howdah* would normally be, 50cm long to the tip of its raised trunk, 46cm high and 25cm wide, so over-decorated it was hideously beautiful, horrendously expensive, totally frivolous and utterly irresistible.

There were also stalls selling bolts of cloth, carpets and rugs (these from Morocco, whose owners have cornered this particular place in the market), confectionery, pictures and kitchen tools. Sometimes there were 'run-out' merchants, keeping a weather eye open for the police, selling puppies, chicks or ducklings, but our favourite stall was the one displaying every conceivable kind of herb, set out in sacks and marked clearly with the potential benefits: 'for gout', 'for piles', 'for rheumatism' and even 'for depression' - so much for the politically correct rules about not making medical claims!

Once a week, about mid-morning, we also heard Pan pipes being played in a strange, repeated, falling cadence. The first time I heard it, I rushed to the balcony to see if I could locate whoever it was who was performing, but I could see no-one except for an old man pushing a power-assisted bicycle along the street. Then, as I watched, he lifted one hand from the handlebars and wiped the back of it across his mouth, and once again the sound pierced the air. He was a knife-grinder, his saddle supporting the grindstone, and the pipes of Pan are the street-call of his trade all over Spain. Later I saw him, his bike on its stand, busily sharpening a carving knife, but in these days of hollow-ground, serrated edged blades we could not help wondering for how much longer the haunting, pagan sound of his pipes will ring out, and yet another tradition will have vanished forever.

We strolled in the evenings and on Sunday mornings along the *paseo*, 'properly dressed' despite the rising temperature. Spanish families dress up for these occasions, and in this predominantly Spanish resort we felt it would have been singularly discourteous for us to have adopted the 'let-it-all-hang-out' fashion favoured by many foreign tourists in certain resorts on the *Costas*. We joined the scores of Spanish and German families taking the air, just as their – and our – Edwardian forbears did in fashionable watering-places a hundred years ago. And, of course, we tested out any number of eateries.

This was not the contradiction to our need to save money that it sounds, as we found it difficult to average more than £12 between us for a meal out, no matter where we ate, and that included beer or a bottle of wine, so it was almost as economical to eat out as it was to eat in and besides, as Susan pointed out, the kitchen in the flat was exceedingly small. We improved our sun-tans on our balcony, spasmodically studied our teach-yourself-Spanish programme and attempted to practise it when we went out and continued to bring up Eloïse who was growing up into a definite handful in such a confined space.

This routine, for two people who had always worked towards some kind of goal, was mind-numbing in its meaninglessness and nearly had us at each other's throats. It also brought a pernicious consequence: it gave us time to think, not just about the practicalities of our future, but about ourselves, our attitudes to that future, and our attitudes towards each other.

In the film 'The Mask', there is a character who writes a book entitled *The Mask We Wear*. This mask, he says, is a metaphor for the way in which the conscious face presented to the world by many people hides a subconscious reality behind it. That there could be a good deal of truth in this now became abundantly clear, at least to me. I began to realise that, throughout my adult life and probably stemming from childhood, I had built an increasingly impenetrable mental barricade to protect, cam-ouflage or even restrain a sort of mental Pandora's Box in which I concealed my real desires, aspirations, regrets and fears, emotions which were sometimes not even the ones I acknowledged to myself in private, let alone which I displayed to others.

Whether I am alone in this subterfuge I have no idea, but I suspect not, especially for those whose careers have been in public service, as mine had for twenty-five years. If you are dedicated to this kind of service then, certainly according to my upbringing, you have to accept that you have no right to interpose your private feelings into the ministry to which you have been sworn. You are committed to separating your life into two disparate levels of existence, one private, the other professional, whose priorities may conflict. To me there is no dishonesty in this dissimulation: it is an inescapable aspect of one's life. But if, as time goes by, the priorities and principles of one's private life begin to diverge radically from those of the professional arena, then one is forced either to abandon the latter and seek an alternative career, or to remain and, consciously or otherwise, suppress or modify the former. To do that, you need a Pandora's Box.

The practice of keeping your private feelings and your working life separate also requires an abnormal amount of discipline. For some it can be too much to ask; for others, the consequences of sustaining it can be profound. In my case it may well have contributed to the break-up of my first marriage, inculcated as I was with the principle of always placing the demands of the service life first. And having developed the discipline into an automatic behaviour pattern, it is impossible to abandon it overnight when you leave the service.

This can lead to confusion and worse when you find yourself dealing with others who have had no such dilemma with their lives, and whose priorities are entirely self-determined. The concepts with which I had been brought up, such as loyalty to one's employer, support for one's subordinates, hard work and family morality, can be hard to find in the competitive, commercial world in which I found myself after I left the Army, and reconciling the tenets of this world with the principles which had previously guided my life meant that my Pandora's Box was required more than ever before.

But there was a paradox: what I had accepted, or had been required to accept or suppress over the years had changed too and was continuing to change in the light of experiences. The contents of the Box were no longer the same. Now, with time hanging heavier than ever before and life filled with trivia, yet having already jointly taken with Susan the risky step of first considering and then taking action over how, where and with what purpose we wished to spend the rest of our lives together, I could no longer ignore this dichotomy and I found myself confronted with certain searching personal questions which threatened to take the lid right off the Box and swamp me altogether. So the arrival of Herbert, who literally ran into our lives shortly before we left Torre del Mar, was perhaps fortuitous in the circumstances. At least it delayed my having to face up to the questions and, worse still, find answers!

Herbert's arrival was on this wise, to plagiarise St Matthew I, verse 3. Susan and I had set out to walk to a nearby supermarket, a distance of about half a mile. When we were about half-way there, we realised that we would have an immensely heavy load to carry back in the considerable heat of midday, as one of the reasons for our going there was to buy several bottles of wine, which were on offer that week, so I went back for the car while Susan walked on.

When I got to the supermarket, Susan was standing by the entrance to the car-park. She turned and looked at me, clutching a small, black bundle to her chest. I shook my head, but she just went on looking at me. I knew that there had to be a good reason, as we had long since agreed that Eloïse would be the first and last stray we would collect, as we were 'inheriting' five dogs and five cats at the *cortijo*, so I parked the car, got out, and waited for the story.

What had happened, in Susan's own words, was this:

You'd left me to get the car, so that we wouldn't have to carry the bargain booze back from the supermarket up the road in carrier bags, and I had walked on instead of coming back with you, because I was already half-way there. Seconds after you'd left me, I turned to see how far you'd got but you were nowhere in sight. As I turned back, I saw this black bundle in the road. Then I realised it had a face, that it was a tiny puppy crossing the road at speed ... and that a lorry was moving towards it, at even greater speed.

I had an urge to grab it out of the middle of the road and, fortunately, an even stronger urge for self-preservation. I remember crouching down and saying, 'Come on - get out of the road.' Everything then went slow, like when they 'freeze frame' a film. I remember being scared, but not scared for me, and intensely angry towards whoever could have dumped a tiny puppy and was responsible for nearly getting it killed.

I looked away or shut my eyes, I don't know which, expecting the worst, and when I looked back after the lorry had passed the puppy was still coming towards me. How the lorry missed it I shall never know. It wasn't damaged at all. The lorry driver had tried to slow, but he couldn't stop, and whether the puppy just cowered in the middle of the road and the lorry passed over it or whether it had got to the middle of the road before the lorry reached it, I shall never know, but somehow when the lorry had passed, it was still coming towards me.

The puppy made a bee-line for me, strangely there was no other person in sight, and I knelt as it made it to the curb and up into my arms and safety (I felt as if I had 'willed' it across the road). It dug its head into my shoulder and we both stood there, cringing. With the horror which might have been came the emotions: Toby'll be furious - it's safe, it's alive, uninjured - it's mine - it missed the lorry's wheels - it's meant for us - how will Eloïse react? - why me; would this have happened if it had been you instead of me? - and above all, WHERE HAD IT COME FROM?

I looked for any owner, but the only person I could see, a man on the other side of the road, vigorously shook his head, so I walked on to the supermarket carrying it in my arms, both of us still shaking, the puppy from its close escape and me from what might have been, both to it and to me. My legs were like jelly; I have no idea how I managed to move.

I got to the supermarket as you pulled in. I could see your face but, for good or ill, I could do no more than apologise. I couldn't give it up: I had just saved its life. I just hoped you'd understand.

After that tale, what could I do? I took the puppy across the road to the pet shop and bought it a collar and lead while Susan went unsteadily into Dumaya to do the shopping.

The real success story, though, came when we got the puppy back to the flat. Knowing what Eloïse was like, and how she had totally demoralised Jason, the pointer dog found by Helen, the woman who had also found Eloïse in the first place and which she had brought with her when she came to see Eloïse a few days earlier, we had severe misgivings about her first encounter with the puppy. But to our amazement all she did was to hiss a couple of times out of sheer surprise, and then watch in astonishment while the puppy devoured the remains of her breakfast. After that, although there was a certain amount of skirmishing which, in the confines of the flat, became quite dramatic but in no sense fraught, and after another meal which they both shared, they fell asleep, so close together that the only thing separating them at one point was a small towel! It seemed that another lost soul had been accepted into the family.

And the name Herbert? Well, when I first saw him, he was about 23 cm to the shoulder and 49 cm long from the tip of his nose, excluding his tail. He was rough haired, black all over except for a white fringe beard, a white blaze on his chest and the suggestion of a white tip to his tail. He had bright, mischievous hazel-brown eyes, needle-sharp teeth and, despite his obvious youth, an attitude - a cocky, Cockney attitude that seemed to say, 'OK, so you've saved my life, but don't expect me to dwell on it. I've made my way in the world so far, and I don't need you now.' Although we were to learn that this was all show and that he was not quite as sure of himself as he tried to make out, he was, at first meeting, a 'right little Herbert', and the tag stuck.

However, before the arrival of Herbert, while we managed to avoid each other's throats in one way, throats re-entered our lives in another, in the form of an appointment back in England for me to have the operation on mine. This was most welcome, even though it was likely to be a painful experience for at least one of us, as my throat certainly hadn't got any easier over the six months which had elapsed since I had seen the specialist, and on one occasion - when a minute piece of chocolate became lodged in my throat - had become quite critical. As we were on a motorway at the time with nowhere to stop and nothing to drink, it had been over an hour before I could shift it. An experience like that can put you right off your fruit and nut!

Since there was nothing to keep Susan in Spain at this stage, she decided she would come with me; we had been warned that I would need ten days convalescence after the operation, which would almost certainly involve a certain amount of T.L.C. and this, for some reason, she did not feel able to entrust to anyone else. So we set out to make the arrangements for us both to go back to England, and it was at this stage that fate decided to remind us that we had been having things far too easy in our slothful existence in Torre del Mar.

The first shock we got was when we tried to book our flights. Although we had read about the vast numbers of foreign visitors who had come to the *Costa del Sol* for *Semana Santa*, we hadn't related this to anything that concerned us, since with Torre del Mar being a predominantly Spanish resort, they hadn't impinged on us. Now we were to discover that the thousands who had come out from Britain for the Easter break would all be flying back at precisely the time that we wanted to fly, and that virtually all the charter flights (which were the ones we could afford) were fully booked.

We traipsed fruitlessly round the travel agents in Torre del Mar, drawing blanks and becoming increasingly panic-stricken as we went until, typically, we happened into the closest one to us, *Viaje Benamar* on the *Avenida del Andalucía*, next to the estate agents who had found us our apartment. There the delightful and energetic manager made vigorous phone calls for what seemed like hours, finally getting us tickets with a British company for the flight to the UK, and with a Belgian company for the flight back.

With this finally settled we then set about finding a cattery a) which we liked, b) which was near Málaga airport and c) which would take a nine week old kitten which was too young to have its injections. This necessitated any number of phone calls and one or two lengthy journeys before we found what we were looking for, and were able to book Eloïse in.

It was now seventy-two hours before we were due to fly, and all that remained was to book the car into a car-park at the airport and drive up to collect the mail for the last time before we left. It was then that fate dealt us her second, and much more cruel, blow. This was in the form of a letter waiting for us from the hospital where I was due to have the operation, dated five days earlier, calmly telling me that the surgeon due to carry out my operation would not be available on the date for which I had been booked, and that new arrangements would have to be made.

There is a word in English, originally used in connection with removing the innards from rabbits or fish, but which is now often employed to describe people's feelings on the receipt of bad news: it is the word 'gutted'. I had always regarded this as being a trifle extreme, but now I knew exactly what it meant. I felt sick and utterly let down by the health service to which I had contributed for more than forty-five years, and which I had used relatively sparingly in all that time.

The letter explained that the surgeon would be away 'unavoidably for a professional commitment' - a masterful piece of hyperbole - and said that they realised how this upset our plans - no they didn't: they had absolutely no idea what it meant - but if I would kindly telephone their Admissions Office (from Spain!) they would do their utmost to accommodate me in planning a new date.

This cancellation clearly did not affect me alone, and the breathtaking lack of concern for the feelings of the patients involved, patients who, like me, had possibly been waiting for over six months, let alone the practical considerations for people in our kind of situation, left us momentarily floundering, after which a deep and simmering anger began to surface. I wouldn't have minded if the postponement had been due to an emergency - after all, I had waited right through the winter during an emergency, while the hospital beds were put to better use during the 'flu epidemic - but it couldn't be that, could it? You don't have an emergency with ten days' notice. So what could possibly justify the surgeon arbitrarily postponing the operation? We had our own ideas, and they weren't very charitable.

However the first requirement was to see if we could unscramble all the arrangements we had made at such cost in terms of time, effort and money. And here fate dealt her third blow: because we had booked on charter flights, it was not possible to cancel our flights and get any kind of refund: if we decided not to go we would forfeit the cost of the tickets. The best we could do (and here the same travel agent worked wonders) was to get our return flight brought forward, so that we only stayed in England for a week instead of the fifteen days previously arranged, and this we gratefully accepted, following it up with another round of phone calls to the cattery, the car park and to England, to revise all the arrangements we had previously made.

After these tests of character, fate finally relented on one score before we left for England: our legal representatives phoned to tell us that the *Certificado Catastral* for the *cortijo* had been prepared at last, that it showed that the vendors were, in fact, the people entitled to sell the property and that, as predicted, the property had never been registered with the Land Registry, so there was nothing now to prevent the *Escritura* from being prepared in our names. This was wonderful news, and in view of the fact that we would now be back from England earlier than expected, we asked if they could see if Pedro and Luisa would agree to bring forward the date for completion of the sale.

One last action remained before we left, connected with the reason why we had come to Spain instead of France in the first place: this was to write our Spanish Wills. This was neither morbid nor, as superstition suggests, likely to provoke our early demise, but simple prudence. As we both knew from personal experience, the problems of intestacy seldom occur when someone dies in their bed at the end of 'three score years and ten'. It's when they die prematurely, possibly as the result of an accident, that the difficulties arise, and this we wanted to ensure would not be the case so far as we were concerned.

So we put this in order and duly appeared before the Notary in Torre del Mar to sign the Wills – unlike England, where Wills are not registered, in Spain they have to be, and subsequently recorded in Madrid – and finally departed for England on Monday morning at 2.05 a.m., with nothing now to distract our rage at our treatment by the hospital. This was not improved by our experience on arrival at Gatwick.

Before we left, Susan had made arrangements to book a self-drive hire car from the airport through Joe and Irene, a charming couple operating the 'Practical Cars' agency out of Málaga airport. They did everything they could to ensure that a car would be waiting for us, including sending faxes and making phone calls on Sunday when they got no response from the car hire firm in England on Saturday. Unfortunately, this firm, despite presumably having had other air travellers in the past who wished to hire a car at short notice, shut up shop at midday on Saturday and refused to respond to any form of communication over the week-end. This was still the situation when we arrived at Gatwick at 4.00 a.m. and it remained the case for another four hours until another firm finally came to our rescue after we had waited in the South Terminal Arrivals until 8.00 a.m. for something to open. And people still wonder why we left the country!

Despite, or possibly because of, these setbacks, I had time to reflect during the three hour drive to the hospital on my reaction to the postponement of my operation, and I began to see things in another light. Certainly the lack of notice was disgraceful, but was I actually entitled, under the NHS, to any kind of priority for an operation of this kind? My condition was not life-threatening (though, so far as I am concerned, neither is a sex-change, which now seems to have moved up alongside a heart by-pass in order of NHS precedence), and although the operation had been placed on the list long before we left the country, should I now expect the administrative staff to take account of my changed circumstances in their rescheduling of the event?

When the Beveridge Report, which formed such a large part of the post-Second World War Labour Party Manifesto, outlined the principle of 'Social Security from the Cradle to the Grave', it included the provision of 'free' medicines and 'free' hospitals (before this, if you needed to see a doctor, or have medicines, or go to hospital, you had to pay, which invariably meant that a large proportion of the population which couldn't pay went without), and when the National Health Service was created, this was precisely what it set out to provide.

But times have changed, and the whole notion of, and indeed the need for, the Welfare State has radically altered since then. So, in my case, should I have realistically expected to have this kind of operation at all on the National Health? Should I really have been required to pay? I was fully aware that the 'nanny state' has engendered the view that free health care is a right, no matter how trivial its nature, but there has to be a limit to this. Above all, if I wasn't paying for the operation, should I expect any consideration from those whose remit is to administer the efficient running of a hospital, not pander to the private circumstances of patients?

It was with these confused thoughts churning round my head that we finally arrived at the hospital. It took us some time to find our way into the building from its car park, and even longer to find Reception (whoever designed the layout could have given lessons to Daedalus, the creator of the Cretan labyrinth). However when we finally got there I asked the woman on duty to phone the Ward Admissions office and tell them I had arrived; the reaction she got was most gratifying.

We made our way to that office, where a girl greeted me nervously with 'Mr Woolrych, we sent you a letter. Didn't you get it?', while shrinking herself into as small a space as possible in case I became violent.

'Oh yes, I got it,' I replied, 'but you didn't seriously think I could cancel the flight, did you?' From her reaction it was evident that neither she nor anyone else had given the matter any thought at all.

'We've now booked you in for 12th May,' she offered brightly.

'The 12th of May is when we will be signing the purchase contract for our house in Spain,' I answered through gritted teeth. 'I wrote to the surgeon's secretary, telling her this. This is not something that can be done by anyone else. It has to be done by us, in person, in front of a Notary.'*

'Oh dear,' she said weakly, 'when can you come in then?'

'September or October,' I answered.

'Not until then?' she said, almost plaintively.

'No,' I replied, 'there is the small matter of having to save up again for the flight, plus the fact that, in the summer season, it is almost impossible to get a flight at all, and much more expensive if you do.'

She looked at me wordlessly as I left, and I wondered just how she was going to report the conversation to the surgeon's secretary when she returned from lunch!

---

* This is not strictly true; we could have organised someone with Power of Attorney in Spain to sign for us, but we didn't see why we should be burdened with this extra cost, on top of everything else.

Chapter 9

He that travelleth into a country before he hath some entrance
into the language, goeth to school, and not to travel.

(Francis Bacon, *Of Travel*)

*England did not endear itself to us. We found staff in hotels
unhelpful to the point of rudeness. We stayed a few nights in a
hotel near Gerrards Cross where, on asking for a hot lunchtime snack,
we got not only the wrong order but when it was returned in the
correct configuration, it was cold. No attempt was made to put this
right by the staff and when we wrote to the manager (he was not on
duty that day), we received a brush-off letter in return. Here in Spain
when my lunch of fried chicken with too strong a garlic taste on it
proved uneatable, it was immediately removed and the staff at the
hotel in Colmenar, where this occurred, fell over themselves trying to
tempt me to eat something else. What a difference an attitude makes!*

It had rained heavily almost all the time we were in England,
causing flooding and all sorts of grief. It was a great relief to catch
the flight back to Spain a week later, where it was also raining, but
now it was most welcome. Before we had left Andalucía the
authorities were already talking about drought, and it wasn't even
May. And in our absence some thing wonderful had taken place:
the countryside was a riot of wild flowers. Although there had
been some flowers in bloom when we left, they had burst out all
over the place while our backs were turned, especially along the
verges of the road leading to our *cortijo*, which happily the local
authorities refrained from having trimmed.

Great banks of sweet-smelling Spanish broom, common broom,
common ragwort, the confusingly named black mustard and
Halimium halimifolium stretched as far as we could see over
the hills. Amongst them, adding splashes of pink, purple, blue
and violet in contrast to the great swathes of yellow, were
meadow cranesbill, cardoon cotton thistles, field scabious, purple-

loosestrife, viper's-bugloss, wild and field gladioli, and large pink cistus. There were crown and oxeye daisies, red poppies, wild peonies and wild mignonette, mallows, giant fennel, great clumps of borage, wild parsnip, *Coris monspeliensis*, oleander, lesser periwinkle, french lavender, tassel, golden-thistle, and the brilliant blue of chicory. And knitting them all together, ropes and mats of mallow-leafed bindweed ... and these were the ones we could identify - there were as many again we could not!

It was also on this road and at this time that we first became aware of what we now call 'the famous walking birds of Axarquia'. These are grey wagtails, which skitter around in the middle of the road every few hundred metres, presumably in search of food. However their over-riding characteristic is their resolute refusal to be diverted from whatever they are seeking until the last possible second. We would watch, horrified, as the little birds disappeared from sight beneath the front bumper, then sigh with relief when we saw that they had taken to the air, apparently as the tyres were about to crush them, to re-alight behind us and return to their previous, all-engrossing occupation.

In early May the momentum of our lives began to gather pace. It was as if we had spent the last four months in 'stasis', and that we had awoken to find ourselves suddenly faced with the need to take immediate decisions again, and live with the consequences of those decisions. Daily events started to have significance of their own instead of simply being part of an overall tapestry, and the contents of my Pandora's Box subsided in the face of meaningful activity. But they had been aroused, and I had a nasty feeling that they would not rest this time until they had been resolved.

Diary - Tuesday 4 May. We visit the *cortijo* to put into place the last piece in the jigsaw - how to work the *acequia* - the irrigation system. This has been worrying us a good deal. Pedro has been remarkably coy all along about details, and we have been wondering whether the whole thing was simply a sales ploy to get us to commit ourselves back in January, and now that it has come to the crunch there may, in fact, be no irrigation water at all, despite the assurance given on the sales details we took from Judy's office that there is 'as much [irrigation] water as is needed'.

Judy comes with us to act as interpreter, bringing one-month-old Bertram, who has been born in our absence. Judy looks great, but Luisa looks terrible: one of her brothers is seriously ill in hospital in Málaga, she says, and she is drawn and haggard with anxiety, a shadow of the redoubtable lady we had first met. She hopes that they can complete the sale the following Monday, 10 May, but could we not hold her to that, as she isn't sure whether her brother will last the week-end. We are faintly suspicious about this - the timing seems remarkably propitious - but say 'Of course,' (of course), while gently reminding her through Judy that, in any event, they will have to complete the sale by Wednesday 12 May, the date *they* had stipulated in the private contract.

After this, we all tramp along the water channel to inspect the system of 'valves' - rocks, wrapped in cloth, stuffed into the various outlets - then go to look at Pedro's other piece of land further along the 'road', which is also for sale. This is similar to the land which comprises our *finca*, although much steeper, and is very tempting, especially as, since January, they have built a single storey *casita* on it (now we know why they were so keen to get the 2 million *pesetas* from us: they needed them to pay for this). However Judy warns us that it is highly unlikely that this bungalow is legal, as the land measures only 8,000 square metres, and the minimum requirement locally to build a new house is 15,000. Even though the *ayuntamiento* - the town hall - is considering lowering this to 10,000 square metres, it will still not be enough.

What Pedro and Luisa have probably got, she says, is permission to build an *almacén* - a store shed - or something similar, and having built it will now wait and hope that they can get permission for a dwelling retrospectively once sufficient time has elapsed - either that, or sell it to some foreign sucker who isn't too bothered about paperwork! But as they are asking 12,000,000 *pesetas*, it will be quite an expensive risk for any purchaser, so we politely decline. And anyway, we can't afford it.

Before we leave we wring from Pedro an undertaking to supply us with a letter stating what our rights are to the irrigation water and when we are permitted to exercise them - he is apparently the Chairman of the Users' Group for the water concerned. We ask, through Judy, if this letter can be available when we meet on Monday 10th, as otherwise it may be difficult to get it, with them moving to Granada, and after all it does form part of what we are buying. He says he will try to do this, but can't guarantee it, as he will have to get it from Málaga. We don't understand this, but as this is clearly all we are going to get from him at this stage we accept it, and I write a note to our legal representative, summarising what has taken place, and say we will look forward to her confirmation that we will meet to complete the sale on 10 May.

Finally, as we are taking our leave, Pedro asks, as a seemingly throw-away question, whether we realise that the electricity to the house is not entirely 100 per cent. Well, we can see that, so 'Yes,' we reply. 'They are planning to redo it,' comes the slightly surprising rejoinder. We think about this, but it makes no sense in the context of the sale to us, so we bid our farewells and say we look forward to seeing them in Torre del Mar the following week.

Diary - Wednesday 5 May. We go to a superstore in Málaga to fill in time. Herbert comes with us, angelic all the way. Back at the flat, we referee the play sessions between him and Eloïse, as he has discovered that if he squeezes her hard enough, she behaves as a wonderfully mobile squeaky toy!

Thursday, 6 May. Nail-biting day - it is still not impossible that Pedro and Luisa might 'welch' on the sale, especially with the alleged complication of Luisa's brother's illness. With difficulty we restrain ourselves from phoning our representative every five minutes to find out if Monday is 'on', but succumb the following day, only to learn that they have heard nothing from Luisa, and that they are reluctant to make a firm appointment with the Notary until Luisa has confirmed the date. We agree that what will probably happen will be that they will hear nothing, and that Pedro and Luisa will simply turn up on Monday unannounced.

Saturday 8 May. A terrible day of waiting.

Sunday 9 May. An even worse day of waiting. The Torre del Mar week-end routine grates even more than usual and it is all we can do not to take out our frustrations on each other, there being no other suitable or available target. Instead we go for long, improving walks with Herbert … separately!

Monday 10 May. 9.00 a.m. Michael our builder phones and we bring him up-to-date. 10.15 I phone Judy and the office: there is no reply from Judy, and the office has heard nothing. They suggest we turn up anyway at 12.15. At 11.30 the office receptionist phones to say that, as we had predicted, Pedro and Luisa have arrived with all their witnesses! Susan immediately goes to get the equivalent of a banker's draft for the final payment and a certificate to say that we have imported the money from Britain for this purpose. Five minutes after she has left, the office phones again. Because Pedro and Luisa hadn't phoned on Friday, they hadn't made a firm appointment with the Notary. Now the Notary can't fit us in! Gloom and despondency for us and acute embarrassment for Luisa, who promptly blames Judy for failing to confirm her appointment for her!

Our adviser tells us that Luisa has grudgingly agreed, after a somewhat fraught conversation, that she and Pedro will come back the following day at 12 noon, when the Notary has said he can see us, once again bringing their witnesses. Susan and I go to our favourite *chirungito*, and have lunch and several exceedingly strong drinks followed by *siesta*, after which we go and buy two beds for the *cortijo* (with ours in store in England, we will have nothing to sleep on once we leave the flat), and arrange to collect them the following day - we hope.

Tuesday 11 May. We go to our legal representatives' office for 11.40 and are relieved to find Pedro and Luisa and their witnesses already there. We all depart for the Notary, leaving Herbert with the receptionist (Eloïse is still at the flat). Wait forty-five minutes in a crowded, airless waiting room, Pedro and Luisa and their two witnesses becoming increasingly agitated over the delay, partly because none of them are accustomed to offices and dealing with bureaucracy and partly because the witnesses are both farmers who have now lost two days' work.

At 1.10 p.m. we all troop into the Notary's office, where we participate in a ceremony which definitely ensures that all parties are aware of the gravity of the step which they are taking (unlike in England and Wales where, like as not, the only indication that you have bought or sold a property is the exchange of contracts between solicitors, usually by post, followed by a phone call to the parties involved).

The Notary reads aloud (in Spanish) the *escritura de compraventa*, signing across each page as he finishes it with a magnificent, elaborate flourish to prevent fraud. We, Pedro and Luisa then sign it, after which the latter then also swear on oath that they are truly the owners and that there is no mortgage, lien or other outstanding debt on the property, and that only they have right of access to the land.

At 1.30 p.m. we all troop out again, and the *finca* is (provisionally) ours at last. As their last acts as owners, Luisa hands Susan the keys to the *cortijo* and Pedro hands me a letter stating that we are entitled to 21 hours of irrigation water a month for the *finca* between May and October, and the dates and times at which we may take it. He asks me to sign his copy. This is done so quickly and with such perfect timing that I don't pay it much heed: I am so relieved to get any kind of document that I sign it without question. This is to come back to haunt us with a vengeance in the coming months, as is the entirely innocuous request we make as we are leaving the building prior to going our respective ways.

'Would it be possible for you not to leave the Land Rover parked in its usual place,' we ask, 'on the verge directly outside the entrance to the house, only we are expecting a lorry-load of building materials later this week, and this is the only place we can put them?' This doesn't seem to us to be too confrontational, given that Pedro and Luisa are supposed to have moved to Granada, so we are a bit taken aback at Pedro's immediate rejoinder, 'You don't own the road, you know.'

We are slightly reassured when Luisa says, 'Don't worry, I'll get him to move it,' and all seems well when we find on our arrival at the house that the Land Rover is parked on a piece of land directly opposite. However it is parked in such a way so as to make it impossible for anyone to use the entrance to the plot as a means of turning round and while this is no great inconvenience to us, then or later, it is to make it extremely difficult in the months ahead for lorries carrying building materials and, worse, fully-laden concrete lorries to turn round when they make deliveries to the house, as there is literally nowhere else for them to turn.

Back at our representative's office and with the sale complete, she gently points out the small matter of their fees and the disbursements they will now have to make on our behalf, so we part company with yet more money and take ourselves and Herbert off before anyone else can ask us for a contribution! After a hurried lunch, during which my old friends the pharyngeal pouches remind me forcibly of their existence, we pack the car with its first load for the *finca* – the animals, some fencing material, bedclothes and food, and two apple trees we had brought back with us from our April visit to England, much to the amusement of the cabin crew in the aircraft – and set off for our new home on the hottest afternoon of the year so far.

Our arrival at the *cortijo* heralds the start of a week which is to be as dramatically different from the measured routines of the previous four months as the *maelstrom* of mythology was to the Sargasso Sea. For openers, what should have been an emotionally satisfying experience degenerates into pure farce when we can't unlock the front door. The key fits all right; it just doesn't turn anything! After Susan has fruitlessly spun the key in the hole for nearly half an hour, and I decide discretion is the better part of valour and quietly get on with unloading the oven-like car, we finally 'affect an entry', as the police are wont to say, through the metal double doors to the sitting room, which prove to be less robust than the front door, which is made of thick, studded timber. We then discover that the front door key works perfectly well from inside, and will lock from outside; it just won't unlock from outside. Luisa couldn't have warned us of this, could she?

All of this makes us late for the forty-five mile return round trip to Torre del Mar to collect the beds and buy a camping stove, Luisa having taken with her the two-burner plate which had been her sole means of cooking for the forty-five years she had lived at the *finca*. Luckily there is no problem at the shop, but it means that by the time we get back to the *cortijo* it is already growing dark, we haven't prepared supper, and we still have the beds to unload, carry down the perilously steep path to the house and assemble in the gathering gloom. So, after we have slipped, slid, and staggered down with two bed-frames and two mattresses, I endeavour to work out how to assemble the beds by torchlight – Luisa has also removed all the light fittings – while Susan cooks *tortillas* on the gas stove – which she discovers leaks.

While we are fully engrossed in all this Pedro arrives, unannounced and without notice, to invite us down to their *almacén*, accompanied by two of his dogs, which amble in and make themselves at home. Evidently there has been a change of plan about the dogs, as they are now all down at the *almacén*, but the cats are still here, which will need sorting out. Of the chickens there is no sign, except for some tell-tale piles of feathers in the grass. Perhaps they are now in the dogs!

Now whether it is because we are dead tired and conscious that we need to get our tasks finished before the light fails entirely, whether we have a gut feeling that it could be unwise to get ourselves too close to Pedro and Luisa, whether it is our sheer astonishment to find that they are at the *casita* and not in Granada, whether it is the fact that, in any event, we can't understand a word they say and on the basis of past experience, any time spent with them is likely to be somewhat fraught, or whether we simply want to savour our first night at the *finca* alone we never have resolved, but we politely decline the invitation, despite Pedro's fairly hard sell. So off he stomps, more than a little put out, and a second or two later Luisa's wail of mortification can be heard right round the valley. We are to learn in due course just why she feels so mortified.

This is not, of course, the way we would have wished our relationship with the previous owners of our new home to start out, but there is no way of going back. We will just have to see how things now pan out. But the result is that our first evening neatly follows our arrival in its failure to live up to expectations, and after that we are <u>extremely</u> careful not to say or do anything which might shatter the fragile remains of our joy in finally being in the *cortijo*. Still, all things pass, and eventually we have supper inside us and beds to sleep on. This we proceed to do by candlelight, which confuses the animals totally, but not before Susan has taken the precaution of liberally powdering around the beds and everywhere else she feels necessary, against the likely invasion by cockroaches, of which we have seen plenty of evidence.

It sounds terrible but it was a relief to realise that 'they' had taken their dogs to the almacén *with them. Taking on five dogs which only understood Spanish and who were not that friendly had been bothering me, so when Luisa arrived next day at breakfast time with a plastic box full of wet bread and proceeded to throw it about for the cats I decided to keep the momentum going. She could feed the cats, I said, but not here; she would have to feed them at her* casita. *Here, I would feed them. She took a bit of persuading but grudgingly accepted it in the end.*

We settle down to sleep in a silence which is almost tangible. The only sound to break it is a dog barking in the distance, and when this finally ceases, the quiet and the darkness envelope us like a blanket. There is no moon outside, just a canopy of the most brilliant stars we have ever seen, and when we blow out the candles the window frames a picture which is almost primeval: no visible lights, cars or houses, just the mountain tops and the nearby trees - sheer magic. After noisy Torre del Mar let alone overpopulated Britain this is slightly unnerving and it takes us a little while to settle but when we finally do, we sleep the sleep of the dead. We are home.

Next day we are awakened at first light by the dawn chorus, which starts abruptly, right outside the house, at 6.15 a.m. Living for years as we had in Bournemouth and then either in the mill near Colmenar at the wrong time of year or in urban Torre del Mar, we have forgotten about this feature of spring in the countryside. The noise is absolutely deafening, and we lie almost stupefied, trying to identify the various birds which are contributing to this cacophony until it stops, just as abruptly, at 7 o'clock.

After a scratch breakfast, we spend a happy three hours collecting and burning an amazing assortment of rubbish, a task which is to form part of our daily programme for the next few weeks, while we wait for Michael to arrive. At the same time we replan the layout for the downstairs of the *cortijo*, an initiative which Michael promptly squashes when he arrives at 11.30. It is, he says, too ambitious, too costly and, above all, he isn't prepared for it, and as he is planning to start work the next day, do we really want to put this back while he recalculates and orders the materials required, arranges additional transport, and gives us a new estimate for costs? Chastened, we agree that we don't.

After Michael has gone, saying that he will be back next day and please could he have 1 million *pesetas* to be going on with (!), we sit in the sunshine on our terrace, under our vine. It is while we are sitting there that we are startled when small cascades of sawdust fall into our cups of coffee. Investigation reveals great black carpenter bees busy overhead, boring into the timber and canes which form the canopy. They have clearly been at this for many years, in the same way that death-watch beetles do into old church beams in England, and the canopy is in imminent danger of collapse. Its replacement, we realise, is going to be necessary a lot sooner than we had bargained for, and is the first of a whole raft of unforeseen projects (for which, of course, we haven't budgeted) which are to be forced on us in the months to come.

With lunch and *siesta* behind us, we drive to Torre del Mar to buy food for the animals, leaving the latter behind for their first taste of life at the house without us. While there we collect more of our things from the flat and buy a patio table and six chairs as we have nothing to eat from or sit on until our furniture arrives from England. We have taken the precaution of keeping the flat on until the end of May as a shower is not something we will have at the house for some time, never mind that there is no hot water supply there either. The wisdom of this decision comes home to us over the next fortnight, as it also becomes a bolt-hole to escape to during the horrendous early stages of the renovation work on the house and despite our joy at being in the *cortijo*, in many ways we wish we had been able to keep it for longer.

While we are in Torre del Mar we take two calls on our mobile phone (which doesn't work at the *finca*). The first is from my son, who is pleasingly delighted that we are into the *cortijo* at last; the second is from our removals company, which tells us that the first consignment of our furniture will be delivered tomorrow, despite the fact that we have expressly told them that we can't receive anything before the end of the month!

Reeling under this revelation, we drive slowly home with the car groaning under its load. We find that our animals have been angelic in our absence, and after unloading the car we sit on the patio in the fading twilight and debate where to put the various boxes and pieces of furniture when they arrive next day. It isn't until it is time to go to bed that we discover that, in the dark and distractions of the previous evening, I had failed to secure two of the legs on Susan's bed properly, and that it was a miracle that she hadn't been pitched out onto the floor during the night. So once again, by torchlight, I assemble the beds, getting it right this time, and we finally settle down by candlelight for our second night as homeowners in the *campo*.

The next day, Thursday 13 May, was one of many we are unlikely to forget. It began innocently enough, with me driving into town to try to get Michael's 1 million *pesetas* (around £4,000). The first hiccup came when this proved to be beyond the resources of the local branch of our Spanish bank without prior notice, and I could only withdraw half a million. I then went to on to the post office to see if we had any mail and found it was still shut, so I settled down on a wall with the other customers to await the arrival of one of the two staff.

Fifteen minutes later this luckless individual appeared, struggling under the load of several sacks of mail; the delay was due, he explained to the highly vocal Greek chorus of onlookers, to the late arrival of our consignment from the Málaga sorting office. He unlocked the door, and was practically trampled in the rush from the said chorus, which abandoned its place on the wall and, to a woman, surged forward to besiege the counter like hopefuls participating in Harrods' January Sale. This made things interesting inside the post office, which only measures 15 feet by 12, including the area used by the staff to sort the incoming mail and store the outgoing ditto.

Since the entire counter area is only about 4 feet by 9, the resulting ruck of seething bodies, all vieing for attention, made the historic confrontations between the respective scrums of Bath and Leicester RFCs. seem like a vicarage tea party. I waded in since, as any rugby scrum-half knows, it is futile simply to wait for the ball to emerge from a ruck: you have to dig for it. And in due course I was rewarded, in the form of two vast bundles of letters and magazines which were plucked from the pigeon hole marked *extranjeros* by the second member of the staff of the *correos*, who had arrived breathlessly a few minutes after the first and who thrust them into my hands with the injunction to sort them for myself.

As this was my first experience with the postal service in the *campo* I checked it later with those of others living away from the coast in circumstances similar to ours and found it, with minor variations, to be much the same as theirs. The first major difference with the UK was that post offices in rural areas are just that: offices to handle post. There are no racks of greetings cards, displays of confectionery, stocks of newspapers or other unrelated goods, nor even writing paper and envelopes: the staff are there to deal with the post. This also means that they largely have nothing to do with the ancillary services offered through British post offices, such as the payment of pensions or vehicle licensing, which in Spain are generally handled by banks, nor with holding government forms, nor even with selling stamps.

This can come as a bit of a shock, as British logic suggests that this is part of the postal service, but Spanish logic says otherwise: in the *campo* the function of the post office is simply to deal with the receipt, despatch and local delivery of mail. Although stamps can be bought at the larger post offices in major towns, in the smaller ones stamps are only held in sufficient stocks to affix to mail handed over the counter, not to sell in strips or sheets. So where do you buy stamps? In tobacconists, where else!

Tabacalera S.A. is a government monopoly, and one day we passed the tobacco factory in Málaga, which looks like a cross between Hampton Court Palace and something out of the Arabian Nights. No wonder the anti-smoking lobby has an uphill struggle in Spain! Tabacalera S.A. supplies cigarettes, etc. to their official shops – *estancos* – which supply everybody else and because it is a state monopoly, the Spanish government also uses these *estancos* for a number of other purposes besides selling cigarettes. Principal among these is the sale of postage stamps.

A third, and major, function of *estancos* is to supply model forms, such as those for medical certificates or for making rental contracts and to sell *papel del estado* – 'state paper'. This is a kind of stamp which comes in various denominations, and is used to pay the fee which accompanies many official forms, such as the *autorización de residencia* – the Residence Permit. You have to have the exact correct amount of *papel del estado* – they won't accept cheques or 'real' money – when you take your form to the appropriate government office, and they don't give change.

Apart from these superficial differences from the UK there were other, more fundamental, aspects to the mail which appeared to require the need for a flexible attitude. Although subsequent experience has revealed that the service within Spain can be fairly slow, we have generally found that there is little difference between the service to and from Spain from what we had been accustomed to in England; mail takes, on average, three to four working days country to country within Europe. However getting the mail once it has reached the *campo* can be greatly affected by local conditions once it has reached the main postal town.

For a start, there may well be no house-to-house delivery; this will depend on the location of the house. In the *campo,* if a house is within the boundary of a town or village that has a post office, then a daily delivery is likely. However as the postal staff are often also the delivery persons, delivery is likely to be in the afternoon, and then only if the postal staff has time. In the village where we stayed for the first three weeks of the New Year, the post-master – and only member of the postal staff – was also the Deputy Mayor, and as he took both duties very seriously, there was occasionally a conflict between the rival interests of the two responsibilities.

If a house lies outside a postal town or village, as ours does, then there is no delivery; instead, all mail is kept at the local post office, or even delivered to a local bar in outlying areas, for the addressee to collect. The storage facilities in these circumstances can range from a pigeon-hole marked *'extranjeros'* (foreigners) to a cardboard box on the floor. And the procedure at the post office ranges from having your letters swiftly sorted from the others by the post-mistress and handed to you with a smile, to having the entire con-tents of the pigeon-hole or cardboard box dumped on the counter, with the invitation to sort them out oneself (as happens with us).

None of this would be too demanding were it not for the vagaries of the post office opening times, and the consequences of national and local *fiestas.* Opening times vary from town to town. In Colmenar the post office opens from 8.30 a.m. to 12 noon (11 a.m. on Saturdays). Our local post office opens from 9 a.m. to 11 a.m. Since, from our house, it is a winding, uphill twenty-minute drive to the post office, this calls for a fairly timely departure when we need to go there, and puts a whole new meaning on the expression, 'missing the post'. There are also very few pillar-boxes in towns (those that there are are coloured yellow), and even fewer in the *campo,* where the usual recourse is to post your letters in the box at the post office. And there is generally only one collection a day.

The effect of *fiestas* on the postal service can be profound. The word *fiesta* can mean a whole range of things, from private parties to public events closely related to the old English - and religious - use of the word 'feast'. In Spain every day of the year is attributed to a saint, and since it would be unthinkable not to give due recognition to saints, there is a *fiesta* going on in some town or village 365 days in the year. And All Saints Day is, of course, a national *fiesta*.

Local *fiestas* seldom last for just the appointed day: they have a tendency to spill over into the days either side, beforehand with the preparation for the festivities and afterwards because of individual and collective hangovers - these are definitely not occasions for sobriety! When these days also include a public holiday, there can be dramatic consequences to the postal service, especially when other towns along the chain of supply also have *fiestas*. Your own post office may well shut for several days and, if others elsewhere do the same, it can be many days or even weeks until the various bottle-necks are eased and normality restored. So the moral is

If the mail and other services are important to your well-being, consider very carefully before settling in the *campo*.

Back at the *cortijo* I find Michael's workmen ripping up the ground floor and Susan marooned on the floor above! Once we have sorted that out, rescued Eloïse from the vine and repaired one of the workmen's cut eye, it is time to go and meet the removals firm's lorry up on the main road as the big pantechnechon is too big for the lane, and too heavy for the bridge to the house. Luckily this is a situation with which the removals team are entirely familiar, and they have brought two smaller vans into which to unload the pantechnechon and ferry our belongings down to the *cortijo* in more manageable bites. By 1.45 p.m. they are done and depart, leaving us with furniture and boxes piled largely on the terrace since, with the floor up, there are very few places indoors where we can actually put it.

This is faintly alarming. With our ingrained reactions to similar situations in England we are worried, first about security - with no fence around the property and no gate anywhere, and the boxes in full view of the lane, there is clearly a major potential for theft - and secondly, about the possibility of everything becoming wet if it rains. Time is to prove both anxieties groundless.

Eighteen months later we will still have no gate (although we will have a fence), we will still have boxes piled on pallets outside the house, covered only by a tarpaulin, and our total unexplainable losses will be two chimney pots and a box of videos, while so far as rain is concerned, this is Andalucía in summer, for heaven's sake: we shan't see significant rain for another five months!

On the plus side, though, we now have a fridge, and the deep-freeze, and our electric kettle, which all still work, so even though we have only one power point on which to work all three, plus a separate one from which to work the washing machine (which has also arrived, but which has to stand outside on the terrace because it is there that we have our only practical source of water), we at least have some of the trappings of civilisation, and the wherewithal to keep food cold and our clothes clean.

It is while we were contemplating these refinements to our lives that our reverie was interrupted by a shout from indoors; one of Michael's workmen has discovered the hard way that insulation has been provided inside the house by packing the internal walls with straw - he is covered in the stuff, which has fallen out from over the doorway into one of the downstairs bedrooms when he removed the lintel. This form of insulation, Michael says, was common enough in old agricultural buildings but this is the first time he has seen it in a house. More to the point, the straw is infested with fleas, so we are faced with an urgent need to clear it out of the house before we and our animals become similarly stricken.

For the rest of the day Michael's men continue to take up the floor tiles downstairs, ready for retiling - the first priority - and begin laying plastic conduit along the dirt floor for the electric cabling to the power points. In houses like ours, where the floors are solid and there is no gap underneath, this is a favoured technique, both for electricity and for plumbing: the electric cables and plumbing pipework are laid in the concrete beneath the tiles. This is great with the electrics if you can be absolutely certain where you want the power points, as it hides the cables away in a totally safe place, but changing your mind later on - if even possible - can be time-consuming and costly. And, as we were to find out the hard way, it can be much more of a problem with the plumbing if you have a weeping joint.

Diary - Friday 14 May. We escape once more to Torre del Mar, taking Herbert and Eloïse, as Michael's men are using an angle-grinder to chase the walls for electric cabling to the lights and the entire house is filled with brick dust, while the noise beggars belief! On our return we find all the tiles have been removed downstairs, except in the hall and the shower room, and that the floor now comprises a fine tilth and looks more like a bed for asparagus or for bringing on bedding plants than anything remotely suitable for walking on in a house. In addition all the doors except for the outside ones have been removed and carefully stacked outside.

Late in the day the first consignment of building materials arrives. These are unloaded onto the side of the road, after which Michael and his boys depart for the week-end. It is then that we discover that we have no water, the weight of the building materials having squeezed totally flat the plastic mains water pipe under the road. This is fairly unfunny with the temperature at 22°C (72°F) in the shade, so Susan and I set to in the glare of the evening sun to move the piles of bricks, the bags of cement and the pile of sand five metres along the road!

Happily this works, and the water is restored. It would be nice to record that we then have a refreshing shower to get rid of the grime, but we are a long way from having hot water yet, let alone a shower, so in the gathering gloom we pour basins of tepid water over each other and wash each other down, an exercise which results in supper being a bit later than usual! It is just as well I have repaired the beds. Later we watch, fascinated, while Eloïse and Herbert play tag <u>under</u> the downstairs internal walls, which Michael has cut off some 20 centimetres above floor level, leaving them suspended from the ceiling, to facilitate the resurfacing - fascinating. Perhaps we can write to Guinness and invite them to record a new Wonder of the World: the Hanging Walls of Lechano!

Later still, as we are settling down for the night, Susan remembers that we have opened the door to the second lean-to, which we are using as a store, to air it: will I go down and lock it. So off I go, armed with a torch, which I automatically shine into the first lean-to, the one formerly used to keep chickens in, as I go past. I wish I hadn't. In the film 'Indiana Jones and the Temple of Doom', Indy and his two companions have to go along a passageway carpeted with crawling things of various shapes and sizes. Our lean-to is exactly the same. The entire floor seethes. Some of the cockroaches are so large we reckon Pedro and Luisa must have kept them as pets. Unaccountably, sleep is a long time coming after this!

We now know the reason for the low wattage light bulb in the passage to the chicken house: it had been left on at night to deter the cockroaches from coming in! Once Michael had started work in the house and, later, knocked down the lean-to's at the end of the house,

the cockroaches decided it was time to leave. It was interesting to watch. The trail could be followed directly down the road to Pedro and Luisa's casita!

<u>Saturday 15 May</u>. Our first day for irrigation water. When Pedro handed us the letter telling us when we can have our water, we noticed it states 'from 7.00 until 4.00'. Since it wasn't totally clear whether this meant a.m. or p.m., we asked, only to be told (so we understood), 'it doesn't matter'. We now learn that this is not the case at all. As we are eating the last of our breakfast at 8 o'clock, Luisa arrives in breathless haste, and in a torrent of Andaluz plus gestures and actions which make her meaning entirely clear, indicates that we have by now wasted one hour of our entitlement. Since we have already realised that irrigation water is like liquid gold and is the lifeblood of every *finca* in the valley, we leap to our feet and follow her, while she puts in place the broken piece of asbestos roof guttering which serves as the aqueduct needed to divert the flow of the *acequia* from the main irrigation channel to ours.

Back on our land, with a torrent of water now flowing past the house, Luisa seizes a mattock and, after shoving its end up a small culvert and dislodging a large toad which is clearly in the habit of taking up residence there, uses its business end to clear out the various channels which run down into the orchard and generally assist in the free passage of the water to where it is needed. This is exhausting work, as I discover when I take over from her after about five minutes of 'on-the-job' instruction; it is also time-consuming, and it is 11 o'clock before I am able to take a break, by which time the sun is high in the sky and I am dripping with sweat.

The rest of the day is devoted to tending the irrigation channels, and with around two acres of sloping land criss-crossed with these narrow, weed-clogged ditches it becomes abundantly clear that, on irrigation day, this is a full-time activity, one which absolutely nothing can be allowed to interrupt. It is while I am on my hands and knees clearing out a stretch of ditch that I can't reach effectively with a mattock that I first make my acquaintance of our near-neighbour, Isidro, an acquaintanceship which is to blossom into confirmed friendship and is to alter the course of our lives. Isidro has a large house by the bridge, and has farmed here for most of his life. However he is infinitely more worldly and educated than most of the local farmers, and despite his having no English and I no Spanish, we are able to talk about the irrigation system with reasonable success.

It transpires that he has a fully automated, piped system, by means of which he can direct water as required to each individual tree: have I thought of doing the same? Well, frankly, I haven't thought of anything; I have been too busy getting totally knackered, mucking around in our own system which doesn't seem to have changed from the mediaeval one developed by the Moors during their occupation of Spain in the Middle Ages. However the idea appeals greatly, as the open ditches which we have water the weeds more than they do the trees and, on our sloping orchard, cause land erosion into the bargain.

More to the point, they are heavily labour-intensive – my labour – and while I fully accepted that running an Andalucían small-holding would require physical effort on my part, I hadn't bargained on crawling along irrigation ditches on my hands and knees, scooping out debris with my fingers. The only problem is the small matter of the cost, as not only will such a system require many hundreds of metres of black pipe, we will also have to 'cull' a large proportion of our fruit trees in order to make it work, as these are far too numerous and close together to give a decent crop, and appear to been planted entirely at random, and so make it impossible to run hoses to where they are required.

It is while Isidro and I are picking our way through our conversation on this subject that he casually asks how many hours of irrigation water we have. When I tell him 'twenty-one', he throws up his hands in horror.

'That's nowhere near enough. All the other *fincas* on your side of the valley have seventy-two: why have you got so little?'

'It's what Pedro ceded to us when he sold us the *finca*,' I replied.

'You've been done,' retorts Isidro (or Spanish words to that effect). And this is to be confirmed next day.

This was not what I expected life to be like but we both keep saying, 'Think about when it is finished.' Yes, OK, but for now it's very hard to visualise it. While Toby is coping with the irrigation, Michael arrives and starts my day by lending us a gas bottle (the good news) and 'Oh and by the way, you'll have no toilet for a couple of days or inside running water' (the bad news). Luckily we do have the outside tap but have to find buckets to act as our loo for a few days. The wedding vows about 'in sickness and in health' make no mention of your husband having to take the honey bucket down the land and bury its contents. That really is love!

We are having a late breakfast and I am nursing the bruises and counting the cuts I sustained the previous day, especially from the pomegranate trees, which are particularly vicious and of which we have a vast number, when an unknown figure makes its way down the path. 'Good morning,' it says, in unmistakable West Riding accents, 'I'm Don. My wife Liz and I live up there,' pointing towards the skyline above the house. 'We're on the same electricity supply as you. There's a meeting this morning to discuss the new supply to the valley. It's going to cost us about 215,000 *pesetas* [around £875] each. Did Pedro tell you about this?' No he damned well didn't, but now we know the significance of that throw-away remark he made to us a week before the sale.

In Britain we would have expected a solicitor to uncover this kind of thing in the course of the Searches and Enquiries before a property changed hands; in Spain it is not quite so simple, especially in the *campo*. When electricity was first made available here the supplying company, *Sevillana*, brought the supply to villages; if individuals further afield wanted electricity, they had to tap off the *Sevillana* supply and run their own cables to their houses. These privately installed systems varied enormously in quality, and it was not surprising that as time went by, *Sevillana* insisted that they be upgraded by the consumers concerned and then handed over to them for incorporation into their grid. However a good many original installations still existed, and it transpired our supply was one of these.

Mulling over this further example of the varied forms whereby the principle of *caveat emptor* can be made manifest, we agree we will come to the meeting, which is scheduled for 11 o'clock at the house of another expatriate neighbour, a German

who has lived here for ten years and who is similarly affected, where we learn the truth of the situation. Apparently the
poles used when the line was originally installed some twelve
years previously were made of timber, a great mistake in
this part of Andalucía where various kinds of wood borers
abound.

As a result, the line has become physically dangerous, with one
pole on the verge of collapse. At the same time, the demand for
electricity to the houses concerned has risen, with many of them
sold and their new owners, in most cases foreigners, wanting to
use microwaves and electric hairdryers, instead of just lighting. So
now we are all faced with the need to upgrade the supply and,
more importantly, to replace the poles since, as matters stand, we
could find ourselves collectively liable if anyone is injured should
the existing pole(s) collapse.

It is while we are waiting for Pedro to appear - and wondering
how we should behave towards him - that another facet to
the situation comes to light. Hans, the German, is an electrical
engineer; he also knows Pedro and Luisa extremely well. It is
likely, he says, that the quote everyone has received for the
work to be done is inflated, since it has been obtained by Pedro
and will almost certainly include a 'fudge factor' for his
expectation that he will get the supply to his *almacén* either at a
discount or completely free for placing the work with that
particular contractor. So he, Hans, has taken it upon himself to
obtain a rival quote, which he now shows us. This is substantially
lower than the original one, thus bearing out his suspicions,
especially as it is every bit as comprehensive as Pedro's quote.
He suggests that his findings should be put to Pedro when he
appears.

When this happens, half an hour later, Pedro is accompanied by
two of his dogs, which walk behind and on either side of him like
Mafiosi henchmen ... and promptly proceed to eat the food
which Hans has put down for his own dog without Pedro doing
anything to stop them. Instead he settles himself into a vacant
chair and adopts an attitude which clearly indicates that, now
that he is here, we can start the proceedings. We are amused and
intrigued by this display, which seems out of keeping with an
Andalucían farmer in the presence of, and completely out-

numbered by, a group of reasonably educated foreigners. Later we are to learn why.

However he now gives a display of statesmanship under duress which would draw applause at the United Nations; it could certainly be viewed with envy by many who grace the corridors of power in Brussels, and gives us a further insight into the character of this complex man. When presented with the rival quote he is not at all fazed: could we, he asks, give him time to discuss this new development with Luisa? Of course, the meeting says: perhaps some of us could come down and see you in an hour or two and get your views?

So off Pedro stomps, flanked by his henchmen, and later Hans and Don, as the two best Spanish speakers, go down to the *almacén* where, they tell us afterwards, although Pedro and Luisa wriggle and squirm, they can do nothing about the situation without admitting their vested interest in the first quote. However Pedro has asked if he can refer the new figures to his original contractors, to see if they can match them and, if they can, perhaps we could still agree to place the work with them? Hans and Don say they agreed to this, and that is how it all duly comes to pass - with us all saving money and Pedro saving face.

Despite this minor success, we are still faced with having to find nearly £900 for which we haven't budgeted, a development which will require yet another re-evaluation of our goals and priorities. It is while we are ruminating on this, and independently coming to certain conclusions as to what we should do, that we learn the background to Pedro and Luisa, a fascinating insight which throws a great deal of light on why they have behaved to us as they have.

It appears that their respective parents owned virtually everything on our side of the valley, so when they themselves married, the dynasty was complete. As a result, for over forty years they had both, but especially Pedro, been accustomed to going where they pleased and doing what they liked everywhere between the bridge over the river and the other end of the valley on our side. In fact, Pedro was the instigator of the building of the new bridge over the river and was a co-founder of the *acequia* system, so he really had stamped his personality on the area - stamped being the operative word, as until recently he had an unenviable reputation for settling any dispute in which he was involved by what could be politely described as 'direct action'.

Now, although many of the properties that were originally in the family had been sold - including their own - it seemed neither of them could accept the notion that taking the money meant relinquishing the rights to the properties concerned: they still felt they had suzerainty over them. This, we conclude, is why Luisa felt so slighted when we declined her invitation to go down to the *almacén* on our first night at the *cortijo*: we had failed to bend the knee to them as *soberanos*.

It also explains why they both still feel entitled to come onto our land and even into the house whenever they please, and occasionally to take away things that take their fancy. Although we have already discovered that Andalucían countryfolk have no inhibitions about coming onto other people's property to satisfy their curiosity about anything new taking place, especially when it is initiated by foreigners, they usually stop short of actually taking things. This is far from the case with Pedro and Luisa, who clearly feel it is still their property. And it explains why Pedro has only ceded us 21 hours a month for irrigation, though there is actually more legal justification for this.

While we were waiting for him to arrive at the meeting, Don showed us a piece of paper which he had been given when he bought his house. This shows that when the *acequia* was built in 1985, the 24 hours a day available for its use were divided up between those who had contributed to its construction; the rights were vested in people - one of whom was Pedro - not the properties which they owned. Had Pedro and Luisa moved out of the valley and gone to live in Granada, as we expected, and had he ceded the rest of his water entitlement to someone else, we might have had a case. But since they still have a plot of land equal in size to ours, we realise we will have great difficulty in challenging his retention of the larger portion of his allocation, no matter how valid our cause might be in the light of the description of the irrigation given in Judy's details or that 21 hours were insufficient to sustain the commercial viability of the *finca* under its existing irrigation system. This is another lesson learned:

Never make assumptions on what is described in property details, and even when you check them out thoroughly, accept that you will still be caught out some of the time!

It also explains why ex-pats who buy out in the campo *erect fences. It's eight in the morning, we have just finished breakfast and there is Pedro walking across our land with his two dogs. The first thing I want done once we can get the trees sorted out is to have fencing on both sides and the front of the property. Not to keep our animals in but to keep wandering former owners and their dogs out!*

Returning home we settle down on the terrace in the afternoon sunshine, to enjoy the rare silence in the absence of Michael and his men. The carpenter bees continue their tunnelling into the bamboo supports to the vine branches overhead, and more cascades of sawdust fall into our coffee. Periodically the sawdust is augmented by bits of palm branch, which have been placed over the bamboo by Pedro to supplement the vines. This is because Eloïse has just discovered that she can CLIMB, and is busy making up for lost time by doing just that at every opportunity. And once in a while, both sawdust and palms are joined by a falling, furry feline, when Eloïse finds that she still has a bit to learn about getting down again!

We find that the carpenter bees bother no one if left alone; this cannot be said for other, tiny ones, which have a nasty sting. The wasps, too, are a challenge, being meat-eaters, to the extent that they will drive Herbert or Eloïse away from their (tinned) food to get to it. And we have discovered a huge millipede which bites you at the front end or stings you from the back end if you tread on it.

On Monday we discover one possible reason why Pedro and Luisa had been reluctant to return phone calls: the telephone in the house is faulty, the 'zero' staying down whenever it is depressed. Michael kindly telephones *Telefonica* on our behalf to tell them about it, and they agree to send a man out the next day.

With our experiences of the service from BT in similar circumstances, we feel we will rely on this when it actually happens, so we are agreeably surprised when, at 10.30 a.m. on Tuesday, an engineer duly appears, closely followed by Pedro, who can't wait to get in on the act.

After about half an hour, while the engineer diagnoses and then fixes the problem, he turns to Pedro and asks - and despite our lack of Spanish, his meaning is unmistakable - 'Who are you?', to which Pedro replies, 'I used to live here. I sold the house to "the English".'

The engineer thinks about this for a moment and then says, 'So, this isn't your place now?'

'It was until a few days ago,' replies Pedro.

'Yes, but it isn't now?' insists the engineer.

'No,' Pedro reluctantly admits.

'Then why,' demands the engineer triumphantly - he has clearly encountered situations like this before, and is enjoying every minute of this one, 'are you here?'

Pedro is so stumped by this question that he makes no reply; he just turns on his heels, storms out of the house and, collecting his two henchmen from outside the front door, marches off up what has been, until a few days earlier, his path.

Watching his receding back we can't help feel sorry for him. He is an anachronism, a legacy from an older way of life. The world is changing around him, and he has absolutely no precedent on how to deal with it. So far as we know, until his daughters persuaded him to buy the flat in Granada, he had never ventured further afield than Velez Málaga - about twenty miles - in his whole life. Take him to Málaga Airport and he will be totally freaked.

In his life he has done what his whole upbringing has conditioned him to do: amass money to leave his children secure. Now he has done that, but it hasn't turned out as he expected: his daughters don't need the money, and have no intention of working the land. So he has become rich for no good reason, and he has no idea how to enjoy it himself with the money he has acquired.

He has no books, no pictures other than photos of his children and grandchildren, no vision of what his life, or even his former home, could have become, no interests other than working the land as his father had done and going for his afternoon drink at the local bar with his friends, all men and all of similar age and outlook to himself. It isn't that he loves the land; emotion doesn't come into it. It is simply all that he knows, and now it is slipping away from him. It seems a sad testimony to a life.

We are to discover later, too, certain other aspects about *Telefonica*. Although its monopoly has now been broken, it is still pretty much as British Telecom used to be – 'nuff said! Our telephone is a radio telephone, this being the preferred solution by *Telefonica* in the *campo* to running expensive lines all over the place. It usually works perfectly well, although there can sometimes be a time-lag or a 'ghost' echo in the response by the person we are talking to, especially when both of us are on these phones, or one of us is on a mobile.

This can be irritating, but is liveable-with. The real problem is with the Internet, as the system is generally too slow to permit connection and can be disrupted in certain circumstances by the use of mobile phones near its line-of-sight signal. We also discover the hard way that *Telefonica* charges for each call as it connects into their system, not when the person phoned responds; we are charged over £8 on our first telephone bill for conversations we haven't had!

These thoughts are all very well, but they don't get the shopping done, so after we make the discovery about the phone on Monday, I make my way into town for my first visit to the *ferreteria* – ironmonger – in the town. This Aladdin's Cave is very similar to the establishment run by Mr Ronnie Barker in the TV series 'Open All Hours'. It stocks absolutely everything, apart from food. Among its trophies are: nails (not in sealed packets, but available in whatever quantity you want, even down to one!), jubilee clips, axes, mattocks, antkiller, plugs (both wash-basin and electric), electric heaters, water pipes of every conceivable gauge, wire mesh, hammocks, padlocks, the list is almost endless.

All I want is some Camping Gaz for our burner, a saw, a pair of secateurs and a giant, two-handed version of the same so that we can start on the over-due pruning of our trees. These are all produced with alacrity and much merriment after my mimed display to augment my meagre efforts at Spanish and I return home in triumph to put the new tools into use...including pruning fig tree suckers from around our opencast toilet drain – fun!

Chapter 10

Love is not just looking at each other,
it's looking in the same direction.
(Antoine de Saint-Exupery)

Deciding to move to Spain had been, for us, a major step, if not geographically, then certainly in the realms of mind and emotion. At fairly advanced ages we had forsaken a familiar way of life in England and had embarked on something almost entirely alien in a country where we couldn't even speak the language, let alone know whether we had an empathy with the culture. We had also left behind children and friends, whose reactions to our going were extremely mixed.

Although, of course, this had been entirely our own choice it nevertheless brought with it considerable apprehension as well as excitement. Had we done the right thing? Were we totally mad? Would we really like it? What if anything went wrong? All of these questions rattled around our heads with growing momentum, massively exacerbated by our twenty-three-week wait in limbo. It would have been so much easier if we had been able to get stuck into our new way of life immediately, when the sheer effort of it all would have made sure that we were too tired to worry. As it was, the wait had allowed undercurrents of anxiety and tension to develop of which we were totally unaware.

What we had failed to realise was that not only were we experiencing anxieties and apprehensions collectively as a couple, we were also suffering from another range of worries as individuals, and were each unaware of the nature or extent of these worries in the other. This was unfamiliar territory, since one of the great blessings of our relationship has always been an ability to talk to one another, and by talk I don't mean the ritual exchanges that unhappily characterise so many marriages (including our own previous ones); I mean share ideas and, more importantly, reveal feelings, including the negative ones which crop up periodically in all partnerships and which, if not dealt with in time can, like a grain of sand in a shoe, become abrasive and cause an infection.

This had been so much the pattern for the ten or so years we had been together that we had come to take it for granted. Now, faced with the prospect of an unfamiliar way of life while simultaneously worrying about how the other felt about a situation for which each of us felt responsible, we found ourselves unable to reveal our feelings at a time when to do so was perhaps more important than at any time previously.

And this was the point: we now had to face up to the practicalities of living our dream instead of merely talking about it, a dream which marked not only a fundamental change in any lifestyle we had experienced before, either separately or together, but also represented the way of life which would be ours for the rest of our lives. Although this was what we had been waiting for and so welcomed it with open arms, it was also alarming and we were each of us preoccupied about how the other viewed it, especially after so long a waiting period in circumstances which had scarcely been ideal. All these individual anxieties had been maturing during that waiting period, unrecognised and unresolved. Now we found ourselves having to reconcile them while simultaneously accommodating ourselves to the practicalities of life at the *cortijo*. This was to test our relationship as few things had done before.

When we met, Susan was married to someone else and I had a live-in lady-friend, and while the sun was setting on both these relationships, we were neither of us remotely looking to replace them. At the same time, neither of us had jobs in the conventional sense. I was self-employed, as was Susan in a part-time way besides being a housewife, both of us in the same network marketing company, so when we got together and set up in business for ourselves, we never had the 'housewife-stays-at-home-waiting-to-welcome-the-bread-winner-after-a-long-day's-work' syndrome which typifies so many (men's) attitudes to their marriages. We were both faced with running the same business and home, together.

These two factors, plus our respective ages, meant that our relationship was based from the outset more on mutually compatible attitudes than on lust (though, happily, that was there too), and we started off our lives together sharing ideas, aims and ambitions (and misgivings, doubts and anxieties) as well as the mundane practicalities of running a business and a household. This meant discussing everything that affected us, whether at work or at home. It also meant that keeping secrets from one another was virtually impossible - try doing that when there is no demarcation about who answers the telephone, opens the mail or pays the bills - so we never even thought of it. This pattern was now to be searchingly tested.

If ever there was a bogeyman in our lives it was a 'what if' factor. We both quietly got on with the waiting game but each of us was wondering 'what if we don't like this, that or the other?' I wanted livestock on our farm: what if Toby didn't? What then? The place cried out for restoration, and not just the house; the land needed to be brought back to life but how, what with and when? And if we had some animals or poultry (which was what we had in mind originally), how much would Toby like that idea when it came to the crunch?

The first indications of what lay ahead came with the realisation of just how insulated we were from the world around us. After the euphoria of moving into the *cortijo* had died down, it slowly dawned on us that we were totally dependent on each other for all mental and emotional needs, and for most physical ones as well. It wasn't that we were isolated, as on a desert island, with no-one else around. It wasn't even that we were so remote that we never saw anyone: we could see plenty of people if we drove into town, and even in our valley the occasional car passed and there were people living within a few hundred yards of us. Our problem was that we were unable to communicate with them, or understand what they were saying in their own daily intercourse.

To anyone who has never been in this situation, it may seem that I am overstating the problem. To them I can only say, try it, and see for yourself. Speaking is a major sense; we humans now depend on it massively for communication and, as those advertisements for British Telecom which featured Mr Bob Hoskins clearly stated, 'It's good to talk.' It is even better to listen - why else were we given two ears but only one mouth? - since by listening we can not only hear what other people are trying to tell us, we are also passively part of the exchange of information between other people. And when you cannot understand a word which anyone around you says, you inevitably feel segregated and apart.

When there is only one of you, there is no option but to get stuck in and start to pick up the rudiments of the language as quickly as possible, and as those who find themselves in this position are generally also among lots of other people, social interaction is inevitable. This may be exhausting - it usually is - and can be frustrating at first, but it is seldom oppressive. For a couple, on their own in a fairly remote valley, with limited contact with anyone else at all, let alone anyone with whom they can converse, the consequences can be very different.

In different ways, Susan and I are both very self-sufficient, and when we met we could each do, and did, the full compass of activities which in many households are the jealously guarded domain of one or other partner, from managing the family's finances to doing the ironing. However there is a power balance which exists in any relationship and ours is no exception; even in a partnership of two, one person has to take the initiative - and the blame - in almost all situations, whether it is buying a new car or doing, or failing to do, the washing up.

In our case the power balance has always shifted back and forth according to the prevailing circumstances and challenges. We didn't consciously adopt this practice; it was an almost inevitable consequence of the merging of our particular individual personalities, and the way of life we had adopted as a couple. However what had worked in England now revealed itself to be both a blessing and a curse in our new-found circumstances and relative isolation, and we found ourselves instinctively reverting to the habits and attitudes which had served as our respective refuges before we got together, and it was our saving grace that we are also strongly interdependent on almost all levels and that there are relatively few secret parts which that interdependence does not touch.

We have always had a greater influence over each other's feelings than is perhaps customary in most relationships. Why this is so I have no idea: perhaps through past experiences we are more acutely aware than is usual of the penalties attendant upon riding rough-shod over a partner's emotions, but the effect is that we have always tried to take into account the other's possible wishes in almost everything we do. This may sound laudable – it probably is in the conventional circumstances of most relationships – and possibly, in the extreme, cloyingly sentimental, but under the limitations which we were now suffering of virtually no other single human contact with whom we could adequately communicate for days at a stretch, it engendered a state of near emotional paralysis.

In most adult relationships the main priority, once the initial surge of passion has died down, is to learn the unfamiliar crafts of living with someone other than one's parents and siblings, and of coping together with the routines of running a home, bringing up children and earning a living. The adjustments required to do this successfully are considerable, and it is unsurprising that many people fail, and take refuge in power-plays over the person who, only a short time before, was the finest thing since sliced bread. A large part of this personal power-play has to do with our fears and hopes, secret or expressed, about how other people will react, but when there are only two of you around there is no forum for public shame, judgements or back-biting, or indeed public acclaim, recognition or reward. There is no-one to attack or defend, revile or praise either of you except the other, and there are no witnesses or scapegoats.

This can be confusing to those who are accustomed to these things. As humans we are pretty much conditioned to the need for some kind of reaction from someone – or, better still, lots of ones – other than our partner to what we need and do; a common manifestation of this is the sad practice of parents at variance with one another who try to recruit the sympathy of their children towards their side of a dispute. So when you find yourself with the very same partner as your only audience then no matter how well-adjusted and devoted to each other you are, no matter how considerate towards the other's feelings and no matter how restrained you are in your reactions to what they say, do or think, you are deprived of a very necessary human outlet and are obliged to make some rapid adjustments to your normal instincts or risk the collapse of the very relationship you are trying to preserve.

On the other hand, when these power ploys are eliminated, or when a situation arises which temporarily suspends them, isolation can engender a strong pull towards uniting together either towards or against those other people with whom you do come into contact, a reaction which may result in the birth of yet another power base, that of the united clan. If this is not resisted it can make one's isolation no longer a matter of choice, and we were acutely conscious of this very real possibility in our case, given our respective temperaments!

As if all this were not enough, at the same time that we were facing up to these challenges, we also had to agree on major policy decisions with regard to our newly acquired home, the first of which was whether we were going to focus initially on working the land to generate an income, or on getting the house more or less as we wanted it, bearing in mind our slowly gestating plans for a B&B. I kept being drawn to the land and its trees and a wish to make them productive; Susan, reasonably, not only wanted somewhere acceptable to live, she also covertly wanted to prevent me from doing too much. This immediately put another strain on our relationship, and made for some interesting exchanges between us before we finally revealed, and understood, our respective priorities.

I am not, and have never been an easy person to live with! Like a small child I have a never-ending curiosity to find out why and the next thing to 'why' is 'why not' and 'why not <u>now</u>'? This makes it hard to control my impatience to have everything done by yesterday! Toby has had to live with it for ten years and sometimes he underestimates my determination. This caused our first major row, with both of us stomping off in opposite directions to cool down. In particular I felt that priorities had been accepted and jobs agreed and that now he was arguing that we hadn't agreed this or that or was changing his mind without talking about it. And because we had no proper accommodation, noisy builders all day, and the constant, appalling mess, patience was in short supply and we forgot to talk. Until this time we had never had so much as a raised voice at each other, now suddenly boom! It was a sharp reminder not to take our good fortune for granted.

Looking back, it seems strange that we should have waited until we had already been a week in the *cortijo* and had actually begun the work of renovation on the house before we faced up to this decision, but at the time it wasn't possible to resolve it beforehand. For one thing, we had been held back by the superstition that we could somehow be tempting fate if we made too many plans too soon; that somehow, we might prejudice the entire sale. And for another, it was four months since we had last walked round the *finca* and, while we had gained a sufficient impression to know that we wanted the place and roughly what we wanted to do to the house, we didn't know nearly enough about what the land produced, how it produced it or whether to rip some of the trees out and start with new ones.

As children we had both been brought up on dairy and arable farms in the south and west of England, and our dream had included keeping livestock in Spain. We hadn't bargained on fruit farming, and largely unfamiliar fruit at that, on land which was, to put it mildly, extremely strange to those brought up in Dorset and Cornwall. The land at the *finca* is almost pure clay ('thixotropic' I believe geologists would call it). It is so hard when it is dry that you stumble on any clods you happen to step on, and are quite likely to turn your ankle. It also crumbles, and is so frictionless that anything loose slips away from under you on any kind of slope, with the high possibility of you ending up on your rear end. But after only a couple of minutes of irrigation, or five minutes of heavy rain, it becomes slurry and you slalom on the paths and tracks and sink to your calves off them. It also holds the water, so that after prolonged rain any badly-drained plateaux become lakes, and banks and roads give way without warning owing to the build-up of water behind them.

While this can be aggravating on a personal level, it is infinitely more significant – and serious – when it comes to buildings, as a nearby German owner discovered during the last serious rains here: his house slid a metre down the hillside! Spades and forks are useless as tools: the ground is too hard for a spade to penetrate when it is dry, and it simply slips through a fork or jams in the prongs, while with both tools it is too heavy and clinging when it is wet. The tool favoured by the Spaniards is a mattock, a cross between an axe and a hoe, and with this, as Luisa had demonstrated, they do all their ground preparation, and very successfully too.

This meant we had to learn new techniques for working the land; we also had a lot to learn about our trees. We had a riotous mixture of pomegranates, pears, peaches, quince, apples, almonds, figs, cherries, apricots, plums and olives and even a walnut tree, seemingly planted without any kind of system. Most were far too close together to grow to any height or give a decent crop and needed to be culled, and all required pruning. There was also the question of whether we should try to rationalise this profusion, and concentrate commercially on just one or perhaps two species, with the rest reduced to what we might need in the house. With an olive-oil processing co-operative only two kilometres away, there was a clear case for focusing on olives, but with our limited Spanish and no prior knowledge about olive-growing, it seemed intelligent to wait and watch while the year unfolded, and learn from observing our neighbours before we started anything radical ourselves.

There was also the small matter of wanting a garden. This will come as a surprise to those who know us well, since for most of our lives, while we have been very happy to enjoy and praise other people's gardening efforts, the last thing we wanted was to do them ourselves. However, as with life, so with gardens, and now we wanted one, too. And this presented another snag. There was plenty of evidence that things would grow at the *finca*; the problem seemed to be to get them to stop! But the challenge was, what form would the garden take and what types of plants would we grow? Our experiences, such as they were, were with 'English gardens' whose lawns, roses and herbaceous borders demanded – and got – almost unlimited water and thrived under a benevolent – and often infrequent – summer sun. Here, clearly, the situation was almost the opposite; already we could see that the heat and intensity of the light and the absence of summer rainfall demanded a radically different approach, but with neither of us having any experience nor prior knowledge of Mediterranean gardening, it seemed prudent to gain a little of both in order to avoid any number of expensive mistakes.

Our conclusion therefore was that the house should come first. We still had a reasonable balance left from the sale of our home in

England, and I did have my occupational pension which, while not generous, at least meant that we had something coming in each month, so the land could actually wait. Obviously we couldn't simply ignore it: we knew that if we let it lie fallow, it would 'go back' at an alarming speed, and we would be faced with a mammoth task in the future. But it did mean that working the *finca* commercially would be the project for the new millennium, as would the garden, and the immediate priority was to renovate ('reform', as the Spanish so nicely put it) the house. However this meant that, far from coming to terms with our new home and reconciling at our own pace our respective dreams for our future in it, our timetable would now be governed by the needs of our builder, seemingly for an indefinite future.

Diary – Friday 21 May. We have now been *terratenientes* for ten days. Isidro calls after breakfast with a wonderful present of half a dozen grapefruit and a bag of extremely rich potting compost and some flower pots (we couldn't help comparing this gesture with the attitude of our English landlords at the mill, who not only counted the spoons when we left, but expected us to pay for the marks made when we moved their faulty butane gas fires on the concrete floor and demanded a full bag of compost to replace the half-bag we thought they had given us). When we show him 'cockroach city' we elicit the rejoinder (in Spanish), 'I hope you don't think we all live like this?' No, we certainly don't, and a visit to him and his family later in their spotless house by the bridge justifies this.

After he has gone we meet Pedro's elder brother who also has land in the valley, a delightful seventy-two-year-old who keeps his land beautifully, so our faith in Andalucían country people is restored. There is more tile-cutting with the angle-grinder by Michael's *niños*, making the front terrace untenable, so I trim and prune more trees until my enthusiasm and knees give out. This is a better fate than Susan's, as she is obliged to remain near the house to respond to the continual cries of 'Susanna' from Michael or his workmen, demanding cold water to drink or other assistance.

At end of the day we have a discussion with Michael about the future programme. We had intended the initial phase of work on the house – the one we could afford – to follow a definite programme. Michael had intended this too, his aim being to get the *reformación* done on enough of the original house as quickly as possible so that we could then live in relative comfort while he got on with the rest. Silly us: we have none of us taken into account the frequent non-availability of building materials when they are required, nor the vagaries of the subcontractors with whom Michael is obliged to share the work, such as plumbers, electricians and the like.

I often thought it would be nice never to have any housework to do. I am now lost: there is no routine, nothing is free of dust and as wherever I go a builder is sure to follow and want something, it can become quite fraught! Even going to the loo is not without its problems!

There is also the small matter that when we drew up our plans for the house so that Michael could give us a cost estimate on which to work, they had been made following our visit to the house back in early February, and we had had no opportunity to revise them, nor to make detailed modifications in the light of the experience of actually living here. Now we have and, of course, being us, while mercifully content with the basic concept, we have began to sprout ideas for 'improving' it.

Luckily we are constrained from being too radical by the fact that the first consignment of building materials has already arrived and the quantities for the balance have been carefully calculated to complete the initial work on the ground floor – and to fall within the cost estimate – but there is still time for us to reconsider things like doorways and doors, the route of the staircase and the number and positioning of power-points and lights (though the latter possibility is being rapidly eroded as Michael completes the floor and wall in each room). These we offer to Michael who, sensible man that he is, tempers them with hard commonsense before we all finally agree or reject them. From this comes our first lesson so far as builders are concerned:

In a project of this kind, chose a builder with whom you can communicate your ideas, who understands your vision and who can and will 'go with you' and 'roll with the punches'.

There is another lesson we are learning with regard to Spanish builders in the *campo* and where Michael, despite being Dutch, is no exception: they never seem to have any tools of their own. True, Michael does have his own cement mixer; we haven't had to hire one as an unexpected extra outlay after the estimate has been agreed, as happened to one British couple we know, although we have had to provide the plug for its electric lead. And he does have his own shovel for moving the end product from the mixer to where it is needed (though he has also borrowed - and broken - one of ours). And he has a hammer and cold chisels for hacking bits out of the walls. But of ladders he has none (luckily we have two), nor hose, saws - either timber or hack - screwdrivers, nor spirit-level (until much later). He has even asked to borrow a pencil with which to mark a level on the walls - and we have to find a sharpener as well!

Now it may be that we are being had for suckers - there is plenty of opportunity for that - and that if we put our collective feet down, he will go and get whatever he needs. But as Michael is so transparently honest about everything else it seems unlikely, and we have come to the conclusion that jobbing builders in Spain do not expect to have to have the same inventory of tools as do their counterparts further north, and that they rely on their clients to provide the necessary hardware. Therefore,

Make sure that you have enough tools to enable your builder to do the job you have contracted him to do or, at the very least, much time will be lost while he goes to get them.

Saturday 22 May. Up at 6.30 a.m. as usual to let Herbert out, then self to Torre del Mar after breakfast to buy the first of the fittings for the house - the downstairs lights. Meanwhile Susan has another visit from Isidro bringing more grapefruit, and who then stays to give valuable advice on how to treat our land which, he says, has had nothing in the way of fertiliser for as long as he can remember. He also gives her directions - which she follows with some difficulty - on how to find the agricultural wholesaler in Velez Málaga. He really is a gem, and we hope he may become a valued friend as time goes by.

Next day we have our first experience of a problem which is to become a familiar adjunct to life in this part of the *campo*: the mains water goes off without notice. As we are soon to learn, mains water in the *campo* is very different from the system in the UK, or indeed on the *Costas*. The supply comes from large, Council-installed *depositos* (storage tanks) sited on strategic mountains, from which local communities/houses are supplied through black rubber pipes. These can be laid on the ground alongside the road, or buried under someone's olive grove. Either way, the supply is highly vulnerable to interference and disruption, and makes 'trouble shooting' extremely difficult for all concerned.

Whether because of this, or for more fundamental reasons, the supply in the *campo* can also be cut off without warning and for indeterminate periods. To allow for this, most houses have their own *deposito(s)*. Unfortunately Pedro and Luisa had not felt this to be necessary when they lived at our *cortijo*, and we were to discover the shortcoming of this deficiency many times during the summer, so the moral was:

**some kind of safeguard against domestic drought
is an absolute priority in the *campo*.**

<u>Monday, 24 May</u>. Michael's *niños* arrive early and proceed with sledge-hammers to knock the archway we have asked for through the half-metre thick original outside wall at the top of the stairs to give access from inside the house to the upstairs back storeroom. This storeroom we are turning into *en-suite* accommodation for guests, plus a bathroom (with a real bath) for ourselves. We hadn't actually anticipated them starting upstairs quite so soon, since the intended archway stands directly outside our bedroom door – what was it that Michael had said about getting the original house reformed so that we could live in relative comfort while the rest of the work was being done? – and negotiating the resulting pile of rubble (you get an awful lot of rubble from a half-metre thick wall made of mud and boulders when you are bashing a hole through it a metre wide and two and a half metres high) takes some doing, though Eloïse and Herbert find it great fun. While this is going on, Michael fits the new doors for the downstairs rooms, which at

least make the place look less like a cave dwelling even though, after he has departed for the evening, we find that one of the doors won't open!

Tuesday 25 May. After the now customary Tuesday trip to collect the mail and go to the *ferreteria*, we spend the rest of the morning drawing detailed plans (on the wall) for the rise and tread for the revised staircase, and the layout for the downstairs loo and shower-room. At 2.00 p.m. Don and Liz come down for *paella* and drinks to celebrate Liz's birthday. I make *sangria* with red wine, brandy, *gaseoso* and Málaga wine but run out of *gaseoso* after a while, so continue with the remaining ingredients on their own – wonderful! Just as we have reached almost total incoherence, some friends of theirs turn up unexpectedly – how they managed to find our lane is a mystery and a miracle – so Don and Liz have to totter off to entertain them, leaving us goggling at the washing up. Despite this we reckon we have the better part of the bargain.

Wednesday 26 May. A rare trip out for us both together (right now we normally don't go out together during the day, as we suspect this could be fairly unwise with builders in the house and our belongings all stacked on the front terrace). After going to Torre del Mar to collect our copy of the Notarised sale documents, buy a new tap for our outside (and only) water supply, do our washing at the flat and generally have a day away from it all, we return home to find Michael and his *niños* gone and the ground floor of the house under about an inch of water.

A moments investigation reveals the cause. The *niños* have re-rigged the water supply to by-pass the faulty tap, so that the open branch they are using for the cement mixer and the house branch are controlled by the same stop-cock. This they have left partially open, so the open pipe has irrigated the road-facing wall of the house which, being porous, has let the water into the house like a saturated sponge. It takes us an hour to clear up the mess, and a few seconds to resolve <u>never</u> to go out together again while they are on the premises. Thank heaven for tiled floors!

Thursday 27 May. Have an interesting conversation with Michael about last night's fiasco, his response to our aggrieved bleating being to comment how clean the floor now looks! We then go with him to look at the downstairs shower room, where it appears the cistern has never been connected to the lavatory and the drain from the shower tray has never been installed, so for forty years the water has simply drained away under the house. There is a mammoth rats' nest in the cavity underneath the shower tray, which shows precisely how often the shower was used.

Our inability to live in, let alone do anything to, the house by day inevitably meant that, despite our basic plan to spend money on the house and not on the land, we inevitably turned our attention to the latter despite the consequential inroads into our rapidly dwindling finances. Chief among our concerns was what to do about the fact that, as matters now stood, we would not have enough irrigation water to ensure the survival, let alone the fruitfulness, of our trees come the summer. Our thoughts crystallised when we saw on the back page of a flyer from one of the super-stores outside Málaga a swimming-pool measuring 4.5 metres across and 1.5 metres deep with a capacity of 17,000 litres. This, we realised would make a wonderful *deposito* for irrigation water, and since it was marked down by £40 I went to the super-store to buy one.

Finding the superstore proved interesting. Although it was clearly visible from the *Autovia del Mediterranio*, reaching it was quite another matter, and I was reminded of the title to a poem by, I think, Ogden Nash, 'You can't get there from here!' I learned a good deal about the outer suburbs of Málaga city before I got there and managed to locate the swimming pool in its box. Buying it proved even more difficult, and getting it to, let alone into, the car a major challenge. Because it was not something one person could lift, let alone fit into a shopping trolley, I had to have help, which proved elusive. After some twenty minutes of waiting it eventually arrived in the form of one Juan Carlos, a name easily remembered in Spain. He organised a flat-bed trolley and two helpers. That it needed all four of us became evident when we tried to move the box onto the trolley - it began to topple and nearly broke the leg of one of the helpers!

I now began to have serious doubts about the wisdom of the purchase as not only was there the small matter of whether it would fit into the car, I was faced with a forty mile, mainly uphill,

SPAIN - A NEW LIFE

drive with this load and, when I reached home, with getting it out again. Still, of such problems life is made, and having gone through a complicated process of paying for the pool, since it wouldn't fit through the normal check-out, and having helped Juan Carlos and his team load it into the back of our estate car where, with all the seats down, it just fitted, I set off for home.

The journey proved interesting. The car fought its way gamely up the considerable gradient without over-heating, albeit at a pace which had impatient drivers behind apoplectic with frustration, but the final leg along the extremely bendy C-road tested the suspension to the limit. This was followed by the last two kilometres down the lane to the house. This is extremely 'down', so much so that I had definite fears for the brakes. However I made it in the end, to be faced with the final challenge: how to unload the pool and put it somewhere safe, a task quite beyond Susan and me on our own. Mercifully Michael hadn't finished work and when shown the problem he responded with a cry of 'niños - to me' or something like that and with much heaving and shoving, they manhandled it down the path to our front terrace. Now all we had to do was to manufacture somewhere suitable to put it, where it could irrigate the trees and also, with summer coming on and the sea twenty-five miles away, where we might even use it for the purpose which the makers intended.

Next day Susan and I went back for a second one! We had worked out that with only one, we would have to run miles of tubing to reach the whole orchard, and that there would be certain challenges with regard to gravity, so a *deposito* at either end of our land would be a more efficient solution. And as if this wasn't enough, we had also decided to get a second dog.

We had come to this conclusion because Herbert had revealed himself to be an extremely sociable animal, both to humans and to other dogs. So far as the latter were concerned, instead of acting as a deterrent, he frequently invited them down to the house to share his good fortune! As a result, Pedro's animals had become semi-permanent 'familiars', lurking at the top of the path down from the road, waiting for food. This in itself, though irritating, was bearable; what was not was their habit of defecating all around the area, including onto the piles of sand and cement that Michael was using, while their nightly, highly vocal chorus, right outside our windows for several hours at a time, as they greeted the moon-rise, other dogs across the valley, the odd passing owl, and anything else that took their fancy, was trying in the extreme.

There was also the fact that, irrespective of Herbert's temperament, he was simply too small to act as a realistic deterrent to anyone or anything. What we needed, we felt, was a *mastin*, a large, rough-haired creature endemic to this part of Spain, generally of an equable demeanour but also aggressive towards strangers, both canine and human. So Susan phoned several animal shelters and finally located what sounded like what we wanted, at a 'refuge' down on the coast on the way to the superstore selling the pools.

When we got there, we were so appalled we wanted to rescue every animal in sight. The 'refuge', we learned from the single attendant present, was only staffed for one hour a day; for the rest of the time, the forty-odd inmates of both genders roamed free in a large compound scattered with old beds, armchairs and other household furniture. With the number of dogs on the premises, this meant that packs had formed, with inevitable consequences to the smallest and weakest.

The *mastin*, we discovered, while quite young and eminently suitable, had caught one of its legs down beside the arm of one of the chairs only the previous evening. In its distress it had wrenched it badly, and because the place was unattended, had remained in this state for several hours. It now required urgent veterinary attention and possibly an operation, for which the attendant looked at us hopefully. Well, we know we are suckers, but not quite to that extent, and knowing also the propensity for large dogs to suffer from hip-displasia and rheumatism in later years, we regretfully declined.

So what else was there on offer? Well, said the attendant, since we wanted a large dog, but one which was still young, there was really only one option: a eight-week-old German Shepherd-cross. This was having to be fed on the table because otherwise all the other dogs took its food (surprise, surprise). Now the very last dog we had in mind was a German Shepherd, not because we dislike them but because we know the breed to be exceedingly demanding. German Shepherds are highly intelligent, responsive animals, and can be found co-operating with man in many different ways. But to get the best from them - and, conversely, to avoid getting the worst - they need a lot of human interaction, and we were far from sure that we could, or even wanted to, devote the necessary time and energy to such a commitment.

However we said we would look at the puppy - what was that about being suckers? - and when confronted with this terrified bundle which resembled, at first sight, a miniature Serengeti wild-dog, but without the 'ping-pong' bat ears (though her ears and feet were her most prominent features), we were lost. So having duly made a contribution to the refuge's upkeep (!) and put the bundle on the back seat with Herbert, whom we had brought so that the meeting between them could take place off 'his territory', we set off for the superstore.

Once there we took turns to dog-sit while the other went into the store. We put a bowl of water down outside the car and sat with the doors open (fortunately the car-park was shaded) with the dogs by our feet, wondering how they would get on with each other and how the German Shepherd would react to being restrained by a collar and lead. We needn't have worried. Herbert, with his usual sociability, tried to get her to play but she, poor little soul, was so traumatised she simply sat, staring into space, hardly moving or reacting to anything.

With the shopping finished the real fun began, since not only did we have the boxed swimming-pool which was the primary reason for us coming to the superstore in the first place, we were also two people, two dogs and several bags of groceries. With the back seats laid flat we (or rather, the three assistants from the store) loaded the pool. Then we packed in the groceries, filling the front passenger space in the process (the front seat was actually taken up with a new dog bed). Finally, Susan crammed herself into the minute space in the back left beside the swimming pool and, with a dog on either side of her and her head against the roof, we set off for home.

I kept thinking that it would now be just our luck to have a puncture, and all the way home I rehearsed how the two of us would cope with trying to unload about a quarter of a ton of swimming pool while simultaneously controlling two puppies on the side of the motorway. However the gods mercifully appeared to approve of our mission, and we made it home without incident.

Once home, though, and with Susan trying to work the cricks out of her neck, we were still faced with the task of unloading the pool without help, as Michael and the boys had finished work, while simultaneously trying to prevent the latest canine recruit from fleeing to the hills. Once again the gods favoured us with their blessing by causing Don and Liz to drop by at that precise moment to discuss the lack of irrigation water. Poor them: we immediately pressed them into service, after which we all collapsed in a state of exhaustion and had to be revived with several glasses of *sangria*, which we had prudently made up and put in the fridge before we left.

After they had gone home, suitably anaesthetised, we ourselves mulled over a possible name for the new recruit. After several false starts, it came to us both almost simultaneously. We have a huge collection of Walt Disney videos, the inevitable consequence of having seven children between us. Among them is one which was a particular favourite, 'The Rescuers', which features a little orphan girl named Penny who has been kidnapped. Penny, despite her experiences and though alone and afraid, is both resourceful and courageous, and it seemed to us from the little time we had had to observe our newcomer that she was the same. So Penny she became and, although often now addressed as 'Dollop', being also 'beautiful but dumb', the name has stuck.

Aside from these forays, the remainder of May followed a familiar pattern. The preliminary work on the house continued apace, with much use of sledgehammer (ours) and bolt-chisel and angle-grinder (Michael's) to enlarge doorways to accommodate someone's 1.96 metre frame, rough out archways, chase electric conduits into walls and under floors, and cut tiles. This made the place untenable for much of the day. Additionally, because Michael was laying the new floor tiles as he went along, large portions of the floor became out of bounds for twenty-four hours to allow the cement to harden. Because these portions changed daily, we found ourselves hopping from tile to tile, in fear for our lives of stepping on the wrong one and having it slide out from under us, not unlike Indiana Jones on some of his many adventures, though perhaps with less drastic consequences.

The dust and rubble resulting from all this was beyond description and belief, so while we still had the flat in Torre del Mar we took ourselves there every third day – separately, of course, in view of the water fiasco – as much to escape the continual hammering and grinding as to enjoy such minor amenities as hot water and a toilet, though we were already beginning to become adjusted to the lack of the former. However we each made sure we were home every evening before Michael left, there to contemplate the results of his day's labours, commiserate with the one left behind, and to shovel the brick-dust and assorted fallen masonry off the front terrace, which was the only place we could call our own.

Our lives were now very much *al fresco* (in Italy, where this expression originated, it means 'in prison', not 'out-of-doors' – fascinating; one wonders which meaning came second, and why!). Michael took pity on us and lent us a gas bottle from his home so that we could dispose of the leaking single burner camping stove. We bought a four-ring hob which would ultimately be installed in our kitchen (whenever we actually got one) and this now stood over a gas bottle, supported on my Black & Decker Work-Mate (and I bet B&D never thought of that particular use for this admirable device). So cooking was done in the hall in exactly the same place that Luisa had done her cooking for forty-odd years, and washing up was done in a bowl on the terrace, in exactly the same way that Luisa etc., etc. What was that about *'plus ça change'*!

We had elected to cook with gas, despite the somewhat unsophisticated design of all but the very expensive stoves, because the frequent cuts in the electricity supply can play havoc with *choto al ajillo* (or *paella*, though this is a Valencian, not an Andalucían dish), or even bacon and eggs, and at least with gas you are assured of the supply. The gas is butane. It is supplied in orange-coloured bottles all over Spain, with paint that comes off on your clothes (there are new bottles being introduced which don't have this endearing characteristic!). It can be used not only for cooking but also for water heating. Although it is possible, if your house has sufficiently good access for a lorry to deliver to the door, to use very large bottles or even a tank, we did not have this facility and had to use the more commonplace 14 Kg bottles which, because we didn't live in a town, we had to collect – and carry – ourselves from the nearest agency. And here we struck a major snag.

Although empty bottles can be exchanged for full ones at official butane gas agencies, of which every town generally has at least one, or at some supermarkets and bars, the problem is getting hold of bottles in the first place. In Spain, you can't just go out and buy a bottle: you have to have an official contract with the supplying company, *Butana*, to get your initial supply, and this involves a visit to your house and the approval of your installation by the accredited engineer in your area. Only when you have this approval can you get your initial stock. This was the 'Catch 22' situation which faced us, one which was resolved only by Michael coming to our rescue (again), by lending us a second bottle from his own stock until we qualified for a stock of bottles of our own.

Our outdoor lifestyle was helped enormously by the fact that it was already hot by British standards (around 30°C or the high 80s F), so this was scarcely a hardship; in a sense we were now on an extended camping holiday instead of a flat-based one. But few people chose to go on holiday to a building site, no matter how hot the weather (though, of course, this is what many holidaymakers so often discover to be the reality instead of the 'luxury accommodation' which they thought they had booked through their travel agent) especially when they find themselves the logistic support for, if not being actually part of, the work force.

This was another feature of our daily life with Michael and his '*niños*': all the time we were at the house we were constantly assailed with cries of 'Susanna' from the 'boys' (Spaniards have great difficulty with 'Susan'), wanting water or a plaster for a cut or some other assistance, or 'Tobi' from Michael, who needed to resolve some obstacle to further progress. As a result, we could never concentrate on anything ourselves; instead we found ourselves impotently herded into an ever-decreasing corner of our front terrace, hemmed in by our furniture and boxes and by the advancing tide of water, bricks and cement which the team mixed and wheel-barrowed into the house to carry on the *reformación*. It was only after the team had departed in the evening and at the week-ends that we could begin to shake off the sense of being besieged in our own home, and emerge like troglodytes to actually do anything for ourselves.

However during this time we did manage to take out shares in our local *ferreteria*. The last time we had been in there we had picked up a flyer with their summer *offertas*, which had shown a number of things we badly needed. These included a chain-saw for the excess trees, a commercial, two-handed strimmer for the bamboo and other ground clutter, a back-pack spray for weed-killer, 100 metres of black hose and two water pumps (there's not much point in having *depositos* for irrigation if you can't get the water out again to where you want it). These we collected from various parts of the shop and gathered round the counter, watched wide-eyed by the other patrons and with mounting anticipation by Juan and Anna, the proprietors.

When we had finished, the latter totted up the total on a piece of paper, and shunted it towards us with their heads averted. It was big, yes, but no more than we had expected, and they had even rounded it down to give us a further discount on the already discounted prices. So I went to the bank's cash-dispenser, handily placed directly across the street, and withdrew the necessary money after which, aided by Juan, we processed up the street several times, ferrying the goods to our car. It made a good talking point in the various bars we passed along the way.

June kicked off with the arrival of the electrician/plumber. Michael, bless his cotton socks, had tried to save money (though whether for him or for us we never did resolve) by employing a young man who assured him that he was skilled in both trades - two specialists for the price of one, an irresistible bargain. It seemed to be too good to be true and as is usually the case, it was. His first trick was not to come when he said he would; he first arrived on Tuesday morning, 1 June, and having seen what was immediately required, said he would be back in the afternoon. So we waited for him, and he never came back. He didn't come on Wednesday, either, but on Thursday, while we were out, he did, and excelled himself by breaking one of our chairs by standing on it, instead of using one of our two step-ladders already sequestered by Michael. He had also broken one of a pair of lights we had just bought for the sitting-room. As a result he didn't reappear at all on Friday.

Still, we now had lights (well, some of them), controlled by switches (though one was wonderfully eccentric and created a fascinating *son-et-lumière* effect whenever it was used), a shower (which leaked), with hot water (sometimes), a toilet (installed so close to the wall you had to be a contortionist to use it) and a washbasin whose outflow terminated directly under the walls of the house, necessitating the digging (by me, at the week-end) of an emergency trench to take the water away from the outlet, a mucky and totally knackering job as it meant kneeling on a steep slope of unstable earth, trying not to fall into the open-cast sewer which had yet to be 'reformed', scooping out glutinous lumps of clay with a mattock and bare hands. Well, you can't expect miracles, can you, and at least now we no longer had to go down the orchard with a shovel and a roll of toilet paper, as we had to do all the previous week!

By now summer had definitely arrived, a very different affair from the same season in Britain, where saturated summer is frequently indistinguishable from soggy spring or arctic autumn, never mind water-logged winter. In Britain fine summer days are often a rarity: more commonly the sky is a uniform grey from horizon to horizon, 'like living,' as Bill Bryson so eloquently describes it in *The Lost Continent - Travels in Small Town America*, 'inside Tupperware'. By contrast the Andalucían version was drawn in primary colours, each day dawning into a cloudless sky which turned, as we watched, from limpid egg-shell to blazing cobalt while the shadows shrank into pitiful pools of ink to escape the ferocious glare of the awesome Mediterranean sun.

Diary - Thursday 3 June. After another dawn bonfire to clear the land in front of the house, we plumb-in the washing machine (cold water only) and jury-rig an electricity supply to it, then sit in front of it holding hands, watching our first load of washing at the house go round - amazing the things that can provide entertainment in certain circumstances. We are joined by Eloïse, who is fascinated by the whole procedure - we shall have to watch that she doesn't get into the machine when the door is open, to satisfy her curiosity about where the clothes have all gone. The dogs have now settled down together and Penny is already more confident and recognising her place in things. However with summer in full swing they have to be inspected and checked for ticks every time they go down into the undergrowth in the orchard, which is a bore.

<u>Friday 4 June.</u> To town for mail, where we watch a man riding a high-stepping horse with no saddle and only a halter for control down the main street - amazing - and to the *ferreteria* for the things we forgot on our last visit. We now discover what we now firmly believe to be the secret of the astonishing output of the average Spanish workman (except, of course, for our plumber/electrician): blue trousers. We notice a rack of them in the *ferreteria* - I did say it sold everything except food, didn't I - and it was then that it dawns on us that we have seen almost all artisans, *peons*, farmers and labourers in Spain wearing these admirable garments. They are virtually a uniform. If they aren't blue, they are green (except for street sweepers in towns, who wear orange), and it now becomes clear that they contain some kind of magic formula where work is concerned.

There is conceivably another reason for their popularity. A pair of these practical, comfortable, hard-wearing and washable items costs around £5, and since they are almost indestructible and can last for years, they make an exceptional investment. By fortuitous happenstance, as I once heard an American colleague wonderfully say, there is a pair on the rack which fits even my elongated frame. These I acquire on the spot, and while I cannot claim they have significantly increased my work rate, they have definitely paid greater dividends than some shares I have owned.

Back home to more lopping and pruning. Have late bonfire as 'no wind at all' - result: house full of wood smoke - highly popular! Finish work as light falls, only to find mains water supply 'off' - typical: now that we have a shower at last, we can't use it, so to bed exhausted and filthy.

We have now established a routine. Up at 6.00 a.m. to take the dogs out, then tea and work on land till 9.00 a.m., when have breakfast, then continue work till 11.00 a.m. After 11.00 it is too hot to work outside until late afternoon, so work inside if can (week-ends only) or feel like it. After lunch and siesta, resume work outside till 7.00 or 8.00 p.m., then shower (if any water), supper and bed.

Fluid-loss and heat when working mean that we have to be aware of the risk of possible salt-deficiency and dehydration during the day: symptoms appear to be loss of energy and appetite, head-aches and dizziness. The bonus is that we are both losing excess weight without trying to and are generally becoming vastly fitter and healthier than we were in Britain. We have also discovered that an Andalucían summer means that washing hung out after dark is dry by the morning – try expecting that in Britain, ever. We finish the day with cup of tea on what remains of the front terrace, watching the western sky-line change from washed pink through lavender to dove grey, followed by the gradual emergence of brilliant stars in a velvet black, totally cloudless sky.

Monday 7 June. Michael's *niños* arrive at 8.00 a.m. while we are doing the customary 'burn' of loppings done the day before. They start to demolish the two lean-to's, in anticipation of the arrival of the JCB which we had been warned on Friday to expect today. This prompts us to continue with clearing the whole area in front of the house where the swimming-pool will go, as Michael wants to use the *machina* to dig the hole for the pool while it is here. By the time we have done that the wind has changed and once again the house is full of smoke! After this the morning is enlivened by three things, all involving Juan, the principle *niño*:

1. He captures a sitting pigeon, which he proudly presents to me. He is dismayed when I let it go, though what he thought we would do with it in our circumstances remains a mystery.
2. He then disturbs a wasps' nest, with predictable results. We spend an enlivening half hour treating his stings.
3. Finally a wall on which he is standing to remove the lean-to roof collapses under him, dropping him nine feet onto the rubble from his previous exertions. This results in major abrasions to his upper arm and sundry lesser cuts elsewhere, though luckily nothing is broken.

At the time of Juan's fall I am well away from the house, refuelling the chain-saw, and the first thing I see from a distance is Susan and the other *niño* half-carrying a fainting Juan to the armchair on the front terrace normally used by the dogs. I gallop up the slope as quickly as I can, and assist Susan with some fairly advanced First Aid, after which shock sets in for Juan and he and the other *niño* (who was as much use as a wet week-end in Worthing in the crisis) take themselves off to find Michael, who is working on another site elsewhere.

I now realise that far from leaving my children behind I have gained more! Michael and his workmen all look on me as a curer of troubles, real or imagined. Calls of 'Susanna' are usually for water from the fridge (it's warm out of the tap) or plasters for cuts, otherwise it's to move some of our belongings out of their way. Life here is never dull even if it's a bit rough and ready at the moment.

Since the JCB has failed to materialise, this gives us an un-expected free afternoon with no-one around. We put this to good effect, though a Muppet-like audience of two dogs who uncannily resemble Rizzo the Rat and The Great Gonzo does inhibit us a

little. Oh for some internal doors! Later I cut down, and up, and stack the remaining pear trees in front of the house, watched with dismay by Pedro, who has come down from Granada with Luisa for their turn for irrigation water. This makes fifteen pear trees I have cut down, originally crammed into a space measuring 6 metres by 10 - no wonder they were all stunted. Early to bed and sleep like logs - cannot begin to imagine why.

<u>Tuesday 8 June</u>. Michael and *niños* arrive at 8.30 a.m. and begin tiling the downstairs – and only – shower room. I go in to the *ferreteria* to see if Juan can re-wind the starter rope on the chain-saw, which I managed to pull right out last time I used it. He does, after fifty-five painstaking minutes, and doesn't charge me a thing. Back home, Susan gets the strimmer going and clears umpteen square metres of weeds in minutes. However, as this is the sort of strimmer normally used to clear the sides of public roads in Britain, and is suspended from the operator by a substantial harness, she looks not unlike a Samurai warrior as she goes about her work, clad in a comprehensive suit of protective clothing, including hard hat, visor and reinforced boots!

While Susan is engaged in devastating fifty square metres of weeds, I resume lopping and pruning with chain-saw and shears. This gives me time to ponder a curious fact: for many days now there has been minimal water in the *acequia*, but since Pedro and Luisa's arrival it has returned in full flood. As this coincides with their turn, we can't help wondering if there is a connection. We shall await our own turn in forty-eight hours time with interest, to see if it continues, and will also watch out to see if this pattern repeats itself next month.

<u>Wednesday 9 June</u>. Michael and *niños* arrive at 8.00 a.m., together with the JCB operator but not the machine itself. While Michael and the *machinista* reconnoitre the ground, the *niños* proceed to take out the rest of the upstairs arch (now why did we think they would finish tiling the shower room, begun yesterday? Shows how mistaken you can be). Later Michael does get on with the tiling, and later still Hans, Don and I meet with Pedro to sign a letter produced by the latter, protesting to the Water Authority about other people illegally taking irrigation water out of the river upstream from us all. We don't expect too much from this, but are amused that Hans is expected to sign the letter, not alongside his name, but by an entry describing him as 'the German', while Don and Liz are 'the English' and Susan and I are 'the other English'. We debate the likely reaction to anyone trying to describe co-signatories to a letter to a similar authority in politically correct Britain as 'the West Indians' or 'the Pakistanis'!

<u>Thursday 10 / Friday 11 June.</u> Up at 6.00 a.m., for our turn for irrigation water. Spend most of day crawling under overhanging pomegranate trees, clearing dropped fruit from the ditches by hand. This has to be the most inefficient, and destructive way imaginable, to irrigate sloping land. Later we move the deep-freeze indoors, where at last there is a space for it, connect it up and, wonder of wonders, it starts without a murmur after six months in store. The irrigation water begins to dwindle after about twelve hours – isn't that strange!

With the tiling of the shower-room only half finished we have been unable to use it for three days, so we go to bed filthy and utterly exhausted, to be woken by the dogs wanting to go out at 1.30 a.m. Later, at 4.20 a.m., Penny gets into the upstairs back storeroom through the newly-made hole in the wall and proceeds to do there what she clearly failed to do when she went out earlier. Back to bed after clearing it up, only to have Eloïse come and sit on my head and purr loudly in my ear - oh, the joys of animal ownership!

The morrow is not improved by Michael and *niños* arriving at 7.30 a.m., together with the plumber/electrician, and we discover the *niños* are taking tools from our toolbox without permission. Gloom all round when we speak to Michael about it - we have to make ourselves scarce by working on the land to allow time for 'face' to be restored. When Michael and team leave at 5.00 p.m., we discover the plumber has 'bodged' the drain in the shower room which he has replaced after his earlier efforts, resulting in a leak. We name him Frank, after the character Spencer, famously created by Michael Crawford. Later we learn that the Spanish have a similar television sitcom called 'Manolo S.L.', so Manolo he becomes.

With our turn for irrigation now over for another month, we take time to consider once again our options for the trees. We are beginning to formulate the idea that we shall dispose of most, if not all, of our pomegranates. For one thing, we have learned there is virtually no market now for the fruit. For another, they are not unlike teenage girls at a dance: although they are extremely pretty, with bright scarlet flowers and a delicate green foliage, they cluster together for support and are prone to making sharp digs at anyone approaching them without caution. If we do cut them down, we shall have room for a respectably-sized 'house' orchard which we can plant with the trees we want but haven't got: oranges, lemons, peaches, nectarines, and so on, while the bulk of the orchard will be left to the olives, for which we have learned the area is famous.

'Dad,' said my son, 'there's a cat in the basin; is this normal?'

'Turn the tap on and let it drip,' called Susan, 'she wants a drink.'

'Of course,' replied my son, 'what else?'

Simon had arrived on Saturday 12 June for an impromptu visit, his flight finally arriving at Málaga Airport at 4.30 a.m., having been delayed for two hours by a drunken passenger. After a couple of hours' sleep we took him to experience the post-office, then on to Torre del Mar to show him round. Back home later in the day he revised his plans to sunbathe, do some gentle rugby training and explore the local area by mountain-bike, and instead seized a mattock and proceeded to clear a patch of ancient and enormous radishes left behind by Luisa. This required us/me to keep pace with him, no easy task as his idea of a little gentle exercise would cripple most people, made no easier by the house water drying up completely, so no possibility of a wash, let alone a shower. Welcome to Andalucía, Simon!

However it was fascinating - and revealing - to see our home through his eyes, and reassuring to find that he not only didn't think we were totally mad, he actually approved! We duly consecrated this approval with a succession of bottles of varying degrees of strength, resulting in our taking a slightly different perspective of our enterprise the following day.

What a rush! It didn't matter if our room wasn't looking its best, but we did feel we did had to have at least one decent bedroom to put our first guest in. At last doors are finally being put in place, which is a novelty and puts an end to being woken in the middle of the night by a lonely cat or dog. But that still left us with stripping layers of old paint off walls, putting back plaster as it fell out, and painting. The room was finished with only hours to spare before Simon arrived. It was the best bit of bullsh*t we have ever achieved and it still looks good!

Midway during Simon's visit, the JCB finally arrived. We all got up at 7.00 a.m. to receive it, but it got lost on the way and didn't turn up until 10.30, whereupon the *machinista* went to work at frantic speed to make up for lost time. His first task was to clear the access onto our land and level an area for materials on the future site for our hard-standing for cars, after which he set about demolishing the two lean-to's and redeploying the rubble to act as hard-core. He then levelled out the ground in front of the house as a preliminary to digging out the swimming-pool.

It was at this stage that his enthusiasm overtook him. We had agreed with Michael the dimensions of the pool, and these we heard him pass on to the *machinista*. However instead of 1.10 metres at the shallow end (about 3 ft 7 in), he proceeded to dig out 1.40 metres (about a foot more). This made it definitely too deep for non-swimming children, and chest height to many adults. Still, it certainly made it a swimming pool, not a paddling pool, especially as the *machina* did dig the deep end out to 1.80 metres as instructed (just under 6 feet), to allow for my 1.96 metre frame.

As a final gesture, the *machina* towed out the 'dead' Fiat 500 from under the fig tree below the house, and dragged it up to the road-side, whence we could have it removed to a dump, and dug out a plateau for one of the swimming-pool *depositos*. The house now stood alone in the midst of a desolation of highly dangerous rubble, but the prospect was wonderful. We had reached the bottom of our *reformación* project, and the only way forward was up.

Junk! They have taken away the old car but under it are bottles, tins, bits of the car engine, wire and all manner of assorted rubbish. One design of bottle – there were about a dozen – that did cause a talking point was funnel-shaped, and had a hole in both the top and the bottom. It looked like an old type electric insulator. It turned out to be a fly trap, only needing to be hung from a tree with a protein solution in it. It would lead many fruit-attacking insects to their deaths. Unknowingly, since they could have been very useful, we ditched the lot!

We were now faced with the decision of whether to get the real swimming pool finished, if we could afford it, or to build a new terrace at the front of the house, necessary sooner than we had planned as the digger had successfully demolished a good deal of the original one. In the end the pool won, not just because we would like to have it for the summer but because, with the hole now dug, the vertical sides would be extremely vulnerable to subsidence if it should rain, and although this was not on the cards, it would be little short of catastrophic if the unexpected should occur. So we resigned ourselves to sitting amidst a pile of rubble for the foreseeable future, and focused instead on the prospect of swimming in our own pool . . . sometime.

On Simon's last night we celebrated with a barbecue beside the pool, a surreal event more like something out of Mad Max than the image created by Paul Hogan in his famous ad. for a well-known Australian beer. The pool, of course, was simply a vast pit, a trap for monster cockroaches and unwary dogs, while the area round it was a mixture of upended tree-roots, concrete slabs and bare earth. We built the barbecue with two piers of broken bricks supporting a metal tray from an old refrigerator, and beneath it lit a fire of olive and almond twigs.

As darkness descended we sat on the ground, eating with our fingers, wine glasses jammed between the tree-roots, while the sun slipped behind the mountains and the stars came out one by one. Soon we were sitting in almost total darkness, lit only by the light from the fire. The dogs slept beside us, while Eloïse prowled in the undergrowth. From where we were sitting we could see no lights of any kind. There were no sounds beside our own voices and the monotonous hooting of a distant Scops owl. We could have been alone in the world.

With Simon gone we resumed our former routine, modified by the developments of the past week. We now had one basin indoors and one tap outdoors. The water supply almost always ran dry at around mid-day until late evening, and during the morning it was needed by the building team for the cement mixer. Although we now had a toilet it didn't have a drain (it had been the first casualty of the JCB's shovel) and the new septic tank hadn't been dug (its intended site now comprised a builder's yard covered with bags of cement, stacks of bricks and piles of sand and gravel), so once again we were back to trips down the orchard. And, of course, we still had nothing resembling a kitchen. This gave a definite direction to our day.

At around 6.45 a.m. I collected our bucket of 'night soil' and disposed it at the bottom of the orchard, once again giving a whole new twist to the vow to 'have and to hold, for better and for worse'. Then we washed ourselves, usually in a bowl on the front terrace, brought in the washing which had dried overnight, put on another load of washing so as to have it done before the building team arrived, had breakfast and awaited the arrival of Michael and his *niños* any time between 8.30 and 10.30 a.m. After that we did whatever we could around the place (including making trips down the orchard with a shovel whenever we had to 'go'), always mindful of the need to be at the beck and call of the team and so unable ever to do anything constructive ourselves.

Toby is one in a million. No way was I going to be caught with my pants down, last time or this time. It was bad enough just keeping up with the demands of our builders without making a spectacle of myself, so when needs must I used a bucket. Life had been a bit trying for the last two weeks; not only did we have no toilet again but running water was in short supply too. I never did go much on camping and now I know why!

After the team had departed at around 6.00 p.m. our own day began. First we disconnected the builder's hose and reconnected the washing machine which stood, unprotected, beside the outside tap with its electric lead run through the window and its outlet hose watering the palm and the vines over the terrace, washed clothes the moment we had water again and hung them out to dry. At the same time we prepared and ate supper - cooked and eaten outside - disconnected the washing machine and used the tap for washing the dishes, after which we filled bottles with water for ourselves and the builder's team for next day. Finally we had showers if we could, reconnected the builder's hose for the next day, walked the dogs and went to bed.

The relentless mindlessness of this routine was bearable only because of three things: First, every day was sunny and hot. This was such a joy after uncertain, but usually cold and wet, England that it was a pleasure in itself and although neither of us is inclined towards camping holidays this was, in effect, what we were enjoying, though spending our time and our money in rather different ways than in lying on the beach or on ice-cream for the kids. Secondly, we were witnessing the birth of our dream, a metamorphosis no less dramatic than the change of a chrysalis into a moth. And thirdly, because of this we were caught up in a sort of on-going 'soap', one in which, besides having walk-on parts, we were also the Directors and Producers, responsible for the financing and ultimate success of the series. This factor, on its own, was enough to concentrate the mind wonderfully especially as, with the demolition phase complete, we could now hope to begin the construction of the kitchen/sitting room extension on the site of two lean-to's.

Before we could do that, we had to get the plans approved. This required, in turn, having the plans I had drawn up redrawn by an architect, at a cost of 230,000 *pesetas* (approximately £950). This was a stiffish sum by any standards, and we were fascinated to see what we would get for it. At first, it seemed, very little: all that materialised was a massive bundle of papers tracing the history of the property, with a relatively small section devoted to the construction work we wished to do (including the swimming pool), incorporating, unchanged, the drawings I had made at the mill all those months ago, using a simple ruler and a sheet of graph-paper! Clearly technical specifications had a different significance to similar plans for alterations to a property in England!

However before the architect submitted the plans for approval, he did visit us 'on site'. There he had a revealing conversation with Michael in which, amidst much good-natured banter and chat, he insisted first, that Michael build a separate wall parallel to the existing outside wall of the house to support the concrete joists for the roof of the new extension – he was adamant that the original wall would not be suitable for this – and, secondly, that Michael use rather more substantial joists than he had originally intended, in view of their span and the possible weight they would have to bear should we ever hold a party on the roof terrace. So maybe the attitude to technical specifications wasn't so different after all, merely the way in which they were stipulated.

It was after this visit that the real advantage of using this architect – and the justification for his fee – became evident. Because he knew how the authorities operated, and also who to submit the plans to and the appropriate procedures to be followed, we had our plans approved in less than four weeks. Since this approval is an essential prerequisite before any kind of new construction work is begun this was a huge benefit, and Michael was able to start building the new extension one month after the architect's visit.

This business of knowing the correct procedures and having the correct forms was, as we were to discover later for ourselves, no small benefit. In Spain you need a permit for virtually any activity which impinges on authority, the most immediately obvious, beside those required for house building, being the entitlement to continue to live in the country as a foreigner and obtaining a Spanish driving licence and Spanish registration for your car. And to get the permit you need the correct application form.

The word 'bureaucracy' was, I think, like so many other things, coined by the French, and is described in my Longman's Dictionary as being '3. a system of doing things officially which is annoyingly and unnecessarily difficult to understand or deal with.' This seems to put it nicely, and certainly the French are the ultimate professionals in putting such a system into practice. But the Spanish run them close, and dealing with Spanish bureaucracy can be, for the north European visitor, a deeply frustrating experience, requiring patience, stoicism, a well-developed appreciation of the ridiculous and unlimited time. For the British, who possess the first three of these qualities from birth, and who invented the art of queuing, it is much less of a trial than for many others, though in our case, several inconclusive round trips of fifty or sixty miles to visit the various offices to which we had been referred stretched even the famous British sense of humour somewhat.

Readers who, like me, are devotees of Asterix the Gaul, and who possess the film 'The Twelve Tasks of Asterix' will be entirely familiar with the problem from Asterix's experience in the eighth task which he and his friend Obelix were set, and the storyline is no exaggeration whatsoever. However the Spanish, being ever-practical, have evolved a way to circumvent the problem which even the redoubtable Gallic warrior would have envied: this is through the creation of a system of specialist 'gofers' called *gestors*. These admirable citizens not only have all the forms you need in order to get your permit, they will even get you the permit itself, fully authenticated in all respects. Unfortunately, few *gestors* speak English - they don't have to - and of course, being in private practice, they don't come cheap, but then neither are the wear and tear on your car and your person if you insist on doing it yourself and, above all, *gestors* will actually get the job done, which is often more than can be said for DIY.

It was a similar expertise to that possessed by a *gestor* which our architect brought to our circumstances, an expertise which should have had us on our knees, expressing our gratitude to the deity of our choice for getting the permit within a month, instead of whinging about the cost, especially as, with our usual sense of timing, we had submitted our plans during the run-up to the Spanish and European elections and, had we not got the permit when we did, we would have had to wait at least three months before we would have seen it. And the work could not have begun without it, as we found out when a policeman appeared at our house and demanded to see our permit shortly after Michael had started on the foundations, on penalty of being ordered to cease work immediately had we not been able to produce it!

However all this was a month away, and in the meantime there was plenty to do elsewhere, the most immediate requirement being the construction of a septic tank. In fact, 'septic' would be a breach of the Trades Description Act: it was, and is, a cess-pit, the difference being that while the former is a highly sophisticated affair in which body waste matter is treated chemically and turned into harmless liquid, the latter is simply a collecting tank and soak-away, a less savoury but much more realistic system, since the former can be turned into the latter by even a hint of bleach or other detergent in the fluid.

In either case, the need was to build a brick-walled 'tank' of about three metres cubed in a hole already dug by the *machina* for this purpose. This is a simple enough task for a skilled builder. However the weather was now approaching its fiercest, and the temperature in the shade on our front terrace was 40°C (103°F) where Susan and I sagged limply in our chairs during the day, dragging hot air in and out of our lungs, our bodies feeling - and probably smelling - like grubby, damp leather. But the hole for the cess-pit was in the full glare of the sun round the back of the house and resembled nothing less than the ante-room to hell. Michael and his *niños* toiled for two days in this inferno, in temperatures of around 120°F, giving a realistic impression of extras in a Hollywood biblical epic, and we had to maintain an almost constant supply of water to prevent dehydration.

However, by 4.00 p.m. on Thursday 24 June we had a toilet again, and our shovel was relegated to its more normal use. At the same time, we took a delivery of a lorry-load of sand as a base for the construction of the first of the swimming-pool *depositos*. This we started to shift down to the plateau we had levelled for it below the lane at 6.30 a.m. the following morning, as we knew that once the sun broke over the ridge the other side of the river, it would be a race against time before it became too hot for us to work there.

We worked as a team, with Susan on top of the pile of sand, creating an avalanche for me at the bottom. From there I moved the sand by wheel-barrow, tipping each load into a succession of hillocks across the plateau. As the sand here is greyish-white, this created a landscape in miniature just like the Cornish china-clay hills of my childhood. Then we both spread the hillocks across the plateau, like icing a giant Christmas cake, and we were ready for the task of assembling the *deposito*.

This we did on Sunday, to avoid being a source of profound amusement for Michael and the boys – again starting at first light. First we laid on the sand some of the blankets in which the removals firm had packed our belongings. Then, we took the wall for the *deposito* down to the plateau. This was not accomplished with quite the ease that it takes to write it. For one thing, the wall was a tight roll of corrugated steel, weighing around 160 kilos; for another, it was as unwieldy and as fragile as the Venus de Milo before she lost both of her arms.

We wrapped it in a blanket and balanced it precariously on a sack trolley. This we trundled up, over, and finally down the extremely uneven, rubble-strewn and steeply-sloping thirty-odd yards between the front terrace, where it had been standing ever since we had unloaded from the car, and its final resting place. It was like trying to restrain a giant Swiss-roll from running amok, while maintaining the momentum of its supporting trolley which we knew, with its minuscule wheels, would have the utmost difficulty in starting again if we ever let it stop. When we finally reached the plateau we reverently laid it down, and then sank down ourselves on the sand, weakly waving our arms and legs in the air as we totally succumbed to the mounting hysteria which we had had to keep under tight control throughout the course of this epic, for fear of damaging the pool wall.

By now the sun was well up, and it was already uncomfortably hot but, despite being fairly exhausted and dripping with sweat, we knew we had to press on immediately with erecting the pool, or otherwise wait until Monday and undertake the task under the gaze of a fascinated audience. So after demolishing two litres of water each, we assembled the sections of rigid plastic tubing which formed the base ring for the pool. This ring incorporated a raised groove along its top edge, about 2 mm wide, into which it was now necessary to slot the bottom edge of the metal wall of the pool.

Imagine, if you will, a tightly coiled watch-spring. Now increase it to 1.2 metres in height and 14 metres in length. Realise, too, that while it is all too flexible along its length, it is totally rigid in its vertical plane, so that it cannot be fed into the groove gradually: it has to be slotted in 'all-of-a-piece'. This is what we had to erect, in gradually rising wind and rapidly rising temperature - and tempers - all the while holding the wall up and restraining its natural impulse to roll itself up again. It took just under two hours, by which time the sun was well up, the temperature was around 35°C/95°F, and we were on the verge of collapse and hardly speaking to each other! Still, it was done and, most importantly, it stayed up, and we could thankfully have showers and recover.

Well, not quite: first I had the fun of carrying a 15 kilo gas bottle round to the back of the house, across the rubble-strewn assault course which passed for the site of our future kitchen, and connecting it to our temporary water-heater. After that I had the even greater fun of watching Susan trying to tighten a leaking water joint on the heater without first turning off the water. And finally we had the joint fun of clearing up the interesting floor decoration in the hall, put there by the dogs which we had had to shut in while we dealt with the pool - they otherwise played happily on the sand which we had carefully levelled to form an appropriate surface. We had no difficulty with the notion of *siesta* this day.

Monday 28 June, saw the start of a quite unbelievable forty-eight hours. It began predictably enough, with us starting to fit the plastic liner for the pool – the thing that actually held the water – at 7.00 a.m. This involved the meticulous and seemingly endless task of smoothing the floor and sides, to take out the wrinkles and ensure that the liner was vertical against the steel wall, and not hung on a bias. Once this was done we pulled the liner tight over the top of the wall, and fitted a duplicate of the bottom ring over the overlap, to hold it in place. Since it was now well past sun-up, this was done in a rapidly rising temperature, so the liner stretched continuously as we worked, and we had to be extremely careful not to tear it.

By 9 o'clock it was done and we faced the moment of truth: would the pool hold water, or would we see a slow seepage from underneath, meaning we would have to dismantle the whole thing and try and locate the hole. We ran out thirty metres of hose from our one and only tap and switched on. The water splashed out of the pipe and slowly crept across the floor of the pool. We peered anxiously around the edge of the bottom ring for any signs of a leak; there were none. Gradually the water rose up the sides, and still the underneath remained dry, so with a huge sigh of relief we hurriedly assembled the ladder which came with the pool and climbed in, and spent an hour smoothing out the bottom before the weight of water made this impossible. After that, it was pure fun. We sat in the rising tide, splashing each other like kids, revelling in the cool of the water and the sun on our faces until, as we knew it would, the water supply failed just before midday.

We had imagined that with the cessation of water, that would be the end of it for the day, and after a relaxed lunch we had a short *siesta* before turning our attention to more tree trimming. It was then that Don phoned to say that there was so much water in the *acequia* that he had done all the irrigation he wanted, and would we like the balance of his entitlement, about three hours-worth. Gift horses like this are never to be looked in the mouth, and we downed tools immediately and set about clearing our channels of the inevitable fallen pomegranate fruit and other debris in anticipation of this bonanza.

Don opened our sluice at 6.00 p.m., and instead of the normal trickle, we heard the unfamiliar rustle of leaves and branches being pushed aside as the water thrust its way down the hill towards us. Then, in an instant, it was on us, bursting out of our feeder pipe with the force of a fire hydrant! It built up a head of pressure behind every obstruction, breaching the banks of our channels and cascading free-fall down into the orchard. We worked like demons in the blazing evening sun to keep ahead of this flood, frantically raking the channels with mattocks and scooping out the debris with our fingers to clear them as the tide advanced. Soon the water was reaching into places where it clearly hadn't ventured for years, and we were forced to hack at the iron-hard soil to create new channels to contain it. By 9.00 p.m., when the flow finally stopped, Susan was so hot she had sweat pouring down her spectacles, and my camel-leather hat was so saturated that sweat drops were raining from the brim! Mercifully the mains water had come back on in the house, so we were able to have showers, but by now we were too tired to eat, and sleep took a long time coming.

This experience forced us to think hard about bringing the irrigation system up-to-date. The great American business philosopher, James E. Rohn, at whose feet I had been privileged to study for a while, used to give a talk entitled, 'The Day That Turns Your Life Around'. In his case it had been his inability to find $2 with which to buy cookies from a girl-scout selling door-to-door, a fund-raising process which I gather is commonplace in the USA. Jim had vowed there and then, 'Never again.' So it was with us now: never again would we crawl on our hands and knees in the mud and filth cleaning out irrigation channels when there was a perfectly good alternative, the only requirements being to take the plunge and clear the orchard of all its unproductive or unwanted trees and find the money to buy the necessary pipes.

Next morning, at 9.00 a.m., the electricity went off! Like the water supply, the electricity supply had been cut off periodically, sometimes for a few minutes, sometimes for several days and always without warning. While we were staying at the mill it was cut off twice: once, for eighteen hours, as the result of a ferocious overnight storm; the other, for a few minutes. In neither case did we ever receive an explanation, much less any warning, and we had already experienced several similar cuts at the *cortijo* since we arrived here. As a result, we rapidly came to two conclusions:

First, it is prudent to have candles and/or torches available for immediate use at night; and, secondly, it is even more prudent to have a generator as a standby!

We were now faced with the need to implement the second of these, as the lack of electricity was making work difficult for Michael, whose cement-mixer was electrically powered, so at 4.00 p.m. after he and his boys had left – there was still no electricity and of course the water had gone off again – Susan and I drove into town together and explained the problem to Juan and Anna at the *ferreteria*. By now the situation was beginning to approach crisis-point, as we also had a deep-freeze full of food, and with the ambient temperature in the house at around 32°C/90°F we were in danger of losing the lot unless we did something to restore power. Juan and Anna were horrified at our plight, and sold us a Honda 4-stroke 2 Kv generator. This was a fairly sizeable beast, but we knew this wouldn't be the last time we needed emergency power, and next time we might well have to supply the whole house, so 2 Kv was by no means excessive. We loaded it into the car and drove to the nearest garage, 17 km away, where we had to buy a can as they refused to fill the generator with petrol in the back of the car.

Back at the house by 6.30 p.m. we unloaded the generator – sixty kilos of it – staggered down to the house with it, filled it up with petrol and oil, consulted the hand-book on how to start it, pulled the cord ... and nothing happened. Half an hour later, once again dripping with sweat and by now frantic, we lugged the generator back up to the car and headed back into town. By amazing fortune we saw Juan coming the other way and flagged him down. 'Ah,' he said, when we explained the problem, 'you haven't put enough oil in. There is a float-switch in the oil tank which operates a cut-out, to prevent the engine from being run with too little oil. Put in the full litre which I sold you. If it still won't start, call me at home – here's my number.' We thanked him profusely, cursed the hand-book, which made no mention of this refinement, turned round and set off home at a speed sufficient to scatter a herd of goats on the road-side, and earn us a few choice Andalucían observations about our driving from the herdsman.

By now it was getting dark, but no cooler, and we had appalling visions of the melting contents of the deep-freeze. When we reached home we humped the generator down from the car once again, searched frantically for a torch so that we could see to fill the oil tank, found one at last, filled the tank and pulled the cord...and were rewarded by a loud bang from the flooded cylinder, followed by the wonderful sound of an internal combustion engine working as it should. I connected up the generator to the deep-freeze and we breathed a sigh of relief when the latter's motor cut in. Ten minutes later the mains power was restored!

However there was still no water, so despite being able to reconnect the deep-freeze to the mains and hide the generator away where Michael wouldn't be able to find it, a shower was impossible, and we crawled into bed, hot, grubby and disgruntled at 10 o'clock, hoping that the following morning would bring a respite. It didn't. When we turned on the tap at day-break it gave a faint hiss and fell silent. We could wash neither ourselves nor our clothes, and we resigned ourselves to another day of less-than-romantic squalor, and to cursing Michael for not having put the installation of a *deposito* as a more urgent priority. He wasn't too chuffed either when he arrived, as he desperately needed water for mixing cement to get on with the tiling, and after a morning of mooching about, measuring up and calculating the materials required for the next phase of activity he and his boys left at 1.30 – and shortly afterwards the water came back on!

Chapter 11

The cumulative effects of the last six months, and the conditions under which we had been living for the past two, now began to take their toll. Our former lives in England had always allowed for both physical and temporal space between us, but these were possible at neither the mill nor the flat. At the same time we had had no meaningful routines for the four months we lived in those two places, yet both of us had been creatures of routines all our lives. This combination of a lack of space and an absence of any purpose had caused pressures which resulted in us trying much too hard not to do or say anything which might upset the other, yet quarrelling over trivia, nit-picking generally and getting on each other's nerves.

Unfortunately the habit created by this pattern meant that by the time we arrived at the *cortijo*, we were somewhat apprehensive of each other's reactions, so instead of turning to each other during these first, crucial weeks we instinctively turned inwards, at precisely the moment when we needed all the mutual support we could receive and give, to face the challenges of our new lifestyle. Unconsciously we were drawing further apart and becoming increasingly critical of each other. This came to a head at the beginning of July, when we had three full-scale rows in a matter of days, something which we had never done in the previous ten years.

Part of the problem stemmed from the cultural background to the business life we had shared, which was grounded on the mind-set that job satisfaction and financial reward were directly related to results achieved. It had permeated all levels of our working together, and inevitably overflowed into our private lives as well. Now we were faced with the urgent need to reappraise this.

The first step was to accept that there could be other goals to life than material or intellectual accomplishment or the attainment of higher office or rank – that satisfaction could possibly be attained from other, less thrusting ambitions. Even to consider this notion was, for me, a virtual heresy, and I was constantly having to pull myself back from instinctive reactions based on upbringing and previous circumstances. But the more I did this the easier it became, and it then became possible to consider not just whether this alternative could be possible, but whether it should.

It gradually dawned on me that we were, for the first time in our lives together, in a situation which demanded, as nothing had done before, the childish question: why? Why do it this way? Why do it now? Why do it at all? And instead of the response which had become ingrained in us over the years: 'Why not?', I began to see that if one could adjust one's priorities from those normally considered paramount to Anglo-Saxons, then an entirely new set of equally rewarding priorities hove into view. For instance, when things didn't go according to plan, or didn't even happen at all, there was an alternative to getting tense and over-wrought which might be not merely acceptable, but possibly even preferable. And I began to accept the idea that, instead of just observing (and criticising) the Spanish approach to life, we should try, at least occasionally, to see things through Spanish eyes. As a race they hadn't done so badly over the years, so who were we to say that the Anglo-Saxon way was necessarily better. After all, things did get done in Spain, and satisfactorily too, if not necessarily quite when or how we expected them to.

Another major problem was that, after more than four months of simply 'marking time', there was the sudden strain of having rather too much going on at once, most of it not under our control. This resulted in any number of conflicting priorities requiring rapid resolution, not easy when we had got out of the habit of making any important decisions at all. Professor C. Northcote Parkinson once wrote, 'If you deny a person the right to make important decisions, then he will make important those decisions which he is allowed to make,' and this had been the inevitable consequence of our lives at the mill and in the flat: we had come to give an entirely disproportionate level of importance to matters which were, almost without exception, trivial.

Now we were having to face up to making decisions which concerned our final home in which we had invested most of our money and all of our hopes, and which would have long-term consequences on our lives. This was our house we were dealing with, our land and our future, where even failing to make the right decision about the height and depth of the steps on the staircase or the position of power points and switches could have long-term consequences for our future well-being. At the same time, we were having to reconcile the differences between our expectations and the reality which had now brought us down to earth with a vengeance, while simultaneously coping with our own individual reactions to it, as well as anticipating each other's, and with reassuring one another that we were still happy about what we had done in coming here.

These problems were challenging enough in themselves but in my case, unbeknown to me, they were aggravated by factors rooted much further back. My late childhood and early teens had not been the happiest of times. My father, who had taken to 'gentleman farming' in Cornwall after a career in the Royal Navy encompassing two World Wars, was an Edwardian personality with little ability to relate to his wife and none at all to his children. My mother, who had run our home and brought me up single-handedly throughout the 2nd World War, was a sensitive person with an obsession for animals, particularly dogs. How, and more to the point, why, these two utterly disparate personalities had met, let alone married, remains a mystery, especially as my father's family lived in Hertfordshire and my mother's in Edinburgh!

When the three of us moved to Cornwall in 1947 (my brother, being a decade older than me, had already fled the coop and followed our father's footsteps into the Navy), the cracks in this relationship became all too obvious and the two principals adopted their own measures for emotional survival, my father by immersing himself in the task of running the farm, my mother in a succession of dogs, while I became an introverted small boy as a result of having to find my amusements on my own, there being no other children within several miles. At the same time, in the early stages at any rate, the farm had been primitive in the extreme, with neither electricity nor mains water, and we had lived for a substantial period of time in semi-derelict conditions. There had also been difficulties with the previous owners, and my parents had bickered constantly over matters which, at the time, were incomprehensible to me.

In an article I once read in a newspaper, the hypnotherapist author stated that the subconscious mind retains all emotional happenings from life's inception to the present, with the same intensity of emotions as when they were first put in; it only needs a trigger of similar situations or events to throw up and relive the traumas of the past, always with the same intensity. Now, unwittingly, we had provided that trigger for me by replicating at the *cortijo* the conditions of my childhood, at least so far as the physical aspects were concerned, and unsurprisingly I reacted to them. Of course, I didn't realise at the time that this was what I was doing; all I knew was that I felt a violent antipathy to the way certain aspects of our lives were developing, notably the attitude of the previous owners and the demands made by the dogs, and I made my views known in no uncertain fashion. Susan, being a woman of spirit, responded accordingly, and because we were both deathly tired three, full-scale rows erupted as a result.

Looking back, it is perhaps remarkable that we survived this phase at all; certainly we know of other relationships which have foundered on less. However, after a number of 'full and frank discussions', as a former British Prime Minister was famous for saying, we happily realised that deep down there was nothing fundamentally wrong, and recognising that we would both be a lot worse off if we had quit at that stage, we managed to reach a suitable compromise. Still, while it lasted it was an uncomfortable passage, and served to point to another moral about ventures of this kind:

Be prepared for any emotional baggage you bring with you to be exposed and fully tested.

It was at about this time, too, that we began to realise that there were deep, subtle changes taking place in us, both as a couple and individually, as a consequence of our new lifestyle. This was fairly scary; it wasn't what we had anticipated at all. We had simply envisioned taking up residence in our *cortijo*, working our smallholding and generally enjoying the Good Life as practised by Tom and Barbara in the famous BBC sitcom, though in infinitely more suitable surroundings. We hadn't given any thought to the possibility that the smallholding and the Good Life might affect us in ways other than providing an escape from the rat race. We should have known better.

We have long admired the attitude of native North Americans towards the land, as is wonderfully encapsulated in the Testimony of Chief Seattle given in 1854 and which is reprinted in full at the end of this book. So we were open, albeit unconsciously, to the influences of the countryside around us. And our first acknow-ledgement that this was taking place was when we began to recognise that, while the pace of our new way of life was vastly slower from the one to which we had been accustomed, there nevertheless beat beneath it a rhythm which, though still indistinct to our ears, was one to which we would need to become attuned if we were to reap its full benefits.

We also recognised, with something akin to dismay, that this was likely to take a fair amount of time. We had become so attuned to the high pitch of the business life with which we had previously been involved that we now saw that it was not going to be easy to escape the less admirable attitudes that went with it. Leaving Britain and finding a new home in Spain was the easy part; winding down was going to be a good deal harder and would be just as demanding as winding up had been in the first place, and we now had rather more sympathy with Sumo wrestlers who, after years of endless eating, training and ferocious competition in an almost monastic environment, have to accept virtually overnight the no less rigorous disciplines required to bring them safely down to a normal weight and size and to adapt to a conventional lifestyle once they retire.

These self-analyses didn't happen overnight; they were part of a process that evolved along with our other preoccupations with our new home, the first of which was the recognition that if the pattern of our first few weeks as home/landowners in the *campo* was going to be continued to any extent, then our new pastoral life was certainly not going to be dull. It came as a distinct shock when we realised that, although it was clearly going to be as radically different from our working lives in England as we had hoped, it was likely to be no less demanding, albeit on a different scale: putting our feet up was not going to be an option. Still, that was what we wanted, wasn't it? Well, yes, it was, and now we were beginning to realise just how absorbing, fulfilling and time-consuming owning a smallholding in Spain was going to be.

The most obvious, unexpected and immediate demand was the constant need to trim and cut back our trees. Despite, or perhaps because of, the lack of water other than the once-a-month flood, these sprouted shoots and suckers with astonishing abandon, and with altogether far too many trees crowded together, keeping them under control was as ceaseless as the reputed task of painting the Forth railway bridge. Every day I tramped further and further down onto the land, clutching secateurs, bow-saw and other assorted paraphernalia, and settled down to another session of snipping, lopping and cutting away the excess timber. Within a few days I had moved far enough away for the house to be completely obscured from my view by the intervening foliage, and I was in a different world, only distantly connected to the hammering and banging and the rumble of the cement mixer to which Susan remained subjected.

There was, however, a limit to how much of even this pastoral activity I could accept each day once the sun began to make its presence felt and, besides, it was hardly fair for me to absent myself from the house for too long, since there were two further activities which demanded our involvement each day. The first was the frequent need to move furniture around to allow Michael and his team to make progress. As with so many renovation projects, getting the necessary sub-contracted help to appear at the time required by the programme was a forlorn hope; the best one could hope for was that it wouldn't be necessary to undo half the work already done to allow, say, the electrician to do his thing when he finally appeared. But in the meantime, Michael and the boys were steadily moving through the house, tiling floors, building walls, creating archways, inserting windows, plastering and making good, all of which required the furniture to be moved to where the mess was least, and then often moved back again at the end of the same day to enable us to go to bed.

The second was the ever-present need to maintain a supply of drinking water. Neither Michael nor his boys ever thought to bring bottles of their own, and with our source liable to cease without warning, it behoved us to pay constant attention to our stocks, and replenish them on every occasion that the supply was working. We had literally dozens of two-litre plastic bottles ranged along passageways, with a few in the fridge, and these we had to use in strict rotation each day, as otherwise they became stale and unusable.

We also now began to paint the interior walls of each room as Michael and the team vacated it. This was a great step forward, as at last we were not only making our own contribution to the proceedings, we were also actually preparing the house for civilised occupation. It was too soon for pictures and curtains, of course, nor could we make up rooms as they would ultimately be; they were still needed to serve as stores, and beds and tables had the habit of becoming platforms to support boxes as soon as our backs were turned. Nevertheless it was a definite advance, and the boost to morale was immediate.

While all this was going on in our own little world, welcome changes were occurring elsewhere, notably that, for the first time in its existence, the main road from our nearby village to Periana was properly surfaced. It was while travelling this road twice a week during this time to go to the Post Office that we experienced a magnificently 'low tech' system of traffic control for each section of road works. Traffic lights were simply not an option; with the opposite ends invariably out of sight of each other, no-one would believe that the lights were working properly if they had to wait for more than a minute. Instead, a 'mandraulic' system was used, involving the use of an olive twig, held by the 'Stop/Go' operator at one end of the road works.

When it was the turn for the traffic at his end to proceed, he handed this twig to the driver of the last vehicle in the column as it went past. When this vehicle reached the other end of the road works, the twig was handed with due ceremony to the 'Stop/Go' operator at that end, who then allowed his waiting line of traffic to proceed. The system was totally fool-proof, as neither operator would allow the traffic at his end to move unless he held the twig in his hand, and was reminiscent of the 'key' system for points control used on single-line sections of railway in much of the UK in the vintage days of steam.

We became familiar birds of passage to the men working on this 8-kilometre stretch of road, as it was also at this time that we set out to obtain *Certificados de Empadronamiento* from our local town hall, an exercise which gave us our first, personal experience of Spanish bureaucracy. These certificates are rather like being on the electoral roll in the UK, and are a prerequisite to getting Spanish registration for your car. It is not enough simply to give your address to the licensing authorities: you have to show that you 'belong' somewhere.

As it is to the financial advantage of the town hall to have you do this, I imagined that getting the certificate would be relatively easy. I was wrong. It took me three visits, clutching passports, NIEs and proof of ownership of the *finca*, and even then I was greeted with utter astonishment when I said I wanted certificates for both of us. '<u>Both</u> of you! Whatever for?' 'Because we have two cars, one each.' 'Your wife has her <u>own car</u>!' 'Yes.' The shrug of disbelief was almost Gallic. Still, in the end we got them, and I made a number of acquaintances at the town hall, who were to prove extremely valuable on future occasions.

I also found that our town hall was staffed with generally delightful people who took a pride in their town and were at pains to try to help, not at all the conventional image of local government officials. That they were unable to help immediately often gave them deep regret and sometimes, it is true, they preferred to let you go away with a feeling of unjustified optimism about the outcome of your interview, rather than with the sour taste of the unpalatable truth, but this was entirely human and understandable. It also became clear that, certainly where matters involving our house were concerned, they knew exactly who we were and where we had bought – and for how much – and what we were doing with it, and were deeply sympathetic over our relationship with Pedro and Luisa, who were clearly well-known in certain quarters.

This weather now was extremely hot, and gave us three further definitions of summer in the Andalucían *campo*.

1. Washing from one load would be dry by the time the next load was ready to hang out;
2. At 10 o'clock at night we would still be warm wearing just a T-shirt and a pair of shorts; and
3. *Cava* bottles filled with water and placed in the sun could provide an excellent – and free – source of hot water for washing up, especially useful when you had no gas ... or mains water, come to that.

We also found ourselves becoming tired to the point of exhaustion more quickly than was customary for us. We put this down to three factors, too, from which we learned another useful moral when undertaking an enterprise such as ours at relatively advanced ages:

1. Despite ensuring that we consumed enough water and salt, the heat was such to sap all energy from us emigrants from colder climes, especially as we couldn't fully escape it. This was to be sharply emphasised when I, who should have known better, spent a morning in the full sun clearing brambles without stopping for water, resulting in the classic symptoms for heat-exhaustion and salt-deficiency, which required the consumption of freshly-squeezed lemon juice laced with salt and a spell in bed before I recovered.
2. With me at sixty-three and Susan approaching fifty, the 'we-aren't-as-young-as-were-were' syndrome was definitely having an effect, particularly on strength and stamina. This was exacerbated by
3. Our four-month enforced lay-off, which had resulted in us both getting badly out of condition. At our respective ages, this was not as easy to correct as it had once been, burdened as were both were with injuries and ailments from the past. So the moral was:

**If you are of 'riper years', be prepared for everything you do,
never mind what other people do for you,
to take infinitely longer, and be vastly more
physically taxing, than you anticipate.**

All this time Michael and his boys were making steady progress, despite being hampered by the frequent lack of water for mixing mortar, and the non-availability of electricity throughout much of the house, the latter due to the reticence of the 'electrician' who, despite having been 'coming tomorrow' for ten days, still hadn't put in an appearance. This made the use of power tools impossible in certain places without running yards of extension cable (which we didn't have and neither, of course, did Michael), thereby also risking blowing the main fuse, since we were still on our old mains supply of about 1.9 Kv.

It was now that Michael and I discovered one possible reason for the electrician's continued absence. When he and I tried to prepare one of the light circuits upstairs for connection, we found the electrician had randomly used whatever wires he had available to take the supply up to the first floor, with no thought whatever to colour-coding or consistency. One junction box joining three separate spurs consisted entirely of black wires! Without a meter, which again neither of us had, it was impossible to determine which wires led to or from switches, which were earth/ground (and if they were actually earthed), and which led direct from the mains. This discovery gave us food for thought about the rest of the wiring, especially when Susan discovered the hard way that a metal wall light fitting downstairs was 'live', despite being switched off!

However it was also now that we discovered one of the major benefits of our old-fashioned way of life. Because so many local Spanish families still didn't have cars, making a trip into town a half-day's walk each way, delivery vans made the rounds of outlying areas instead. These made it very nearly unnecessary to go into town at all. The Bread Lady came every day except Saturdays, the Fish Man on Tuesdays, Thursdays and Saturdays. Carlos, bringing frozen food from the *congelados* called on Thursdays, making a supplementary visit on Friday to deliver anything which he didn't actually have with him the day before. Since the shop from which this van came stocked items like bleach, eggs, tonic water, chicken food and *vino de mesa* as well as frozen food, it could supply virtually all our needs on its own, except for fresh meat and vegetables and dog food.

Diary – Tuesday 13 July. We decide to take a break from the house and walk up the bed of the river which flanks our land, since by now this has dwindled to little more than a large stream. After some fairly hazardous scrambling down, and subsequently up, the bank through a near secondary jungle, avoiding the predatory and highly tenacious brambles which lurk in the undergrowth, we find a magical place like an Arthur Rackham illustration. The stream meanders between massive boulders and slides beneath moss-covered branches overhanging rock pools in which terrapins and even fish lurk. The air is marvellously cool and we watch fascinated as clusters of strange black dragonflies hunt over the shallows. Progress on foot is far from easy, and we are both wet, muddy and exhausted by the time we have traversed the 200 metres between our southern and northern boundaries. But we are exhilarated too; who would have thought that we would find a river such as this, still running in July, in a land where the summer temperature averages the mid 30s Celsius/90s Fahrenheit, and where most *rios* are such in name only, being dried-out water courses for most of the year.

We are not the only ones fascinated by the river: Herbert is there with us, busily rootling through the undergrowth, seeking suitable trophies. But for Penny, the experience is rather more traumatic - and dramatic. She becomes separated from us when we first scramble down out of her sight, and after about half an hour we hear her piteous whimpering as she rushes to and fro along the top of the bank, looking for us. When she finally locates us, her relief is almost tangible, and she launches herself down the slope without giving too much thought to how or where she is going to stop. I manage to catch her before she falls headlong into the river, but she then sees a nice patch of unbroken green duckweed which clearly offers a safe, dry lawn on which to recover her composure.

She wriggles out of my arms and leaps onto it, and disappears completely into the pool hidden underneath. The expression of outrage on her face when she surfaces speaks volumes. However we are entirely wrong in thinking that this experience might put her off the river, and we have since categorised her as an Andalucían Terrapin Hound, owing to her insistence on catching these unfortunate creatures and bringing them back to the house in her mouth, quite unharmed, as loving tokens of her esteem.

Mid-July also brought two visits which definitely indicated that progress was being made. The first was from a woman from the firm Michael had contracted to build the swimming pool. We had calculated that we would have enough room for a 8 x 4.5 metre pool, and had had the hole dug accordingly. The pool firm's preliminary estimate was based on this and the fact that we would paint it ourselves rather than have it tiled by them. However after her visit this estimate was revised upwards, since apparently the relative inaccessibility of our property and the narrowness of our lane meant that the firm would have to use more, smaller trucks to bring the raw materials than the fewer, larger ones they customarily used.

This revision caused a lot of heart-searching. The first estimate was at the limit of what we felt we could afford. However the alternatives to finding the extra funds of either reducing the size of the pool or not having a pool at all were, to us, simply not acceptable, the latter because we were in no doubt that we needed one, especially if we were going to have paying guests, and the former because the construction of a swimming-pool really was a one-time thing and we were determined not to compromise; we knew the pool would confront us with our parsimony for the rest of our lives if we did. So we concluded, inevitably, that we would have to find the money somehow, even if it meant postponing another part of the *reformación*, and we gave her the go-ahead.

The other visit was much more prosaic but infinitely more significant: a representative from the liquid concrete factory in Colmenar, to view the site for the new kitchen/living-room extension, to determine the quantity of concrete required and whether the vehicles and equipment required to lay the footings and floor could actually reach us. This was a huge step forward: at last the hazardous bombed-site aspect at the end of the house would be no more, and we could begin to contemplate the possibility that some day we would actually have a kitchen, and a place indoors to eat our food!

At the same time as these visits, the firm of electrical contractors we had all engaged to replace the old mains 'grid' finally reached us. They had been wending their way across country, connecting the overhead cables to each house as they reached it, ever since 22 May, and we were the last house to be connected. This was another great moment: the day was now in sight when we might even be able to run the deep-freeze and the microwave simultaneously, or even a hair-dryer, without blowing the main fuse and plunging the house into total darkness!

Diary – Monday 19 July. Swimming-pool construction begins. No, it doesn't – this day a total non-event, as neither Michael, his boys nor the swimming-pool people turn up. Michael phones later to say that he and Antonio, his building materials supplier, should be coming in the evening to deliver the box-section steel rods to reinforce the footings of the extension, and the steel wire 'mat' on which to lay the concrete for the floor. Inevitably, they don't.

Tuesday 20 July. Michael and his boys start to build the walls for the *en-suite* shower room in our main guest bedroom in the former storeroom in the 'upstairs back', as there is still no sign of Antonio or the swimming-pool people. Michael leaves at lunchtime to sort out his Land Rover, which is 'kaput', and at 2.00 p.m. the liquid-concrete representative arrives to say that the trucks with our concrete will arrive at 8.00 a.m. tomorrow. Michael doesn't come back in the afternoon, so his boys are faced with the challenge of somehow getting home without transport. We do not offer a taxi service, as know this will be the thin end of the wedge. At 6.00 p.m. Antonio arrives at last with the steel, and with several pallets of bricks with which to start building the walls to the extension, one of which bursts in mid-hoist – most spectacular! Later I phone Michael to tell him of these developments.

Wednesday 21 July. Michael and boys arrive at 7.30 a.m. to lay the box-section steel rods into the footings, and the steel 'mat' over the floor area. 8.00 a.m., ready for the concrete lorry. 8.45 a.m. Michael goes to look for it, finds it waiting by the bridge. Tells it to get on up to the house! This is followed by Antonio with his lorry, so chaos while both lorries manoeuvre, one behind the other, off our very narrow lane onto the area at the back of our house. The procedure now is fascinating. The concrete lorry discharges a load into a funnel-shaped hopper suspended from the crane on

Antonio's lorry. When full, this hopper is then swung up and over the roof of the house, narrowly missing the chimney, and down to the floor area of the extension.

There Michael directs it to where he wants it, then opens a trap-door at the bottom of the hopper, to allow a flood of liquid concrete to pour out. This he and his team push and flatten with wooden paddles, to make a completely even surface alongside the previous load, while the hopper goes back for the next one. Neither Antonio nor the concrete-lorry driver have a helper, yet the whole process moves without pause at a systematic pace which matches exactly Michael and his team's ability to deal with each load before the next one arrives.

By 1.30 p.m. the job is finished and everyone departs, including Michael and his boys who say they have done enough for one day! At 5.00 p.m. the electrical contractors arrive to do the final work in preparation to switching us over to the new 'grid' tomorrow, including fitting a vast and hideous new box for the meter at shoulder height, right outside the front door! At the same time a representative from the Gibraltar branch of a British building society arrives to discuss the possibility of a mortgage, to help us complete the landscaping work outside the house sooner rather than later. He describes our venture as 'courageous', and says he normally never contemplates a loan on a property not adjacent to a metalled road. Since ours lies two kilometres from such a road, we suspect this visit will come to naught. Fool!

Thursday 22 July. While I go to the coast for shopping, Susan stays behind to fill holes in our smallest first-floor bedroom ready for painting – she has discovered that paint mixed with wet plaster is a brilliant combination for filling cracks. I get back at lunchtime to find the new power source connected and switched on, and that Michael has seized the opportunity to retain this firm to pick up where his present, unlamented electrician has left off, and to rectify some of his worst failures where possible. At the same time Michael and his boys have started to build the foundations to the extension over the footings laid yesterday and, when this got too hot, have moved indoors to continue building the walls for the *en-suite* shower. We only hope this won't interfere with our bringing some of the rest of our furniture and boxes through the outside door to the 'upstairs back', and storing them there – we have just been told by our removal company that these will arrive next Tuesday.

<u>Friday 23 July.</u> In the evening, after Michael and the boys have finished for the week, I dye Susan's hair. This is something I have never done before, so it is slightly nerve-wracking for us both, and is not helped by the arrival, slap in the middle of the proceedings, of one of the three German co-owners of a house further down the lane which they use for holidays, to introduce himself. What he thinks of his first meeting with the English permanent residents can only be guessed. What I do know is that the dyeing is an unqualified success: perhaps I have missed my vocation!

After the last visit to a hairdresser in Torre del Mar where I had my perm shower, I decided it had to be DIY where my hair was concerned. I had cut and trimmed all my children's hair and regularly cut Toby's. Mine I had coloured, cut and permed myself over the years, sometimes with spectacular results when interrupted by the telephone or some crisis! I have been going grey unwillingly for the last twenty-five years and prefer to disguise it. I gave up the struggle here what with the water problems and no mirrors to hand but then dragooned Toby into being my personal colour changer.

<u>Saturday 24 July.</u> We go into town to buy assorted ironmongery at the *ferreteria*. On our return I carry down into the orchard the heavy, timber ladder which was formerly used to reach the 'upstairs back' storeroom from inside the house, and succeed in tripping and falling fairly heavily. Luckily nothing is broken and I suffer no more than injured pride and cut legs, but it is a sharp reminder of how vulnerable we are here to any kind of accident, however innocuous, and I suspect I shall pay for my inattentiveness the next day. Meanwhile the dogs rediscover the river, necessitating showers for us all!

<u>Sunday 25 July.</u> I am right: I am stiff and bruised all over, so we abandon ideas for work and instead do some much-needed planning about the future for our land. We finally decide that we shall create a fenced 'dog pound' for our pack at the back of the

house, so that we can leave them secure when we are out for the day without necessarily having to shut them in the house all the time, and create a 'house' orchard directly below the house, with fruit trees whose crops we will actually use. The rest of the land we will give over to olive trees, to supply to the *co-operativo* up on the main road for processing into its renowned *virgen* olive-oil. This will mean cutting down most of the vast number of pear and pomegranate trees which at present stand far too close together to bear a decent crop, and for which there is no cost-effective commercial outlet. They will make several years' worth of fuel for our wood-burning stove. We finish the day with the first grapes from our own vine, over which my throat closes like a vice, reminding us sharply that the problem still needs to be dealt with.

Tuesday 27 July. Our furniture arrives at 3.00 p.m., mercifully after Michael and his *niños* have left. This time there is a team of four, and they unload the lot in three hours. There are now more boxes than space here: the big bedroom is full to within eighteen inches of the ceiling (thus demonstrating that its floor is stronger than we thought!), the small first-floor room has bed-space but otherwise is also full, the front terrace has a new wall, one-box thick, three boxes high, stacked against the front of the house, and a two-box thick wall, same height, against its outer wall, leaving a corridor two metres wide for access into the house. The dining room has just enough space left to walk through it, there are boxes under every bed in every room, and our leather-covered three-piece-suite and a truckle bed are in the 'upstairs back', where we hope Michael, and especially his *niños*, won't use them as convenient places for lunch!

Wednesday 28 July. Irrigation Day. Up at 6.30 a.m., to discover flow at full bore, thanks to rain the previous day in Granada Province. Open both arms of sluice and send water to both ends of our land simultaneously. We can practically hear the trees slurping up the moisture – they have had nothing for eight weeks as, on our last Irrigation Day, there was no water at all. As usual I spend the day clearing the channels of twigs, leaves and dead pomegranates ahead of the advancing flood, even more determined to improve on this mediaeval system next year, while Susan tries to track down a smoke alarm in one of our boxes plaintively, and penetratingly, going 'beep' at regular intervals, like a lost Scops owl.

Boxes, boxes and more boxes! I can see me getting to know the contents of these things very well indeed. When they were stored in England we managed very well without but now they are here we must find so-and-so to use it; why? The very first job is to buy some insect powder and cover the outsides of the boxes and the floor around them with it, to stop any crawly thing setting up home in our belongings. The main culprit is a hopping job similar to a grasshopper but smaller and chunkier which appears to love cardboard boxes.

Thursday 29 July. Poetic justice: irrigation water stops; we only wish it were Pedro and Luisa who are affected, not Pedro's charming brother Antonio. Later: a miracle! The pool people arrive at 1.00 p.m. and dump off a cement mixer and a wheelbarrow. They then bugger off till 4.30, when they return with two van-loads of bricks, which they proceed to try to lay in the pool pit as the start of the outer supporting wall, without the benefit of either a ladder to get down there, a spirit level or a long tape-measure. In the end they borrow the first two from us and the last from Michael. They also connect their cement mixer's power cable into the house mains with two bare wires held in with matches. We shall watch the rest of their efforts with interest!

Friday 30 July. No sign of pool people; later they ring to say they will come, *seguramente*, on Monday. We then try to go to Torre del Mar for shopping, but discover the car battery is flat and there is a slow puncture/leaking valve in the near front wheel. The battery appears to have a dead cell, and automatically triggers the car alarm. Susan finally discovers where to turn it off, but not before we have woken up the entire valley and deafened ourselves – fun! We are now marooned in the house till Monday.

August is the month when all of Spain goes on holiday, which was why we were so relieved when the pool people said they would start on 19 July. Even allowing for 'hiccups', ten days should have been enough for them to complete the job before the onset of the holiday season. Now we were faced with a situation where, not only had they barely started but Michael (who, as our builder, was the overseeing contractor) was taking his family to the Netherlands for two weeks to visit his mother, and would not be here if they delayed much longer. If this occurred they would not start until he got back, and it could be October before the pool was finished and we could paint it, let alone put any water in it ... just in time to close it down for the winter.

Diary – Monday 2 August. After our first lie-in on a Sunday since we got here and a rest day in preparation for the pool people starting work today, absolutely no-one turns up at the usual start time of 8.00 a.m., so Susan goes to work unpacking and checking the computers while I assemble a new, flat-packed kitchen corner bench-seat, attempting to follow the world's most unhelpful instructions. Then at 10.30 the pool people arrive and begin building, at amazing speed, the brick screen walls and floor against which they will lay the pool concrete ditto, three Germans from down the road arrive for coffee and a chat, and our removals firm's Alicante office phones to say that they have located most of the items we had noted were missing from our furniture, including the treasured portrait of my mother, painted by her father when she was twenty-three. Things are looking up, and we are further encouraged when the pool construction team leaves at 6.00 p.m., with all four screen walls almost complete. They say they will do the bottom tomorrow, and then the iron-work. We shall see.

Tuesday 3 August. Juan, Michael's chief *niño*, arrives at 8.30 carrying a puppy which, he says, he has just found on the back road to Periana. It is a totally fearless, energetic, fat fluffy bundle. I admire it and hand it back. 'No, no!' says Juan (in Spanish, of course), 'it's for you.' Hmm, just what we need, a third dog, especially right now. However it proves irresistible, and we accept it. So does Herbert, but Penny is petrified. Eloïse thinks it's a splendid toy. We wonder how long it will be before it thinks she's the splendid toy!

The puppy looks to have been dumped or abandoned for only a few days; it is in reasonable condition, looks much too young to have left its mum and has blood-sucking ticks in both ears. Out come the butter and then the disinfectant and first aid kit. Butter the ticks (it stops them breathing so I have been told and it works too) wait a few minutes and then gently remove with tweezers – just the job I needed for today. The puppy adores the attention and lies down like a starfish earning him the name of one of our previous dogs, Enoch!

Michael and *niños* work on the extension, the pool team arrives at 10.30; it's all happening. Then the inevitable also happens: at 3.00 p.m. the water 'dies'. Michael and *niños* quit and the pool team goes to get the metal mesh with which they will line the bottom and sides of the pool to form the base for the concrete. They return at 5.00 p.m., when the water also returns, so we fill up every available container and do a load of washing before it 'dies' again at 8.00 p.m. . . . as does the electricity, so to bed, once again, by torchlight! Luckily the pool team has finished all the brick-work and half laid half the metal reinforcement by this time.

Enoch is extraordinarily precocious. His eyes still have a blue sheen, so we reckon he is only four or five weeks old, yet he knows how to pant, tries to eat dry food, already knows who we are, squeaks when he wants to 'go' outside, knows how to find his way back to the house when he has finished, and plays vigorously with who or whatever will respond. Herbert is amazingly tolerant (except when needle teeth and exceptionally strong jaws close on his ears), Eloïse is respectful and Penny runs away. . . which Enoch thinks is a great game. He is six inches (15 cm) high at the shoulder, ten inches from the base of his tail (which wags incessantly) to his forehead, and three and a half inches from shoulder to shoulder – a tiny, non-stop dynamo!

Wednesday 4 August. Up at 6.20 a.m. expecting to face overnight mess from Enoch, but find none – amazing. Michael and *niños* arrive 8.00 a.m. and begin digging a small pit beside the swimming pool to house the pump and filter. The pool team arrives 9.45 a.m. and begins fitting a 20 cm deep boxed steel mesh frame, similar to the arrangement Michael used in the footings for the extension, against the single thickness mesh liner they have already installed, all the way round the pool and across the floor. This will form the reinforcement for the concrete and will also hold it in position while it sets. Mercifully both the mains water and the electricity are back on, so we can use the washing machine again and refill all the containers for drinking water. By now the temperature at mid-day in the coolest part of the house is 28°C/83°F, while in the shade on the terrace it is 38°C/101°F and an awesome 45°C/115°F in the sun where Michael, his *niños* and the pool team are working. How they do it totally defeats us. No wonder Spain shuts up shop this month!

<u>Thursday 5 August.</u> A new team from the pool company arrives to fit the plumbing and install the pump and filter. They don't get around to the latter until after mid-day, when the temperature in the pit is over 40°C/104°F, so we erect our green and white fabric 'gazebo' over the pit, to provide shade. This causes astonishment while we are doing it, but is greatly appreciated once it is up. When they, Michael *et al.* have gone, we celebrate still having mains water by having a shower - together, to save water, of course. One thing leads to another, and we find we have now added Fozzy Bear to the Muppet-like audience in our bedroom!

The mornings were now becoming quite chilly, although the days were still blisteringly hot - 38°C in the shade - and the nights overly warm. On Sunday we watched with concern as a fire developed just beyond the river up-stream from us, only half a kilometre away, and a strong wind from the *Sierra de Enmedio* escarpment further to the north blew burning embers downwind towards us, threatening to turn a modest blaze into a major conflagration. We took turns to maintain a watch well into the night and were intrigued - and dismayed - at the measures taken by the local authority to deal with the situation. It was not until the fire had really taken hold that a policeman appeared, in a small van, to take a look. He then departed, returning three hours later at the head of a small column of minuscule equipment, whose volunteer operators then stood around for quite a while, discussing the situation, before deciding that there was really very little they could now do, as the fire seemed to have done its worst, and burnt itself out. We wondered what they could or would have done if it had still been blazing as before.

This episode caused us to think rather more urgently about putting our House and Contents Insurance in order, and to ponder in general the means of dealing with emergencies; having had Juan's injuries to contend with and now this, it only remained for us to be burgled to complete the Big Three. So what, exactly, would we do if we were faced with a situation which was beyond our own resources? The short answer was, not a lot.

We had now come to realise that there was a fundamental difference from what we had come to expect in the UK with regard to access to the Emergency Services and what was available in the Spanish *campo*. It was not that Emergency Services didn't exist: they did – and do – and when you could get hold of them they were as competent as any. The problem was how to get hold of them. There appeared to be three reasons for this.

First, there was no equivalent of the '999' system. Each Emergency Service had its own telephone number, and you had to be prepared to do whatever it took to reach the service you required, individually and in Spanish. This might not be so easy when your house was on fire and you were trying desperately to rescue your belongings and your cat. Even the most competent speakers of Spanish might fall to pieces under these circumstances.

Secondly, when you did get through and could make yourself understood, there was the small matter of directing them to your house. Our house has four different addresses: one known to the Town Hall, another used by the electricity company, a third used by *Telefonica* and a different one again on the title deeds to the property. No one knew which was correct, or even if any of them was correct, and it was all academic anyway, since neither the road nor the house were distinguished by any markings whatsoever.

When the cement lorries came to the house, or *Telefonica* engineers, or anyone else for the first time, one of us had to drive up to the main road – about 2 km – meet them outside the olive mill and physically guide them to the house. We still have to do this today since, even with improving Spanish, it is virtually impossible to give someone coherent directions. Trying to do it to an ambulance driver while one of you is lying prostrate with renal colic (as has since happened) is simply one challenge too many!

The third problem was distance. Although there was a town eight miles away with a 24-hour First Aid Post, for practical purposes our nearest source of emergency help was the hospital, over twenty miles away. This meant that it could take literally hours for this help to reach us if we needed it. So with regard to emergencies we came to the conclusion that we had to be prepared, like those attempting long-distance passages in sailing yachts, to deal with them ourselves, and not just the 'big three' either: our car failing to start because of a faulty battery had been just as much of an emergency, living where we did and without a local call-out service.

To us, none of this was a deterrent to living in the *campo*. We both had a reasonable knowledge of First Aid and had already found that a comprehensive First Aid kit went a long way to resolving most medical situations. For fire-fighting we had a fire blanket for the hob and fire extinguishers around the place, and we had already realised that our swimming pool would make a handy water reservoir, given that we now had a suitable pumps, a hose, and an emergency power supply that didn't depend on mains electricity. And, as we had already witnessed, the dogs made wonderful intruder alarms and deterrents.

Our main concern in dealing with emergency situations was to remember to follow the admirable advice given in the *Hitch-Hiker's Guide to the Galaxy*: DON'T PANIC! However we had already developed a suitably 'DIY' attitude to dealing with similar problems in Britain, where we had never had too much faith in the efficiency and benevolence of local councils. We had long since recognised that the '999' services there were over-stretched, and that getting hold of a plumber, mechanic or electrician in a hurry in the UK could be fraught, and could usually cost an arm and a leg, so we had always preferred to deal with situations ourselves, whenever possible. And the benefit of our circumstances in the Spanish *campo* was that, so far as our new home was concerned, the Rates for the house and the land together were less than £50 a year, compared with the £80 a month we were paying for our home and garden in Bournemouth, so creating a reserve of the funds with which to deal with emergencies ourselves was entirely reasonable.

We did realise, though, that there was one major behavioural change we had to make, and quickly, from our practices in the UK: this was our approach to normal physical activities. In this I was helped by my former pastime as a single-handed offshore sailor. Since this is one where there is no 'get-you-home' service and you are on your own so far as emergencies are concerned, it engenders an extreme caution when undertaking even simple, routine tasks since one mistake can, as the advertisement says, turn a drama into a crisis. So now we started to take immense care when using sharp implements, adopted safety procedures when handling inflammable substances, told each other where we were going and when we should be expected back, and generally began to behave in a way unrecognisable from the casual, not to say carefree, approach we adopted 'back home.' In short,

we always wore (and still wear) gloves for gardening!

Diary - Saturday 7 August. Come back from Torre del Mar to find the swimming pool people have delivered a load of special cement mix, an event greeted with enthusiasm by us and even more so by the dogs, who think the small resulting pyramid a wonderful place to play - and use as a toilet! Disabusing them of this notion takes a bit of doing, and sustaining it even more so as in the evening the dogs take themselves down to the river for a swim, then have the bright idea that the pile of cement will make a great place to dry off; they are dismayed to find me sitting beside it, reading a book, awaiting just that eventuality.

Wednesday 11 August. At 10.30 a.m., four and a half weeks late and after a myriad of false starts, the pool people arrive with the equipment to start the construction of the pool proper, which begins at 4.30 p.m. after the morning has been spent setting up and testing. The equipment comprises a trailer-mounted generator driving a compressor on another trailer, both trailers of a size which require lorries to pull them. There is then a king-sized 'food processor', in which the pool compound is mixed with sand and water and transported upwards by a conveyor belt to a hopper, which drops the mixture into the hose from the compressor. The mixture is then blasted away at 60 p.s.i. to the nozzle, where it is mixed with more water and the resultant near-liquid is sprayed into the boxed steel frame to form the floor and walls to the pool. At least, that's the theory. The practice proves to be a little different.

The process clearly works: the pool firm concerned had a long and successful record to substantiate it. However it is undoubtedly complicated and, with an almost predictable inevitability, in our case things begin to go wrong almost immediately. Within an hour of starting the compressor begins to 'hunt', surging well beyond its governed speed and then dropping back to a corresponding level below it. This results in the operator at the nozzle having to contend, at one minute, with pressure not unlike a fire hose, projecting a stream of sand and cement which would serve perfectly for grit-blasting, and in the next with an over-wet mixture which dribbles round his feet like badly-made porridge.

This surging has other effects elsewhere. Because the speed of the 'food processor' is linked to the governed speed of the compressor, the mix being transported to the hopper is either whipped off the end of the conveyor belt like a rat disappearing down a hole, or it backs up at the mixer end, where gradually the effect of the 'down' surge from the compressor takes control, and the porridge mixture begins to clog in the hose. Since the pool compound is designed to set reasonably quickly, it is only a short time before the hose is completely blocked. At this affront the compressor gives up the ghost and dies altogether, which is just as well, because our mains water seizes the opportunity to follow suit.

There are now two distinct groups of people engaged in rituals that would fascinate any outside observer. On the one hand there is the pool team, who take turns to jump up and down on, and then shake, the blocked hose to try to break up and remove the rapidly hardening cement, as though trying to batter into submission a large and over-fed python, while on the other are Susan and myself, rigging our submersible pump into our swimming-pool *deposito* and running a garden hose from it some thirty yards to the large barrel which, until then, has been fed from our mains supply and from which the pool people's own pump feeds it to the nozzle at the end of their hose. Susan and I finish first, at about 6 o'clock, and triumphantly turn to the pool people, only to find that they are still python-wrestling, and won't need our *deposito* water until next day. So we watch them until 7.15 when they finally quit, whereupon, of course, the mains water comes back on!

Thursday 12 August. The day begins well. Michael and his boys arrive at 8.30, the pool team at 9 o'clock together with an engineer who delves into the compressor and, after much clanging and swearing in Andaluz, pronounces everything to be OK. He is, of course, wrong; half an hour after he has departed, a new fault develops, at the point where the compressed air and the cement/sand mixture meets below the hopper. This has probably been caused by the strain imposed by the blocked hose yesterday. However the result is that the mixture is now forced out through the joint, engulfing the two 'coolies' who are feeding the 'processor' in a cloud of choking white dust while the new hose operator stands in a rising puddle of liquid cement. It is a scene which Dante couldn't have bettered and would have even given Hieronymus Bosch some new ideas.

For the rest of the morning, the pool team battles on, with minimal success, until 1.30 p.m. when the final straw is reached in the form of a second lorry-load of cement compound which no-one has thought to delay, and which now arrives with nowhere to put it. After they have unloaded it round the tree at the top of the path down to the house, and watched it pour half-way across the road, they all go off for lunch until 4.00 p.m., leaving us to cope with any passing traffic. When they re-start the team foreman has returned, which is a help, as at least he mops up the excess liquid from where his deputy has let it accumulate on what is supposed to be the pool floor, but it is still not right, so the engineer is called for again, finally arriving at 5.15. At this point the woman from the pool firm phones to ask brightly how near the team is to finishing, and is appalled to learn the truth of the situation. Susan unsurprisingly now develops a migraine, which is only partly alleviated by the team foreman giving us a melon in token compensation for the delay.

<u>Friday 13 August.</u> Today dawns true to its reputation: no water! The pool teams arrives at 10.30 a.m. to pick up where it left off yesterday, with similar results: by 1.30 p.m., zero progress. Michael arrives mid-afternoon to announce that the pool team will now have to work until they have finished, as the equipment is needed somewhere else on Monday. Finally the various problems are sorted, and work leaps forward.

With the continued absence of mains water, our 'jury-rig' for water from our *deposito* becomes critical. The problem is, the pool team turn their pump off with no regard – or curiosity – about where the water is coming from, so the barrel overflows within minutes unless our own pump is turned off at the same time. Then they start again without telling us, and wonder why the barrel runs dry, so perforce I now become part of the team, tending the supply of water to the 'sharp end'.

Our front terrace, and all our furniture and boxes on it, are now covered with a fine layer of gravel, and as the nozzle operator has reached the upper levels of the pool walls, there is 'fall-out' from the jet striking the rim of the pool. This makes it dangerous to stand in the line of fire, as the fall-out can hurt up to twenty feet away. However the bulk of the job is finally finished at 9.30 p.m., leaving only the final surface to be done and we thankfully watch the pool team depart, leaving their equipment to be collected on Monday.

Saturday 14/Sunday 15 August. After fixing the pipes to the *deposito* so that the mains refills it instead of supplying the header barrel used by the pool team, we spend a wonderful week-end alternately watering the concrete in the swimming pool to prevent it from cracking (it's strange, but it doesn't seem to make it grow much!) and watching videos, only marred by the VCR cutting out every time the fridge or the deep-freeze cuts in. We have an unexpected abundance of mains water and manage to do three loads of washing as well as nearly rcfilling the *deposito*, which allows us to have a swim – sort of. I also watch Susan practising the long-jump down to the *deposito* plateau with nearly serious consequences, and on Sunday we celebrate the completion of the pool by having burgers and chips with tomato ketchup for lunch and watching 'Independence Day' – our children would never believe it. However the water goes off again in the evening, so no showers, and the clutter, perpetual dirt and the close proximity of the dogs are definitely beginning to get to us.

Monday 16 August. Surprise, surprise: no sign of the pool people; now we know why they were late getting to us. I go and see one of our German near-neighbours, who says the problem of the VCR cutting-out is due to drops in voltage, and what we probably need is an *estabilasador* which would compensate for this. By coincidence he has one which he isn't using, and kindly lends it to us. He is right; it makes all the difference. In the afternoon two new workers recruited by Michael arrive with the swimming-pool paint and take a look at what they have to do in Michael's absence: tile the top of the pool parapet and build a flight of steps in one corner of the shallow end of the pool, as at present there is no way into or out of the pool: it's just a whacking great storage tank!

Tuesday 17 August. After three weeks of minimal water in the *acequia*, suddenly there is lots. By coincidence, it is also Pedro and Luisa's turn for water. You've got to hand it to them: here we are, educated Brits. and Germans plus a Spanish banker and the rest of Pedro's and Luisa's respective families, yet they alone have the secret of getting water when the rest of us go without (there was minimal water in July as well). All sorts of explanations abound, the most popular of which are either that they have done a deal with someone up-river to sell other people's water rights or that their past reputation for taking 'direct action' still ensures a positive reaction to a visit from Pedro by anyone illegally taking water upstream. Whatever the reason, it's impressive.

The rest of August played itself out largely without drama, except for one incident which served to remind us of what an unusual place it was in which we had chosen to make our home. Thick clouds swept in from the coast one evening, filling the valley and blotting out the stars. Within minutes the other side of the valley vanished from view and from the nature and behaviour of the clouds we began to mutter 'tornado'. We spent a frantic ten minutes bringing indoors anything and everything we felt might get damaged, and covered the rest as best we could, after which, total anti-climax: the clouds rolled away to the north, the view across the valley was restored, and one by one the stars began to reappear. Weird!

Michael's deputies finished tiling round the pool and built the steps, the pool people finally came back on the last two days of the month to trowel on the top surface for the walls and floor, making it six and a half weeks to the day from when they were due to have started, and they still hadn't finished the plumbing! We painted the pool and began to fill it and made the necessary arrangements for me to return to England for my much-postponed operation.

Eloïse decided to investigate the pool while we were not looking! Now we had cat paw prints in the new screed on the bottom of the pool. The dogs alerted us to her wrong doings because they were cross that they, thank goodness, couldn't join her to cause more havoc! We have had to accept, very reluctantly, that the dogs have to be restrained while the builders are on the premises, as they find piles of sand irresistible as play areas and never fail to investigate newly-laid concrete, with predictable and artistic results. When Michael and his boys leave in the evening we have also made it a first priority to cover the sand with a tarpaulin - the team never thinks to do this itself - as Eloïse also finds it an ideal lavatory!

Chapter 12

Cheer up, the worst is yet to come.
(Philander Chase Johnson)

I returned to Spain on Saturday 18 September. The operation had gone off successfully, though I had been slightly non-plussed to find myself looking up at a group of green-clad worthies as I was being wheeled into the theatre which changed seamlessly into a group of totally different worthies as I was being wheeled out, all without the blink of an eye, and to find that forty-five minutes had elapsed in the process. I had convalesced, if that is the right word, at the house of Susan's eldest son and his girl-friend, both of whom were absent for most of the time, being British Airways cabin crew. Still, that gave me the opportunity to complete the dreaded Self-Assessment Income Tax Return for the previous year, something which had been utterly impossible at the *cortijo*, so the time was well spent.

My flight arrived at the wonderful time of 3.00 a.m. and, when I emerged into the Arrivals foyer, I completely failed to recognise Susan at Málaga Airport! She had trimmed and coloured her hair in my absence and hadn't told me as she wanted it to be a surprise. This it certainly was - I walked straight past her. Since these can be emotionally charged events at the best of times, and in this case made more so by one of us having had a moderately serious operation while the other had had to 'hold the fort' alone in circumstances such as ours, this was unfortunate - both the surprise and the response - especially as, given the time of day, we were both also very tired. We laughed it off and made light of it, but it was a while before it assumed its proper perspective, and served to point to another useful lesson for a lifestyle such as ours:

Enforced separation can be more traumatic than you expect, and it is wise to be aware of the possible consequences.

220

We got home as dawn was breaking, so there didn't seem a lot of point in going to bed. Instead we walked the dogs, who were gratifyingly pleased to see me (unlike Eloïse who, characteristically, took the line of 'Should I know you?'), had breakfast and generally pottered, all the while receiving a steady stream of Spanish visitors ranging from Isidro (of course), bringing peaches, Carlos the frozen food van driver, and several others right through to Pedro and Luisa (now there <u>was</u> a surprise). All enquired earnestly about how the operation had gone and whether I was all right now, and while this was exhausting it was extremely touching, given that we had only been in residence for four months and that our neighbouring fellow-country persons seemed oblivious of the fact that I had been away at all!

While Toby was away, I had only the workmen here as company(?) during the day. Our Spanish neighbours were passing by far more frequently it seemed and so it became obvious that I was being 'taken care of' in a distant sort of way. My use of the Spanish language was still minimal and basic but they made sure I could ask for help should I need any and that it would be forthcoming. This was most welcome as our British neighbours kept themselves firmly to themselves, but I think they were all very disappointed that I was coping well on my own.

It was wonderful to be back. Long before the sun appeared, the sky on the other side of the valley was transfused with a wonderful, opalescent light which changed, as we watched, to the palest of blues streaked with high, pink-washed clouds. Clumps of flowers turned their faces east to greet the sun and around us, apart from the dogs rootling in the undergrowth, the chirp and clink of sleepy birds waking to the dawn and the distant tinkle of a herd of goats being taken to browse were the only sounds to disturb the silence. The difference from the M26 to Gatwick the evening before was almost too difficult to accept.

However next day I got a truly British welcome home: it started to rain! At around 9.30 a.m. a steady, persistent and remarkably heavy downpour set in, the first since our arrival at the *cortijo*. Within minutes the rock-hard ground was transformed into a mud-slick and the trees drooped with the unfamiliar weight of water. The *Sierra Guaro* to the north took on the appearance of the Brecon Beacons on a good day, with mist in the valleys and the whole of the mountain covered in clouds.

The dogs were most disconcerted with this transformation, and charged about through the rain, looking to us for reassurance. The swimming-pool, which had reached its high water mark at 11 o'clock, now looked like becoming over-full, and by mid-day there was a definite stream running through the building materials stacked outside the back of the house.

More interesting was how the roof over the main house was behaving, as this was the first time we had seen it tested. Happily it didn't seem to let the water in anywhere, not even through the somewhat doubtful tiles over the rear of the house. Even more happily the end room of the house, the one which had been inundated when Michael's *niños* left the tap on outside, appeared not to be letting anything through this time, for which we gave much thanks as it was now acting as a storeroom. However the kitchen/living-room extension, whose walls had been erected in my absence, had about one and a half centimetres (half an inch) of water across the floor by the time the rain stopped at 5.30 p.m., and we awaited Michael's reaction with interest.

Next day both Michael and his *niños* begin laying the concrete roof joists for the extension. In my absence they had fitted the new *rejas* (window grills) we ordered months earlier to replace the extremely tatty ones which were gracing the downstairs windows of the original house when we bought the *cortijo*. These grills are a feature of all Andalucían houses, though whether they are supposed to keep intruders out or the inhabitants in is a moot point. They can be extremely elegant, the more elaborate ones evoking images of the screens used to hide Islamic women from the gaze of men in mosques, so the idea of them performing a related function here is not so far-fetched, given the Region's history.

With Michael came the swimming pool plumbing team to connect and test the circulation pump and filter. The latter found several leaks in the connecting joints in the pipework and the pump pit was half full of water! Again we had a glaring example of the characteristic of all artisans we have met here: they had minimal tools with which to do the job for which they were being paid, relying on us to provide what they needed. Specifically, they had no means of freeing off and re-tightening the joints, and they spurned the jointing compound which we offered them to seal the leaks, preferring to use yards of plumbers' white tape instead.

By now autumn had definitely arrived; a T-shirt was not enough first thing in the morning, and socks reappeared for the first time since April. The weather was virtually perfect. It was cool enough at night no longer to need a fan on all the time, and the mornings were sufficiently cool to make 'doing things' a pleasure. The afternoons were still hot enough to justify a *siesta*, and in the evenings we were still wearing shorts at 7.00 p.m. Dusk was a time which could be a painter's dream - and nightmare - with the kind of light in which Turner excelled. One evening I stood for twenty minutes just watching the light fade over the mountains, and afterwards we had home-made rogan josh for supper - what more could a man want!

We now embarked on the overdue task of wall-painting, while Michael & Co began laying *bovedillas* between the concrete joists which were now all in place. *Bovedillas* are strange, trapezoid-shaped, box-lattice tiles, 12 cm deep, 63 cm long and 25 cm wide. They are laid on the joists with their long side downwards. This side forms the base for the ceiling of the room below while the raised box section supports the concrete for the floor of the room above or, in our case, a flat roof terrace.

Coming from a country where timber is still used extensively for joists, rafters and floors we were fascinated by this technique, just as we were fascinated, and at first astounded, by the overall technique generally used for constructing new buildings. This involves creating a 'skeleton' of reinforced concrete pillars and joists bedded into a concrete 'raft' and then filling in between the pillars with bricks, laid any-old-how simply to fill in the space, and creating floors and ceilings between the joists with *bovedillas* and concrete, as Michael was doing for us. The, to us, time-honoured crafts of carpentry and brick-laying simply weren't involved; on the other hand the skills of concrete-laying and rendering were in abundance. It was all so unfamiliar that we had to forcibly restrain ourselves from commenting on, let alone criticising, the work now being done on our behalf. The lesson learned was

Just because a technique is unfamiliar doesn't make it unsafe. Spanish buildings are no more liable to fall down than British ones, provided the design is sound and the correct materials are used.

<u>Diary - Thursday 23 September</u>. Dogs and a peaceful time do not go together. Susan says I should learn to ignore them but this I find impossible. So far, before we have even got up: all three have been out to do their business and have a bark; Penny - now a substantial animal - has crawled onto the bed for a cuddle, an activity which, for her, includes lovingly chewing our fingers; she has been replaced by Herbert, while Enoch has seized the opportunity to do his business in the dining room, he having found something better to do with his time when he was out earlier. This necessitates getting up (again) to mop it up; all three have roiled around the bedroom for a while, before demanding to go out again to have another bark. And Susan tells me to ignore this! The problem is, she can; having raised five children, she says it's now in-built!

After breakfast we go to the market in Torre del Mar for vegetables, and to visit the nearby English bookshop. This has to be cut short as my throat starts to play up, but not before Susan manages to buy six Comet goldfish (to keep the mosquitoes at bay in the former swimming-pool *deposito*, what else?), two zebra finches and two Bengalese finches plus assorted plants and food for both species (as she is an authority both on keeping fish and hand-rearing parrot chicks, I guess she knows what she is doing). Back home two friends, Henry and Jackie from Bournemouth, arrive in the afternoon to stay for a month or more, partly for a holiday and partly to help us paint the house. Michael and *niños* have laid the steel wire mesh mat on top of the *bovedillas* to reinforce and hold the concrete for the roof terrace floor, so all is now ready for a repeat performance of the ballet which we witnessed when the extension floor was laid. Unfortunately I have to take to my bed, as my temperature is 102°F/39°C. And to wrap it up, we have several power cuts during the evening, and the water goes off!

<u>Friday 24 September.</u> With me still running a temperature, Susan takes the opportunity to clean and reorganise the outside the front of the house, which now looks like a terrace again and not a furniture store. In the afternoon the tranquillity of the valley and our peace is disturbed by the arrival of a vast, caterpillar-tracked mechanical digger, clanking along the track which runs past our house. This necessitates moving Henry's and our cars to let it past, but even with this it manages to sever the mains water pipe opposite the house. Isidro - who else - comes to fix it, but it serves as notice to us that we need to keep suitable hose couplings in the house to deal with similar emergencies. Later we have several hours of rain: wonderful. Our trees lapped it up.

<u>Sunday 26 September.</u> Having spent all of Saturday in bed, I stagger up and am rewarded with the sight of a fruit rat emerging from a hole below the swimming-pool parapet, having a swim and returning to its hole. Neither it nor Jackie, who is sunbathing by the pool, notice each other, but Henry's reaction is agreeably rewarding when I tell him!

I phone the hospital where Toby had his operation, and explain the problem. The Sister I talk to on the other end of the phone is very helpful and locates the surgeon concerned. He confirms that antibiotics are needed and which ones. My faith in the system is slightly restored. We shall have to see if the farmacia *in Periana has got them.*

<u>Monday 27 September.</u> After Michael and *niños* arrive, we all go to town for the mail and to get me the antibiotics (which they have), then on to Torre del Mar to show the town to Henry and Jackie and go to the supermarkets. We leave the dogs shut in all morning for the first time, and are rewarded with only a small puddle from Enoch - not bad, not bad at all. We are also regaled by Michael with the news that <u>two</u> concrete lorries plus Antonio with his tipper-lorry and hopper should be here to lay the extension roof this afternoon. In fact they arrive at 4.30 and, as the temperature is around 29°C/85°F they, Michael and *niños* have to work flat out to get the job done before the concrete sets! They finish by 7.00 p.m. and depart, leaving us, as usual, to wet down the concrete to

prevent it from drying out too quickly, a task which presents a challenge or two since there is minimal water pressure and the roof is two and a half metres above the front terrace where the tap is.

<u>Tuesday 28 September</u>. The antibiotics appear to be working but the throat is still swollen and inflamed, so clearly there is something wrong. We are debating the possible need for me to go back to England to see the surgeon when Simon calls with the news that he can get tickets for England's Rugby World Cup pool match against New Zealand on 9 October. This settles the debate, and as Henry and Jackie kindly offer to house and dog-sit for us, next day we all go to Málaga Airport to try to get flights, two for Susan and me and another for Henry, timed so that he and we swap over at the airport on our return, so that he can go home for his mother's birthday.

Amazingly we succeed, so back home to try to organise an appointment with the surgeon, though not before diverting to one of the superstores in Málaga (never make a trip to the coast just for one purpose), where we see a large, prefabricated aviary which Susan covets, so buy it as an advance birthday-cum-Christmas present (it's too expensive to serve as only one!). The store says they will have to order it, and will deliver it to us free of charge. This is a great bonus, though it will be interesting to see if they can find us, and we take bets on whether they will deliver it while we are in England. We get home to an ecstatic welcome from the dogs which includes Henry and Jackie and augers well for our absence, and later the final piece of the jigsaw falls into place when the surgeon says he can see me on 7 October so all-in-all, a highly successful day.

At the beginning of October, just before we left for England, I walked the course of the *acequia* with Henry, who will 'do' our last turn for water this year. As we walked back, having set the 'sluice' in the correct position, we found the water running onto Luisa's brother's land above ours, instead of down the channel to us. While we were contemplating the need to remove the dam of earth and stones which was the cause of the obstruction the brother appeared, in a state of some agitation.

'Where the hell did that come from?' he asked.

'Where did what come from?' we answered, in all innocence.

'There was nothing in the *acequia* five minutes ago,' he replied, 'then suddenly, here I am, ankle-deep in water!'

We explained, and he was very good about it; he even got his mattock and cleared away the dam for us. Next day we left for England, and Henry and Jackie's experiences in our absence were revealing:

Diary Extract - Tuesday 5 October. Found Eloïse sprawled on top of bird-cage, acting very suspiciously - hung cage outside.

Wednesday 6 October. Woke to find Enoch asleep on pillow beside us.

Thursday 7 October. Same again - must remember to shut the door! Saw the biggest millipede yet; Henry whacked it to death with a shoe. Eloïse still trying it on with the birds.

Friday 8 October. Think Eloïse believes we do not feed her enough: she is always either lurking round the bird-cage, or has her head in the cat-food bag with just her back legs showing! Strange animal - like her owners? - though at least they don't stand upside down with their heads in a bag!

We flew back on Sunday, I having had the all-too-familiar experience from days gone by of watching England lose gallantly, and unnecessarily, at Twickenham the day before. Still, the evening which followed made up for it! At Málaga Airport we waved good-bye to Henry, who was flying home for his mother's birthday, and drove home. It was wonderful to be back. We never thought we would be so happy to return to a dust-covered, rubble-strewn building site. The dogs gave us another ecstatic welcome, though it was clear they had had a great relationship with Henry and Jackie in our absence. Next day Michael appeared on his own; apparently one of his *niños* owed money everywhere and was making himself scarce, while the other had left for pastures new. Michael was not a happy bunny. And, once again, we had a truly English welcome; it rained heavily for the whole of our second night back. Dawn was dark and gloomy, clouds were down into the valley and there was a cascade of water from the road running down our newly-sculpted front path, straight into the front door!

The following day was Spain's National Day, so understandably, Michael took the day off. However when he failed to show the day after we wondered what to do with ourselves, as it was brilliantly sunny and hot. The prompt came from a millipede, which fell at my feet from the overhead covering to the front terrace. These millipedes are highly toxic, so anywhere that harbours them must be viewed with less than total enthusiasm.

'Why don't we take it down?' suggested Susan. 'We could start at the road end and just clear away the scrubby bushes on the bank and one section of the overhead covering, and then have a break.'

Which is why, without a break (of course), ably assisted by Jackie, we dismantled, cleared away and burned the entire structure, vines, palm fronds, lengths of bamboo, supporting timber and all by early afternoon, rendering us exhausted and a number of carpenter bees who used to live there confused and very angry. The increased light was wonderful, though the sense of space and exposure definitely induced agoraphobia, and we were acutely aware of the need to replace it all before the onset of the hot weather the following year.

Henry returned on Friday 15 October, necessitating a trip to Málaga Airport for 2.25 a.m.! The rest of the day was spent cleaning *cal apagada* (slaked lime) off the front of the house, ready for painting. *Cal* is the traditional form of whitewash used for houses in the *campo* and, while very effective, does flake and crack, necessitating annual renewal. Nowadays *pintura plastica* is available for both interior and exterior use. Since this is invariably of exceptionally high quality and very reasonable price, it is infinitely preferable to the old material and we intended to use it but not, of course, before we had made ready the surface, including filling all the cracks.

Next day, when Henry had fully recovered from his trip, he and I dug up the lane! For a long time I had wanted to re-route the course of the water from the *acequia* where it crossed diagonally under the road to the far end of our land, as the point where it debauched actually required it to run uphill before it could reach the trees. Not surprisingly, this made it less than totally effective.

Now I had the chance to remedy this, but to do so involved digging a trench across the lane ... the public lane.

It's not every day you do this kind of thing, even here, and in Britain I doubt whether you could do it at all, even if you asked permission from the council and took massive precautions. Here we simply got on with it, a task which took from 9.00 a.m. until 3.30 p.m. We then borrowed Michael's cement mixer – a chance to get our own back – and with Susan at the mixer, Henry manfully wheel-barrowing the mix to the trench and me filling it in, we laid a 16 cm diameter rigid tube across the lane, at a depth of about a metre to avoid the possibility of distortion or worse still, fracture from the weight of any passing lorry including, of course, any concrete lorries which might have to come to us in the future.

We finished at 6.00 p.m., and then cleaned up and drove to Torre del Mar for supper. It was our immense good fortune that Pedro and Luisa were in Granada at this time, as they would undoubtedly have gone ballistic at this interference to their rights to free passage – unless of course they had initiated the interference – and in fact only two vehicles came along the lane the whole time we were working. Luckily these weren't lorries, and the planks which Michael used for shuttering the concrete for the extension and which we had purloined for the purpose were strong enough to support them. These we left in place when we went out, guarded by the warning triangles from one of our cars, and by dawn when we cleared everything away no-one would have known of our activities – most satisfactory.

Two days later, as a reminder that all such silver clouds have a black lining, Susan took to her bed aching, shivering and, as she put it later, 'feeling as though she had a steel band round her ribs'. Presuming that the steel band was not a calypso one, this meant a trip to town to the *farmacia* for antibiotics. This was not helped by my also developing a ferocious cold, doubtless triggered by the onset of rain compared with which our earlier experiences were merely an *hors d'oeuvre*s. It started just as I was getting ready to leave. Within minutes it was running in rivers off the roof terrace, and there was a waterfall pouring down the bank on which the extension was built. Part of this gave way in due course, sending a cascade of tiles and other materials down into the orchard, but the extension itself held totally firm and we breathed a sigh of relief.

The rain lasted for three days and gave us a taste of what might be in store for later. It highlighted the need to get the roof terrace waterproofed as soon as possible. We used our 'Vax' - what a wonderful device that is - to take over thirty loads of water off the rubble-strewn floor below when the rain finally eased, out of what was to become the kitchen! The animals were totally confused by this change in the weather. Eloïse refused to go out at all and while the dogs enjoyed it at the beginning, their inability to get dry and the glue-like mud which clung to them (and which they inevitably brought into the house) became very trying for them (and us) after a while.

On Thursday the rain cleared and we emerged like troglodytes into the steaming air. Antonio, Pedro's brother, arrived to tend his strip of land next to ours and, because we had no need for them, we offered him all our pomegranates if he cared to pick them. At first he demurred saying, as we understood him, that they were too far gone. However next day he arrived just after first light and disappeared down onto the land, whence we could hear the sounds of whacking and stacking for the next two or three hours.

Later in the morning, just as the rain re-started, he reappeared, carrying a crate full of fruit, and thereafter he ferried, without a break, a seemingly endless supply of crates up to his Land Rover. Since Antonio is seventy-four, we were totally exhausted just watching him, but more was to follow. When he had finished at around 1.30, he fished out of his cab an old lemonade bottle filled with an interesting brownish liquid. *'Esta vino,'* he said, *'de fabricación casera. Para ustedes.'* And so saying he climbed into the cab and disappeared, leaving us to savour this home-made nectar, with its texture of warm silk and a taste of velvety sweetness, like a million summers caught in a bottle. It was damned strong, too: after a couple of very small glasses, we weren't going to feel any more pain that day. It certainly kept out the damp!

On Sunday the rain, which had held off on Saturday, reappeared, the heaviest yet. The land was now so saturated it began to release the excess into the river, which rapidly became a dangerous animal, a brown torrent two metres deep, surging down towards the lake at about 20 m.p.h. Any dog, or human come to that, which slipped and fell in wouldn't stand a chance. If ever we needed it, we now had confirmation of the appropriateness of the name we had given to the house; we were only thankful that it was over a hundred metres from, and many metres above, the river bank especially when, for a period of around half an hour, we watched it overflow the bank and inundate the bottom corner of our land!

At about 4.00 p.m., during a short break, I slid and staggered across to our northern boundary and opened up the storm ditch which ran between us and our neighbour's field, as the water was 'leaching' down from the land above ours and cascading across the lane. It seemed incredible that less than a month earlier we had been bemoaning the possibility of a drought. Now our preoccupation was with the damp as, with no heating in the house, any clothes not actually being worn were beginning to go mouldy, and the chill was definitely getting to us. What was maddening was that we had a perfectly good wood-burning stove waiting to go into the living room, but we couldn't use it until the extension actually had a floor, nor could we fit a chimney until the roof had been waterproofed, neither of which could be done until the rain stopped!

Next day, while I managed to get out in the car to do some much-needed shopping, Susan found our electric blanket which we hadn't looked at since leaving England and hadn't thought we would need before Christmas, changed the plug and put it on the bed on FULL! She also hunted out the convection heater we had last used in the flat in Torre del Mar and an old, fan-driven heater which she put in the hall, so when I got back at least some parts of the house were drying out. However the rain then restarted in earnest, and Michael and his boys quit for the day... and the work programme slipped remorselessly backwards. This brought home another aspect of living in Spain:

Building work stops whenever it rains.
This must be allowed for in planning.

Joy of joys, next day the weather relented. On the last Wednesday of the month the rain stopped and a gentle south-easterly wind blew in from North Africa, raising the temperature to 28°C/85°F and turning our overgrown orchard into a hot, steaming jungle. The roof terrace surface dried out and we covered it with tarpaulins to keep it that way, and impatiently awaited the return of Michael and his boys, who were unaccountably absent. However the next forty-eight hours were frantic. By Friday evening Michael and his boys had finished rendering the outside of the extension and, more importantly, had covered the flat extension roof with red, rubber sealant. At last, we hoped, the rain would no longer pour unchecked through the concrete and *bovadillas*, and the interior of the extension might dry out enough for us to start painting. And, to cap it all, Susan's new zebra finches had four eggs!

Chapter 13

Winter is i'cumen in,
Lhude sing Goddamm,
Raineth drop and staineth slop,
And how the wind doth ramm
Sing Goddamm
(Ezra Pound, *Ancient Music*)

November started with a very unwelcome telephone call from the office which had represented us when we bought the *finca*. In the past, when a new owner wished to register a property, he or she had to pay only the 6 per cent tax to transfer the property into his or her name. Now, we were told, the Spanish tax authorities had altered the rules with regard to unregistered properties such as ours. Apparently, the penny had dropped that they were missing a trick with this procedure and they had decreed that the tax to obtain the initial registration also had to be paid. The responsibility for this properly lay with the previous owner(s). However in general, property sales agreements in Spain stipulate that it is the <u>purchaser(s)</u> who must bear all costs except for *Plus Valia*, including the cost of all matters relating to registration, and ours was no exception. This neatly let the vendors off the hook and we were faced with finding a further 6 per cent on the declared purchase price.

Whether our advisers should have known about this and taken appropriate measures beforehand was not something we were in a position to explore, any more than were the ethics of allegedly 'shifting the goal-posts' in this way, and implementing the shift after a property has been purchased but before the issue of the *Escritura Publica*; although we could, and did, appeal against the ruling, in Spain the clock continues to tick from the day the demand is issued and if you fail in your appeal (as we did), then you are liable for some fairly hefty penalties if you fail to pay the sum involved by the due date set on the original demand. This meant that our immediate priority was to raise the not inconsiderable sum of money required almost immediately, not indulge ourselves in futile back-biting. Although we could do this from the funds we still had on deposit, we would then have little left to carry out the work we wished to do in the New Year to landscape around the outside of the house.

We were now faced with a 'Catch 22' dilemma, one which required us to come to a firm decision about whether or not we would pursue the B & B idea the following year. If we decided to go ahead with this, then we would have to carry out the landscaping; there was no way we could accommodate guests with the place looking as it did. But this would now require us to raise a loan or mortgage to pay for it, and these were among the very things we had come to Spain to escape. Equally, if we did raise a loan or mortgage, then we would need the income from taking in guests in order to pay for it. Alternatively, if we were prepared to wait an indefinite period to complete the work around the house - in other words, go on living in a house isolated on a building site - then we could simply tighten our belts and save up for the required amount of money, hoping that prices didn't rise too much in the meantime. So the question was: how important was it for us to have the landscaping work complete within a relatively short time frame?

There really wasn't any choice; having paying guests was something in which we had experience and which we generally enjoyed, and it didn't take us long to agree that we couldn't face living on a building site for any longer than we had to. This meant that we would have to raise the money required to pay for the outstanding work, as our existing resources were now running dry, and that in turn would require an increase in income to meet the monthly premiums on such a loan, an increase most easily achieved by taking in guests. So the die was cast, but now we had to find a source from which to raise the money to finance it.

Now, whether it was through premonition or some other influence, on our visit to England in October we had arranged with one of Mr Barclay's representatives that we might have a Barclayloan 'on standby'. This we now activated, and a vital life-belt it was. But such a loan is, by its very nature, a purely temporary measure; the interest rate alone dictates that. And to replace it we made an early appointment to talk to our Spanish bank, to see if they would be prepare to consider a mortgage on the property.

To be frank, we did not have a great deal of optimism; from past experience with British lenders, we couldn't see them being wildly enthusiastic about lending money to people who, at the time of the application, weren't working and had no income other than a pension, and who might have a less-than-average chance of seeing out the full term of the loan, so we were amazed when the bank expressed no misgivings in principle, only requiring as preconditions the regular transfer of adequate guaranteeable funds into our account and the valuation of our house by their representative. Happily we were able to satisfy them on the first, and a date was set for a visit by the bank's surveyor in early December for the second, so the chances were that we would be able, in the end, to go ahead with our plans. However the whole episode all went to show that just when you think you've got it all made, when you've relaxed and unbuttoned your coat (so to speak), loosened your tie and poured yourself a celebratory glass, Fate will be there to remind you that you've had it all far too easy, and will up the ante to see how well you cope with a new test of your ingenuity.

It also confirmed an interesting fact, one that had been demonstrated to us time and time again in our business days, that once you have made up your mind about something and started to take action, then things start to move in that direction almost before the ink is dry. On our next visit to Torre del Mar we got talking, entirely by chance, to an English professional artist, Liz Lewis, who was having coffee with her husband at the table next to ours. When we told her where we lived and what we had in mind she immediately enthused that it could be just the place for members of the art club to which she belonged. She asked if they could come and see us the next day, as they were flying back to England the day after. We had severe misgivings about this, as the place was in no way fit for such an inspection, but agreed on the grounds of 'never looking a gift horse, etc.' and the visit was, in fact, a great success. In the end what she had in mind didn't work out, but the visit gave us all the encouragement we needed to set the B&B enterprise in motion.

<u>Diary - Monday 1 November</u>. Suddenly we are overwhelmed by an explosion of colour. Our orchard and the lane verge are a green carpet of shin-high Bermuda buttercups in which the dogs joyously frolic, pierced by clumps of oxeye daisies and narcissi, and our neighbours are industriously planting vegetables for a winter crop. This is the 'Second Spring' we have been told about. We didn't really believe it, but now that it is here, it certainly beats the hell out of the average British November! For our part, we celebrate with Spring Cleaning or, more accurately, Spring Painting, beginning with the extension walls.

<u>Tuesday 2 November</u>. The first wood-cutting of the autumn - if only we had something to burn it in! Still, we are likely to need it soon enough, despite the wonderful weather now, and if I leave it until the wood-burning stove is actually fitted it is likely to be soggy and uncuttable, never mind unburnable. Antonio has also added to the gift of wine with a bag of broad bean seeds for us to plant, so when finished with wood-cutting I dig a suitable bed in the orchard (watched surreptitiously by Antonio from his strip of land) and heel them in. Michael and boys have finished building the wall to our bathroom upstairs and are now chasing in the electric wiring so, who knows, we may even be able to have our first bath this side of Christmas!

<u>Friday 5 November</u>. Inkerman Day and Guy Fawkes Day. Both fail to register. What does register is the arrival of the proprietor of a shop in Velez Málaga which specialises in fitted kitchens who takes measurements, makes drawings, and asks us to come to the shop next Wednesday to look at the plans and be given their quotation. Highly efficient and all done without a word of English being spoken. We are definitely making progress! The day ends in pure farce. Somehow the mains water pipe alongside the lane has been split, happily for us 'downstream' from our house, but nonetheless irritating, as the water is running down our front path and under the surround to the swimming pool, where it is causing erosion. I try to mend it, and get utterly soaked. In the end I simply bend the two ends back on themselves - how fortunate, now, that the pipe is plastic - and tie them down to stop the flow. All we need now are Pedro and Luisa and the day will be complete!

<u>Monday 8 November.</u> We have the first northerly gale of the autumn over Sunday night. With no windows in the north-facing wall upstairs, only holes, and no doors either, this makes for a noisy and chilly twelve hours. The wind abates somewhat by morning, but it is still 'fresh', as the weather-men would put it. Later we have a 'first': Michael and his boys, the plumber and the electrician, all here together! Michael lays the tiles on the parapet to the roof terrace, the plumber lays the water pipes for our bathroom and the *en suite* guest room shower, the electrician gets on with installing the wiring for the extension and Michael's boys bang the world's largest holes in the outside walls upstairs to take the drains out from the bathroom and the shower. We feel under siege in our own home as work continues till 7.30 p.m. and by the end of the day the 'upstairs back' looks like a battlefield but there is no doubt, a lot has been accomplished in eight hours. I celebrate by being stung by a wasp over my left eye when taking the dogs for a walk.

<u>Tuesday 9 November.</u> Another epic day. Emilio the plumber makes great strides fitting the plumbing to the extension, Michael and boys fit the chimney stack for the wood-burning stove through the extension roof and ceiling (not quite where we want it - ah, well) and to round it off, at 7.45 p.m. in the pitch dark, we take delivery of a lorry-load of assorted items, including the tiles for the roof terrace floor, our bath, the shower tray for the *en suite* guest room, our three 1000-litre fresh water *depositos*, the flooring materials for the 'upstairs back' and a proper water-heater made, surprisingly, by the German firm better known to some for its highly successful World War II night fighter aircraft! Fortunately it doesn't come armed with cannon, and we hope that at last we can have a reliable supply of hot water - once we have approval for the gas and can progress beyond the two bottles still on loan from Michael. The evening culminates at 9.00 p.m. with Emilio, assisted by Michael and illuminated by a flash-light held by me, hanging the water-heater and plumbing it into the system, connecting its gas supply and giving it a test run. When work finally finishes I take the dogs for their last walk under an ink-black sky with hard, glittery stars and a keen, searching wind.

The rest of the week saw massive strides. We had to hand it to them; once Michael and his boys had all the materials to hand, and provided they weren't interrupted by fiestas, domestic crises, medical ditto or just plain hangovers, they really got a move on. By the end of the week they had laid most of the floor in the 'upstairs back', a task which required compensating for a drop of 14 cm over a length of just over 8 metres, plus tiling the extension roof to make it, at last, the roof terrace we intended. Emilio had connected the drain outlets from upstairs, so at last we could actually use 'the facilities' there, and then José the electrician had installed the circuits for the 'upstairs back', so we could even, at a pinch and using make-shift connections, use the said facilities after dark.

We had given the new water-heater ample usage, revelling in a supply of hot water that didn't expire half-way through. We were at last beginning to surface from our Neanderthal existence, a feeling reinforced by our visit to the kitchen company's shop in Velez and seeing a computer simulation of what our kitchen would look like, making some adjustments, being given, and accepting, a price and being told that installation would (not 'might') begin at the end of the month, and would take two to three days. After half a year of purgatory the light of civilisation, if not yet paradise, was beginning to glimmer at the end of the tunnel. I even managed to clear a space between the predatory pomegranates and plant more of the broad bean seeds given to us by Antonio, a task less easy than it would have been in Britain as it involved breaking the solid clay into reasonable sized lumps as I went along, all the while trying to avoid being captured - or scalped - by the pomegranate branches.

We were also visited by neighbours, Pepe and Teresa - he is a banker in Málaga, where they live for most of the time. They also own the furthest habitable house on our side of the valley and a good-ish patch of land, so they are here fairly frequently. Pepe brought a coupling for the mains water pipe, which he and I fitted, so the water supply was restored to his house and the others 'downstream' from us. Teresa also brought us a pot of *melacoton* (peach) jam and a pack of *membrillo* (quince) jelly, both home-made. They proved to be a delightful couple, who talked 'Andaluz' at us a full speed, so we understood about one word in fifty, but never mind. Pepe was a bit suspicious of us when we first arrived, fearing that we might not bring the right kind of attitude and 'tone' to the valley, but seemed now to be reassured. We reciprocated their gifts with a box of sticky fly-papers, which they had never seen and which Teresa clearly coveted.

Diary - Thursday 11 November. We have now been in residence for exactly six months. This is commemorated in the evening by an overture of massive claps of thunder, followed by the rain returning with a vengeance. Susan and I sit in the hall - still our kitchen, but hopefully not for much longer - huddled round the hob for warmth sipping champagne while the thunder crashes overhead and the dogs whimper and moan around us (interestingly Herbert, normally the most placid of our dogs, becomes very apprehensive with Enoch only slightly less so, while Penny, who is very much the 'Beta female' of the pack and who starts at the slightest sound, is totally unconcerned). As the opening scene for a Victorian melodrama it couldn't have been bettered, especially as, by 1.00 a.m., another, more ominous, noise begins to be audible over the thunder: a deep, resonant roar from the river, with the sinister clanking of boulders being forced downstream by the flood.

Luckily by dawn the rain has eased, and as the roof terrace has proved its worth by not letting a drop of water through, Michael and the boys begin laying the floor tiles in the extension. Unfortunately they have forgotten to do anything about the trench they dug for Emilio yesterday at the other end of the house for the permanent arrangement for the mains water inlet, and which they had not told us about. This has filled with flood water which inevitably empties itself through the still-porous outside wall of the house into the downstairs end bedroom. This, equally inevitably, we only discover by chance after Michael and his boys have gone home, by which time the floor is half an inch deep in water, so once again we find ourselves shifting furniture, cursing all builders loudly.

Saturday 13 November. 5°C/42°F at 8.30 a.m., our coldest morning yet. Susan and I huddle in bed, thanking our stars we don't have to:

1. Get up in the freezing dark to bring the cows in;
2. Wash down the said cows in an arctic cowshed;
3. With numbed fingers, try to start a reluctant, petrol-driven Alfa-Laval milking machine by the light of a hurricane lantern;
4. Cart each cow's output to the dairy and put it, so help me, through a bone-cold cooler;
5. Stagger out with a full churn of the damned stuff and stack it on the loading platform for the milk lorry; and finally
6. Wash out each milking pail and its assorted rubber pipes and other paraphernalia by hand, all before going to breakfast.

All of these had been the lot of one or other of us (or both) on all too many days in our early teens. No wonder we wanted to escape! Now our routine problems are the washing and the washing-up, the former because of the difficulty of drying anything and the risk of electrocution in this weather, as the washing machine is still outside on the front terrace and, despite the covering we have rigged, remains exposed to the elements; the latter because of the dark and the wet as it, too, still has to be done outside. What was fun and an adventure in the summer has now become a bore and a chore, made worse by the constant dirt which, like the poor, is always with us, and permeates everything.

Later I take the dogs for a walk round the valley on what has become a beautiful day, photographing the river, which is now a thing of terrible beauty, sweeping all before it on its path to the lake, roiling and surging through the narrows in a foam-capped torrent. Unexpectedly Michael and his boys arrive in my absence and are given a piece of Susan's mind about the inundation of our end bedroom; undeterred they unload two immensely heavy steel doors, one the back door to the kitchen extension, the other the door from the upstairs passage onto the roof terrace. Once they are fitted, we will actually be able to secure the house when we go out - until now it has been a case of presenting a convincing façade and hoping that no-one actually tests it!

On Monday and Tuesday Michael and the boys finished tiling the extension floor, and on Wednesday the ceiling man arrived and, in one day and with one helper, plastered the entire extension ceiling measuring 7 x 6 metres plus our small *bodega* - wine store -

with an incredibly smooth, billiard-table flat surface. Now we knew why he was so difficult to pin down to a date for coming here: with workmanship like this, he was understandably in high demand. While he was doing this, Michael finished tiling the hall and finally removed the ramshackle door and frame which used to close off the access from the house into the old lean-to's with their population of cockroaches, but which gave unrestricted access for those cockroaches into the house. This we were replacing with an open archway over tiled steps down into the extension and, once the kitchen was fitted, the transformation of the inside of the house would be complete.

Now we could begin the fairly mammoth task of evacuating the hall, which had been our kitchen for so long, and moving down into the new pantry the shelving unit which had served us so well as the storage for all our cooking utensils, dry food and other paraphernalia, and finally decorate the walls and ceiling, and fit a proper light. With the extension ceiling finished we could also, joy of joys, at last install and bring into use in our new living-room the wood-burning stove which had been languishing unloved under the stairs ever since we arrived.

This we did on Friday, having given the new ceiling thirty-six hours to dry out. Fitting the internal chimney from the stove onto the stub thrust by Michael through from the roof-terrace proved an interesting challenge, as it required creating an elbow to allow us to place the stove where we wanted it, but we accomplished it in the end and then, the moment of truth: after all this time, would the stove actually burn? In some trepidation we put a match to a bed of kindling and stood back and watched when, glory of glories, it burnt beautifully and, when topped up with logs, heated the extension and much of the house ... and because it was damp and had no bed of old ash, and had an interesting number of unsealed cracks, smoked like hell!

Diary – Saturday 20 November. Our timing with the stove could not have been better: we have rain all morning after which the wind veers and picks up to near gale force, and the temperature drops sharply. This puts paid to our plans to wash and dry the extension floor, but teaches us that we need a taller chimney outside from the stove, with some kind of vane or draught-inducer on top, as otherwise the down-draught puts the fire out! Instead we get on with the boring but inescapable part of living as we have been, that of packing away everything which is standing on or under our one and only table so that we can move it down to the new extension, and with finding the parts for and erecting in the hall the computer workstation from our office in England, connecting the computers and the printer and seeing if they still work!

Sunday 21 November. The weather clears and, in addition to dealing with the extension floor, we begin the long-delayed task of treating the new windows, frames and shutters in the extension and elsewhere around the house against insect infestation. This takes a surprisingly long time, as it requires total concentration and meticulous care for several hours and I, for one, finish with acute back-ache, having painted the shutters on our now-redundant wallpaper table, which is too low for comfort. Still, it all looks good once it is done, at and least we now shouldn't hear the ominous crunching of various wood-borers enjoying a snack.

Tuesday 23 November. Very cold overnight: temperature down to 0°C/32°F. Our gas seems to have become thick in the pipe and won't ignite, so I have a nice, arctic shower before breakfast – shades of boarding school! Go to Velez Málaga in morning with the dogs who are going to visit the vet to be 'done'. They are wonderfully well-behaved on the way down in the car, only one of them being sick and none causing difficulties. After being told to come back and collect them at lunchtime, we go on to the *chimenea* shop to swap the things we bought last week, as they don't fit! Then manage to find the *Centro de Salud* to get my British DSS Form E106 stamped (this will give me temporary entitlement to Spanish state medical treatment until the DSS sends me my form E121).

The place is absolute pandemonium, and we hope we never have to go there in an emergency. We have a fortuitous encounter with a Swiss doctor who speaks English, and who steers us round from the Outpatients department to the office next door and introduces us to one of the duty clerks. This clearly impresses the clerk and we are in and out in ten minutes, with Susan, as my

Dependent, added to the certificate for good measure. This is something which should happen automatically but which, like several other EU directives which are still relatively novel here, can sometimes present a challenge to bureaucracy. Finally the good doctor gives us his card, 'in case we should ever need his professional services in the future.'

With three projects successfully accomplished before 11.00 a.m., it is time for coffee, then back to collect the dogs. Penny, having had much the more complicated operation, is a bit 'sicky' and woozy, but it is Herbert who has problems in the car. Back home, with the dogs sleeping off their respective losses, we fit the new extra pieces of pipework to the stove, seal the various cracks and relight it - major improvement: the fire now burns slow and hot, and we can actually sit in front of it without being asphyxiated, so we move the TV down to the living-room from its resting place in the old sitting-room and spend the evening watching videos in front of the fire. This is more like it.

Michael is amazed at how we looked after our pets. It's just the normal way most English do, but different from the ways here. He expresses his thoughts on this by saying he wants to come back after his death as one of our dogs. The dogs going to the vet change his ideas on this and he decides it isn't such a good idea after all.

<u>Saturday 27 November.</u> Penny back to vet for check-up – OK, but stitches cannot be taken out for another ten days. Leave Herbert and Enoch corralled on front terrace, first time we have left them outside in our absence. On our return find them still there (miraculous), and very pleased to see us. Penny only sick once in the car – just 2 km from home – and then did so into a carrier bag; if only children could be trained so well! Begin painting the extension in the afternoon, in anticipation of the arrival of the fitted kitchen.

<u>Sunday 28 November.</u> Lie-in with the dogs. 'Bonding' with the dogs has become something of a feature ever since Enoch arrived as when he was very little, he couldn't/wouldn't sleep away from us, and he would spend the night tucked into a ball beside Susan's head! This pattern has persisted ever since, and has meant that in the morning, we have to compensate for the other two feeling left out by having them all in with us on the bed before we get up. This, too, was OK at first, but as Penny in particular has grown larger, there has been less and less bed left for us, and as she has also grown heavier, it has become increasingly difficult to move her, especially as she is exceedingly affectionate but remains lacking in self-confidence, and so feels she has to demonstrate her affection for us beyond all doubt before she will get down. When we finally get up, it is cold enough for porridge for breakfast! Spend the day painting the extension ceiling and starting on the walls.

<u>Monday 29 November.</u> We phone the kitchen company, who confirm that the kitchen will start being fitted tomorrow morning. Given the company's track record so far we are inclined to believe this, so the race is now on to finish painting the extension walls – and have them dry – before the fitter arrives. By the end of the day we are totally exhausted, and look and feel like Mr and Mrs Potts, the Painter and his Wife, from 'Happy Families'. Thank heaven we don't have the paint-brush-sucking Master Potts to contend with, though the dogs do their best!

<u>10 December.</u> Up first thing to finish clearing, cleaning and tidying the extension, then self up to the olive mill on the main

road to meet the kitchen fitter. Wait fifty minutes past the allotted time and am just giving up in despair when, thankfully, he arrives. At the house the weather mercifully shines benevolently, as the fitter unloads and stacks everything in the open outside the back door! He then works until 7.30 p.m., assisted by Michael and his boys, by which time he has installed about half of the basic units and Michael *et al.* have knocked holes in the outside wall for the gas supply to the hob and for the ventilation and the extractor hood.

Someone trying to be clever has goofed - here is the man fitting my kitchen and someone has filled in the sink outlet hole! This now means that a hole has to be knocked out again and we will need to wait for the plumber to come back before we can use the sink. Seven months without a proper kitchen, so near and yet so far. I am going to feel odd once it is finished, not sitting down to do the cooking. Having the hob on the workmate was far too low to stand, so all my cooking has been done sitting down. It will be strange to be almost normal again!

11 December. Overnight we have resolved that by Christmas the house must actually bear some resemblance to a home, so the race to get the extension painted before the arrival of the kitchen fitter is now extended to getting the whole house in a civilised condition in the next three weeks. This is no small order. We still have no useable kitchen, no dining-room, no sitting-room or pantry, no storage for china, glass or cooking utensils - and therefore very few of any of these actually unpacked - and although the electric wiring is in place, no lights in the extension, the passageway to it, the *bodega* off the passageway or the hall/office where the passageway starts, so this whole area is uninhabitable after dark. The *en suite* guest room upstairs still has no windows or doors, the roof terrace is untiled, there are no bath, shower or toilet facilities upstairs, much of the inside of the house still needs painting and we are sleeping in two minute bedrooms on the ground floor as the main bedrooms upstairs are still serving as stores and are full to the ceiling with unpacked boxes, furniture and other belongings. There are no pictures or books anywhere.

The day begins with the discovery that the wood-burning stove, after burning for a week, only surrenders half a bucket of excess ash. This really has to be one of our more successful investments. With care it can be made to stay in overnight and as it has a hot plate, it can also serves as an auxiliary hob. The kitchen fitter returns and, with a colleague, hangs the suspended units over the 'pier' and also fits most of the work surface as well as all the cupboard doors. While this is all going on the official gas fitter arrives – he has declined to come until the hob has been fitted in the kitchen – and inspects our installation, makes some minor adjustments and fits two bottles in parallel for the water heater. When we have signed the necessary contract (and paid him 40,000 *pesetas,* about £160) he leaves us with six full gas bottles, so at last we have not only all the ones we need to use, we even have a couple of spares for when any of them run out, and can return to Michael the ones he lent us all those months ago.

12 December. Woken at 4.30 a.m. by the dogs, who have heard a prowler – almost certainly another dog. After rushing out to see it off, they then leap onto the bed with us, though whether to protect us from the prowler's return or to be protected by us is unclear. Later we go to Torre del Mar for Christmas shopping and return to find that Michael has tiled half of our bathroom and that the kitchen team are making good progress. By late afternoon the kitchen is finished, though sadly there is no tap for the sink and neither the water nor the drains are connected. This is a shame, as it looks fabulous, and the evening is faintly surreal, as we can now cook in splendour with the hob in its true setting, but still have to wash up outside under the stars.

13 December. Emilio the plumber arrives at mid-day, fixes the kitchen tap and drain, and plumbs-in the washing machine, which at last we can move indoors. After seeing it on the front terrace every day for nearly seven months, its departure makes the place strangely deprived without it. However its repositioning is not before time, as its chassis has become 'live' with the damp, making it fairly risky to use – we get a sharp reminder if we forget to turn the power off before opening the door! At 2.45 p.m. the kitchen is finally fully operational – it's only been twenty-six

weeks since we last had a real kitchen. Unfortunately I mark the occasion by going down with gastro-enteritis, so the champagne has to wait.

16 December. I am now more or less recovered; we celebrate it by painting round the new front door (which still has no glass) and along the edges of the extension ceiling, and then cleaning the new floor several times. Then comes a moment we have been waiting for: we carry down to the extension our antique corner cupboard, from where it has been languishing in the old *salon* under a dust-sheet ever since it arrived here. It is one of the very few treasured pieces we have brought with us, so we now lovingly clean it, treat it for wood-borers, and position it in what will be our sitting area, making sure that, after all this time, we avoid the irony of getting it scorched by the wood-burning stove!

17 December. Susan is up at 4.30 a.m., something she has been doing for several days now as she is excited and full of ideas and wants to have everything 'right' NOW! We go to Velez Málaga for Penny to have a final check up and all is clear, then on to 'Buffalo', a discount furniture store we have been eyeing for some time, to buy lights for the extension *et al.* Return to find Michael working alone, fitting the window in our bathroom, as his 'mate' has done a bunk. He's the one who apparently owes money all over the place, and is now hiding from his creditors. We commiserate with Michael while quietly cursing the situation, as it will seriously affect our chances of making the house civilised by Christmas. However Michael, bless him, agrees to work late if I can rig up a temporary light for him upstairs. It is now that we discover that, while our bathroom and the passage to it are OK, there is something wrong with the wiring into the *en suite* bedroom: the light I fit there emits a feeble, orange glow, and power tools will not work from the wall sockets. Once again we are beset by the incompetence of electricians, and we can only hope that Michael can get the current one (no pun intended) back in the next two weeks.

We were now on the last lap of our self-imposed race. The first, mammoth task was to unpack our glass and china, washing each item before putting it into its new resting place, and to move items of furniture into the extension, notably the three-piece suite. This took several days and gradually created acres of space in the old *salon* and in the passages where they had stood all this time, and at last gave us access to the walls. This allowed us, joy of joys, to start hanging pictures. These are very important to us; we don't feel a house really becomes a home without them, and between us we have amassed a fair collection over the years. These I now proceeded to deploy on every wall that I could reach, a task that took several days since it involved drilling the walls and inserting screws with rawlplugs, as picture-hooks proved to be totally useless on walls such as ours.

With these task completed, it was time to assemble our still flat-packed bookcases and at last unpack and reacquaint ourselves with our other indispensable collection, our books. This was a reunion with old friends, and our progress was predictably slow as we sat on the floor, emptying the boxes in which they had been lovingly packed and stored for so long and examining the contents. We also moved the deep-freeze from the hall, where it had been a feature for so long, into the pantry which now forms part of the extension and, even more significantly, managed to persuade the dogs to accept the pantry as their overnight accommodation. This in turn meant that, at last, the dogs could begin to perform properly one of their primary roles, that of early-warning system and general deterrent, as the pantry lies between the back door of the house and the main living area.

I now also began the daily task of splitting and sawing logs – not photogenically with a logging axe like William Shatner in the Star Trek movie 'Generations', but sweatily with sledge-hammer and wedges, bow- and chain-saw, like Toby Woolrych in real-life Andalucía. When I had enough of this, it was back to painting the now denuded passage to the extension and the *bodega*, an action which finally 'tied' the extension to the rest of the house and made the whole building as one, plus fitting the overhead lights and generally making good, while Michael fitted the still-missing windows and doors upstairs, finally eliminating the howling draught which seemed to have been our lot since the end of the summer.

There were still individual high (and low) lights to enliven our days, such as when my head had a disagreement with a corner of the new kitchen cupboards. The cupboard won this exchange, resulting in the need for the treatment of a colourful scalp wound. And the morning when we were brought to shuddering wakefulness by a sudden concert of dogs from Pedro and Luisa's orchard down the road. There was no indication of why this should be - killing something, perhaps? - but it certainly upset our gang, who celebrated with a monumental display of incontinence, resulting in the need for an immediate bonfire to dispose of their bedding!

Outside the wild narcissi were blooming (in mid December) and our orchard was covered with yellow Bermuda buttercups in full flower, while inside the extension the overnight temperature seldom dropped below 15°C/60°F even with the stove almost out, yet in England, less than three hours' flight away, we learned that the first snow of the winter had fallen. This brought home to us even more than the sweltering summer had done just how different our lives had become in this fellow-member state of the European Union.

During the time that Susan had worked at arm's length for the Realtor in Florida we had made many visits to that State. During those visits we learned a good deal about its west coast, the climate, terrain, flora and fauna, and it now dawned on us that what we had in our valley was just like the best parts of Florida, with few of the nasties. We had the same sunshine and heat, but very little humidity; we had valleys and mountains, not swamps and creeks; we had birds and butterflies, not moccasins and alligators; and while our land could become water-logged and our lane almost impassable when it rained, at least we didn't have the likelihood of having to evacuate because of a hurricane!

In the week before Christmas Michael, now with a new team of helpers, banged a succession of holes in the outside wall of the extension - so peaceful! - then fitted the *rejas de ventana* - window bars - which are an indispensable feature of Andalucían architecture, so we were finally secure (or imprisoned, depending on your point of view!). We wrapped and sent presents to loved-ones in England, and wrote and despatched a myriad of Christmas cards. We dug out the boxes with our Christmas decorations and our artificial Christmas trees – it was just as well we had invested in two of these back in Bournemouth as they were unobtainable here and Michael promptly borrowed one!

We made trays of mince pies, and took them round to our neighbours as gifts. Isidro and Maria seemed slightly non-plussed, either because the idea of such a gift at Christmas-time was alien or because they were understandably cautious with us being foreigners. Don and Liz were out, so we left theirs at the door, hoping their cat or any stray dog wouldn't get to them first, and Hans the German welcomed us in for a glass of wine.

Then, twelve months to the day after we had first arrived in Andalucía, we decorated the living-room in the extension with greenery and streamers, and erected and decorated a Christmas tree. For us this is the best part of the Christmas scene, and has a special significance. Although it has no real bearing on the Christian festival, if done with love and joy it has always seemed to imbue our various homes with a feeling of magic, and this was no exception. A change seemed to come over the old house. It was as though, by our replacing with a quiet and private sense of celebration the pandemonium of activity and the cacophony of sound that had filled it for seven months, the *cortijo* recognised that a new chapter had begun and that, instead of facing a slow decline with the passing of the years, it had a new life and a new purpose with which to enter the next Millennium.

To be sure, there was still much to do. The upstairs rooms were uninhabitable and the electric wiring still had to be sorted. The mountain of boxes remained to be unpacked. Around the outside of the house was a desolation, the land urgently demanded our attention and the B & B business had to be planned and initiated. But the corner had been turned, the core work done. We were secure in our new home, and the future beckoned with infinite promise.

Epilogue

We all need powerful long-range goals
to help us past the short-term obstacles.
(Jim Rohn)

We have always run someone else's race for them – work, mortgage, even children. Now we are able to set our own goals in our own frame of reference. It's scary, even frightening, and at times very uncertain, but it's our race, and if we want we can stop to pick the flowers or the apples, and have fun. The uncertainty is part of the fun, and there are always helpful people who will stop and give us a hand if we ask.

Very occasionally over the past twelve months we have asked ourselves what the hell we are doing here, what made us abandon the familiar tempo and patterns of life in England and take up residence abroad, but a little quiet reflection has been all that it took to set us straight.

Our decision to leave Britain was triggered by a number of personal factors but these, on their own, would not have been enough to uproot me; behind them, and running much deeper, was the realisation that we were profoundly unhappy with the fundamental order of things as they have become in the country of our birth.

My pre-2nd World War generation was steeped in certain values and Susan's immediate post-war crowd still retained the majority of them. Today it doesn't take an in-depth study of the social history of the past fifty-five years to see what has happened in Britain since the age of the 'baby boomers'; piece by piece the country I knew has been dismantled and in its place has arisen somewhere I can no longer call home.

It's not just the erosion to the point of extinction of the values with which I was brought up; it's also the loss of the physical things which made the country what it was. Where, today, can you find a double-decker bus with the rear platform which lets you jump on and off? What has happened to the trains? Why have they replaced the red telephone boxes? And what are they doing to that seemingly indestructible landmark, the Post Office?

I do not intend to burden readers with views which have no bearing on the title of this book; this is not the place for political polemics. Suffice it to say that we have become so distanced from the country we once called home that, so far as we were concerned, almost anywhere in the civilised world was preferable to life in post-Millennium Britain. Where we have struck gold is in finding those values which we had feared were lost forever preserved almost intact in the Andalucían *campo*.

We have been here a year, of which the greater part was spent in fairly extreme conditions. We have survived, as of course we would, since there was nothing intrinsically threatening about them, though they were sometimes more than slightly uncomfortable. We are now well on the way to realising our dream, and if a minor nightmare was the price to pay for it, it was well worth it.

We have come a long way since we arrived here. We have watched the destruction and resurrection of the somewhat primitive house we bought, and have lived so long with Michael around us (he is still with us) that he has become virtually one of the family. We have learned to cope with the uncertainty of our domestic water supply, the irregularity of the electricity and the limitations of the telephone.

Occasionally we have looked beyond the valley at other houses; we still find it almost impossible to pass an estate agent's window without looking at the pictures, and the grass is always greener, etc., etc. But, at last, we are slowly beginning to realise that in the tranquillity of life in our valley, the wild flowers and birds which arrive in season, the changing shadows on the mountains and the glory of the stars seen across an unpolluted night sky we have found what is, for us, journey's end, and the compulsion to look elsewhere is receding.

We have learned 'survival' Spanish, largely by osmosis, and have developed our own brand of 'Spanglish' for more advanced conversation, a unique dialect which can sometimes result in glorious misunderstandings. We are learning to adapt ourselves to the pace of life in the *campo*, and to adjust our rhythms to those of the changing seasons. We have learned to be non-judgmental about, if not entirely to accept, the local attitude to animals, and to be less emotionally involved with our own. We are no longer inconvenienced by the lack of postal delivery to the door and we have found the non-availability of English newspapers to be no drawback whatsoever: political posturing, British domestic problems, sport and gossip about the lives of the allegedly famous, seem strangely irrelevant here.

Above all we have found immense joy in the process of integrating, so far as is possible, with our local community, a community whose attitudes and priorities are more concerned with personal relationships than the slavish observance of regulations and which are, we feel, infinitely to be preferred to those we left behind. And, of course, there are the additional bonuses of the weather, the freedom from 'Big Brother', over-protection and undue bureaucratic control, the space around us – no small benefit after over-crowded Britain – the weather (have I mentioned that already?), and the price of fish (though this, of course, may change).

In this we realise we are deeply privileged: most people spend their entire lives living where circumstances have placed them, not where they would have chosen. For some these circumstances can be truly horrific, and we are fully aware of the need not to take our good fortune for granted. And my Pandora's Box, the place where I hid the differences between what I was paid to do and the private aspirations, desires, regrets and fears which lay behind: what of that? Well, until I sat down to write this epilogue, I hadn't thought about it for ages; in fact, I hadn't even seen it since those early weeks at the *cortijo* when I was doing battle with the demons from my childhood. It appears that I had consigned it, the way one does with luggage which one no longer immediately needs, to a sort of mental attic.

When I uncovered it and peered into its depths I was astonished to find it empty. The contents appeared to have seeped out while my back was turned and become quietly fused with the emotions and ambitions I now presented to the world. As a former army friend of mine (who has remained a friend despite the penalties of attaining extremely high office and being awarded a knighthood, both of which suggest that he knew where he wanted to go and precisely how to get there from way back) wrote in his last letter to me, 'It looks as though, at last, you have found what you want to be doing with your life.' And if we needed any confirmation of this, while our home still isn't known locally as *Cortijo del Rio* it isn't known as *la casa de Pedro y Luisa* either: its become *la casa de Tobi y Susanna*, and we can't imagine any greater accolade than that.

<u>Note.</u> Since this book was written, Toby and Susan have started their B&B enterprise, now expanded into half-and full board farmhouse holidays as distinct from merely B&B, and have welcomed guests to their home for more than two years. Readers who wish to sample the joys of life in the Spanish *campo* may find out more by writing to their e-mail address **bandb_andalucia@hotmail.com**

Acknowledgements

As we discovered while we were engaged in this adventure, there are many others who have done before us what we are doing now, and many who have been here far longer than we have. Almost without exception, where we have encountered them, these kind and generous people have given freely of their time and their knowledge (and often their hospitality, too), without which we would have wasted much time, money and effort. To them must go our heartfelt thanks.

We must also mention the wonderful openness we have received from the Andalucían people, who could be forgiven had they shown resentment to the swarm of foreigners, of many different nationalities, who have invaded their traditional homeland and way of life. Instead, again almost without exception, we have been greeted with warmth, honesty and friendliness, bearing out something which was said to us shortly after we arrived: truly, the best kept secret about Spain is the Spanish people themselves.

Chief Seattle's Testimony - 1854

You must teach your children that the ground beneath their feet is the ashes of our grandfathers. So that they will respect the land, tell your children that the earth is rich with the lives of our kind. Teach your children what we have taught our children, that the earth is our mother. Whatever befalls the earth befalls the sons of the earth. If men spit on the ground, they spit upon themselves.

This we know: the earth does not belong to man, man belongs to the earth. This we know: all things are connected, like the blood which unites one family. All things are connected.

Whatever befalls the earth befalls the sons of the earth. Man did not weave the web of life, he is merely a strand in it. Whatever he does to the web, he does to himself.